THE MEANING OF BAPTISM

ALCUIN CLUB COLLECTIONS No. 67

The Alcuin Club exists to promote the study of Christian liturgy in general, and in particular the liturgies of the Anglican Communion. Since its foundation in 1897 it has published over 130 books and pamphlets. Members of the Club receive publications of the current year *gratis*.

Information concerning the annual subscription, applications for membership and lists of publications is obtainable from the Treasurer, 5 St Andrew Street, London EC4A 3AB (telephone 01-583 7394).

THE MEANING OF BAPTISM

A Comparison of the Teaching and Practice of the Fourth Century with the Present Day

RAYMOND BURNISH

ALCUIN CLUB/SPCK

First published in Great Britain 1985
for the Alcuin Club
by SPCK
Holy Trinity Church
Marylebone Road
London NW1 4DU

Acknowledgements
Extracts from *Documents of Vatican II*, edited by Walter M. Abbott,
are reprinted by permission of Geoffrey Chapman, a division of
Cassell Ltd.

Extracts from *Christian Baptism*, edited by A. Gilmore, are
reprinted by permission of Lutterworth Press.

Extracts from *Your Baptism*, by S. F. Winward, are reprinted by
permission of the Baptist Union.

British Library Cataloguing in Publication Data

Burnish, Raymond
     The meaning of baptism: a comparison of the teaching and
     practice of the fourth century with
     the present day.—(Alcuin Club collections; 67)
     1. Baptism—History— 20th Century
     2. Christianity—Great Britain—History—
     20th century
     I. Title   II. Series
     265'.1'09015   BV803

     ISBN 0-281-04200-4

Phototypeset by Tradspools Ltd, Frome,
Printed in Great Britain by
Whitstable Litho Ltd, Whitstable, Kent

Contents

vi

Abbreviations

ACW	*Ancient Christian Writers* series
AS	A. Schmemann: *Of Water and the Spirit*
Cat.	Cyril of Jerusalem: *Catechetical Lectures*
Cat. Myst.	Cyril of Jerusalem: *Mystagogical Lectures*
CCD	*A Catechism of Christian Doctrine*
CSI	Church of South India
DCG	*General Catechetical Directory*
DVII	W. M. Abbott (ed): *Documents of Vatican II*
E.M.B.A.	East Midland Baptist Association
FaCh	*Fathers of the Church* series
FLC	F. L. Cross: *St Cyril of Jerusalem's Lectures on the Christian Sacraments*
IFH	I. F. Hapgood: *Service Book of the Holy Orthodox-Catholic Apostolic Church*
Mf	*Montfaucon* series
OICA	*Ordo Initiationis Christianae Adultorum*
PG	*Patrologia Graeca*
PGL	G. W. H. Lampe: *A Patristic Greek Lexicon*
P-K	*Papadopoulos-Kerameus* series
Procat.	Cyril of Jerusalem: *Procatechesis*
RCIA	*Rite of Christian Initiation of Adults*
RR	W. K. Reischl & J. Rupp: *S. patris nostri Cyrilli opera*
SC	*Sources chrétiennes* series
Stav.	*Stavronikita* series
WS	*Woodbrooke Studies*

Acknowledgements

The piece of work which has now reached its published form began life in the form of research in preparation for a Ph.D thesis submitted to the University of Nottingham in 1983. My work has been assisted by a number of individuals and institutions, and I mention here only those to whom I am most deeply indebted, with apologies for any sins of omission.

Academically, I must acknowledge the encouragement and support which I have received from my Supervisor, Sister Charles Murray, SSND. I am sure the finished work has also benefited from the comments and suggestions of my external examiner, the Reverend Robert Butterworth, SJ, who also commended my work to Dr Kenneth Stevenson, who in turn made possible its publication through his recommendation of the work to the Alcuin Club. I am also grateful to those who contributed to the research by answering letters and completing questionnaires, and especially the Right Reverend K. T. Ware, the Bishop of Diokleia, whose help was invaluable in the Orthodox chapter.

Financially, I must acknowledge the support which I received for my research from the Scholarship Fund of the Baptist Union of Great Britain and Ireland, and from the trustees of the Dr Williams's Trust, who were also generous in their support, especially as they had funded my earlier research with their Glasgow Bursary in 1969–70.

The Churches to which I have ministered in the last seven years, Thomas Helwys Baptist Church, Nottingham, and Powerscourt Road Baptist Church, Portsmouth, have been gracious in their forbearance with a minister who wished to pursue academic research whilst in the active pastorate, and have shown their interest and support in their own way.

In the most recent stage, as the thesis has been transformed and reduced to be suitable for publication, I must also acknowledge the help and assistance which I have received from the Reverend W. Fancutt, who proof read the 'nearly final' draft. I am also most appreciative of the help and support of the present editor of the Alcuin Club, Michael Perham. In addition I must acknowledge the encouragement of the Committee of the Alcuin Club for their offer and assistance in the publicaton of this work.

However, in practical terms, I must acknowledge the greatest debt of all to my wife, Florence, who has made great sacrifices to make this research possible at all. She has fended off the potential interruptions of both callers and children, she has given advice on matters of style whenever it was sought, and most significantly of all, she has typed every word of each successive draft and the final copy with a high degree of professional competence, and an inexhaustible supply of patience.

Raymond Burnish

The Feast of St John Chrysostom, 1985
Portsmouth

Introduction

The conversion of the Emperor Constantine in AD 312 formed
the catalyst for the development during the succeeding century of the 'golden age' of catechesis at such centres as Milan,
Jerusalem, Antioch and Mopsuestia, as the church felt the
benefit of its imperial patronage, expressed in the edict of
Milan, granting religous toleration,[1] and the restoration of
property lost during persecution.[2] As the Church realized,
slowly and cautiously, that its days of persecution and
oppression were over, it began to build places of worship
which it considered architecturally fitting for the worship of
God, encouraged actively in Jerusalem, for example, by the
imperial family itself.[3] Within these centres of worship there
was scope to instruct openly those who wished to join the
Church as believing adults, and to baptize them. As the
century went on, large numbers wishing to join the Church
meant that the Paschal Homily developed into its place within
the context of formal catechetical lectures given during the
Lenten and Easter season and baptism was administered
during the Easter Vigil. At first this may seem to be a long
way from the situation today, but when we examine the
developments in the catechetical explanation of baptism
during the period 1960–80 in the light of the fourth-century
material, then a distinct relationship emerges.

The eastern Church produced a neat corpus of material
from Jerusalem, Antioch, and Mopsuestia in the form of
lectures delivered by Cyril, John Chrysostom, and Theodore
respectively. These lectures we shall consider, reflecting as
they do the church situations in those cities. This material is
readily available today both in the original and in excellent
modern translations, and for the reader's convenience, quotation for the most part will be made from these modern
translations. The teaching given on the baptismal theme is
examined under the two headings of:

The Theology of Baptism and its Catechetical Explanation

The Liturgy of Baptism and its Mystagogical Explanation.

In Jerusalem the reference to baptism contained in Cyril's *Procatechesis*, *Catecheses*, and *Mystagogical Catecheses*[4] are collated and considered and additional contemporary background material is obtained from the *Peregrinatio Aetheriae*.[5] A similar method is adopted in considering the extant catechetical lectures of John Chrysostom in Antioch[6] and those of Theodore of Mopsuestia.[7] For reasons of space the literature studied has been restricted to the recognized catechetical lectures, particularly excluding the profusion of homiletic material with which John Chrysostom lived up to his name. Its inclusion would have given a corpus of material so vast as to unbalance the present study.

It seems plain that the vast majority of those attending the catechetical lectures of the fourth century were adults and able to make up their own minds about their commitment to Christ and his Church. Although the baptism of children was referred to by John Chrysostom, the whole tenor of all the lectures, their content and their complexity, points to a committed adult audience. For this reason modern parallels have been sought amongst churches which have a policy of the baptism of Christian adults across a spectrum which reflects both Roman Catholic, Orthodox, and Protestant Churches.

The church situations chosen for comparison on the basis of their teaching on the baptismal theme during the period 1960–80 have been selected to illustrate the diversity of expression of Christian faith during the period, although 'main-line' churches have had to be selected to obviate problems caused in locating material from smaller and less administratively organized denominations. Those chosen are the Baptist Church in Britain, the Roman Catholic Church, particularly in Britain, and consideration is also given to the current practice of the direct descendants of the fourth century, the Eastern Orthodox Church. The Baptist Churches were chosen because they are probably the major main-line Christian denomination in Britain committed historically to the baptism of believing adults, 'adult' being defined as those whom the Church considers mature enough to answer for themselves in matters of faith and commitment. They also represent a denomination which has no great tradition of liturgical worship, but rather an avowed commitment to freedom both of worship and of expression of worship. The Roman Catholic Church was selected because of the changes implied in the Second Vatican Council, and executed in the spirit of that council, whereby the rite of adult baptism has been revised to become what Aidan Kavanagh has described as 'the definitive exposition of what the Roman Catholic *norm of baptism* is henceforth to be.'[8] This change has taken place within the context of the restoration of the catechumenate.[9] Although it is still early days to assess the full impact of this change, material produced by those putting into practice the revised vernacular versions of the *Rite of Christian Initiation of Adults* has been considered and assessed. The Greek Orthodox Church produces almost a time-capsule effect by its adherence to the fourth-century pattern, with nineteenth-century words[10] from the American translation most commonly in use in Orthodox churches in the English-speaking parts of the world, although some recent catechetical material produced by Alexander Schmemann has been studied and contrasted with the fourth-century approach.

The modern period represents problems of its own in locating material, and so it has been necessary to start one stage further back to establish the material used. In the case of the Greek Orthodox Church this has been established by letter to The Right Reverend Dr K. T. Ware, Bishop of Diokleia. The material which he recommended is considered in order to establish the baptismal teaching and practice of that Church. Although the Roman Catholic material might seem, at first sight, to be the most readily available, replies to a circular letter sent to each Roman Catholic ordinary in England and Wales, together with the chairman of each Diocesan Commission on the Liturgy and on Catechesis, indicate that the new rite is only infrequently used. There is evidence of a reawakening of interest in the baptism of adults in some dioceses fuelled by the Sadlier *Christian Initiation Series*, enthusiastically describing the use of the rite in the United States. By their very independency the Baptist Churches provoke problems of analysis, and this study identifies the material and the baptismal practices most commonly in use by means of a statistical survey of some 330 ministers attending ministers' conferences in nine areas of England in the Spring of 1981.[11] The most frequently mentioned titles provide the basis for the study of the current Baptist catechetical teaching on baptism. The liturgy has been identified from the various Baptist Union publications for the period.

This study seeks to show that the formative period for catechetical teaching was the 'golden age' of catechesis in the century following the conversion of Constantine and that the most recent years of the twentieth century have shown a reversion towards that golden age. For the Roman Catholic Church this has been a deliberate reversion, brought about by the reform of the liturgy of Christian initiation commissioned by *Sacrosanctum Concilium* from the Second Vatican Council. The new rite has reawakened interest in the classic period, and shown a tendency to canonize the fourth-century theology and catechesis of baptism, and to return to the theology of the ancient Church. The Greek Orthodox Church retains the liturgy as well as the theology of the ancient Churches which are being considered, almost in a fossilized form, finding its spiritual security in a dogged adherence to the practices of the ancient Church, in spite of the efforts of theologians like Schmemann, to seek a more meaningful understanding of these practices. The Baptist Churches show an unconscious reversion to the fourth century because of a limited number of ways of expressing the truths of baptism to those believers seeking instruction for it. However, far-reaching differences in ecclesiology form an interesting contrast with the views of the Roman Catholic Church. The link between ecclesiology and baptism must be an indissoluble one, as the theology of the Church into which the candidate is being initiated must have some bearing on the theology behind the rites of that initiation. This link will become apparent as the church situations are examined and contrasted.

When considering the subject of baptism and the means of the initiation into the ecclesial community of the Christian, the canvas is so broad that the scope of the subject has had to be rigidly defined to make the study both manageable and worthwhile. Lack of published material available for study meant that the Pentecostal Churches and other smaller Protestant groups would be almost imposssible areas of study, although one booklet favoured by some Baptist ministers is from a Christian Brethren background.[12] Although the Anglican Church and the main line Protestant Churches have a liturgy for baptism of those able to answer for themselves, there does not seem to be a sufficiently large number of candidates to make catechetical material particularly worthwhile or easily available. However, a decreasing number of infant baptisms and a renewal of interest in the Easter Vigil may alter this over the next decade or so. It is also reasons of space which have limited the literature studied in the modern period to that identified by respondents to their respective letter or questionnaire. Similarly the study throughout has been restricted to the explanation of the meaning and implications of the baptismal rite, rather than to a consideration of the whole gamut of catechetical material, which would have vastly increased the material, and made it unmanageable within the restrictions of time and space available.

We therefore begin our study by an examination of the earliest of the fourth-century material available to us, namely that of St Cyril of Jerusalem.

I

St Cyril and the Church
at Jerusalem

Past scholars agreed that St Cyril's *Catecheses* were delivered as a Lenten course in Jerusalem in about AD 350 and probably immediately before or after Cyril had been appointed to the episcopate, which is variously dated between AD 349 and 351.[1] Although a scribal note[2] indicated that all the lectures were given in one year, this is hard to reconcile with extensive variations in the manuscripts, particularly in view of the two recensions of *Catechesis* 2.16–20, and the references to the seasons which seem to reflect a British spring rather than spring time in Jerusalem – at least if they are to be held to refer to only one year.[3] Similarly Cyril's own references to his previous lectures in *Catechesis* 6.21 would either suggest a corpus of instructional material given by the bishop each year following an unalterable pattern, or would suggest that this particular comment was made after 349 which was probably the earliest year in which Cyril would have been involved in the lecturing. However, the scribal note does give a clue to the method of the preservation of the text, in that it purported to be the reporting of Cyril in shorthand as he was speaking. However much stratification is present in the lectures as we have them, we have no reason to doubt their authenticity nor the fact that for our purposes they represent an accurate picture of the Jerusalem catechetical teaching during Cyril's episcopate from 349–387.

However, the position of the *Mystagogical Catecheses* is by no means as clear and we find an extensive division of opinion among scholars.[4] Although we are aware of the main elements of the authorship debate, for the purpose of the remainder of this study, we will refer to the author of the *Mystagogical Catecheses* by the name of Cyril. It may be that as our study proceeds distinct parallels will be discerned between the

I

references to baptism in the credal teaching of the *Catecheses*, and the teaching of the *Mystagogical Catecheses*. In spite of the debate as to the identity of the author, there is sufficient evidence to assume the probability of Jerusalem as the location of the delivery of the *Mystagogical Catecheses*, and to assume that they were given in the fourth century.[5]

The catechetical works of Cyril are to be found in the edition by W. C. Reischl and J. Rupp;[6] and the edition reprinted by J.-P. Migne which dates from the early eighteenth century and was produced by A. A. Touttée and P. Maran[7]. The *Mystagogical Catecheses* and the *Procatechesis* have been edited by F. L. Cross.[8] For the sake of clarity, the English translation from which most of the quotations are given is that in the *Fathers of the Church* series which provides the only translation into English in modern times that I have been able to locate.[9] However, some excellent background material, filling the gaps, particularly in terms of baptismal practice, which Cyril left unspecified, comes from the pages of Egeria's diary. Although many date this diary in the early fifth century, Devos,[10] who is followed by Wilkinson,[11] opts for a date around AD 384, towards the end of Cyril's episcopate. Even if they are wrong, which the author personally doubts, it is unlikely that baptismal practice would have changed significantly, even in a forty-year period, once the liturgy had been crystallized, and so we are justified in referring to the *Peregrinatio Aetheriae* in this study. In the material which follows, we shall treat the *Procatechesis* and the *Catcheses* as the source of reference for the teaching of Cyril on the theology of baptism, and the *Mystagogical Catecheses* as the source of reference for the liturgy of baptism.

1. *The Theology of Baptism and its Catechetical Explanation*
Egeria described Cyril's baptismal lectures to us thus: 'His subject is God's law; during the forty days he goes through the whole Bible, beginning with Genesis and first relating the literal meaning of each passage, then interpreting its spiritual meaning. He also teaches them at this time all about the resurrection and the faith.'[12] Probably Egeria's meaning is that the bishop took the whole teaching of scripture as his syllabus.[13] Within this structure, we find Cyril giving a series of lectures on the mental preparation for baptism, emphasizing pre-baptismal penitence and repentance, and on the

essence of Christian doctrine and the creed of the church at Jerusalem.

Cyril founded his teaching on baptism by speaking of the baptism of John as the end of the Old Testament and the beginning of the New Testament.[14] Because of this he saw John as the greatest of the prophets and he explained Jesus' word 'Among those born of woman there has not arisen one greater than John'[15] with reference to John's greatness in comparison to Elijah, Enoch, and even Moses. Even Jeremiah, sanctified from his mother's womb, was inferior to John who was not only sanctified but even prophesied in the womb.[16] Cyril summed up the reason for John's greatness thus: 'For since the grace of baptism was a great one, it called for greatness in its author.'[17]

John's baptism, however, although it gave remission of sin and was preceded by confession of sins, remained inferior to Christian baptism.[18] As Cyril said: 'Glorious was he who baptized with water, but what in comparison to him who baptizes "with the Holy Spirit and with fire".'[19] Indeed Christian baptism was superior to that of John in Cyril's view because: 'Jesus sanctified baptism when he himself was baptized.... He was nevertheless baptized that he might impart grace and dignity to those who receive the sacraments.'[20] Again when speaking of the incarnation as an article of faith to the catechumenate, he said: 'Christ came that he might be baptized and might sanctify baptism.'[21] At Jesus' baptism, the Holy Spirit descended in the form of a dove, and Cyril explained this: 'The Holy Spirit descended when Christ was baptized to make sure that the dignity of him who was baptized was not hidden.'[22] He went on to say that in Jesus' baptism he vanquished the dragon in the waters.[23] Perhaps even in Cyril's day the Palestinian fear of the open sea was still to be seen in this reference to Job's Behemoth and Leviathan.[24] In any case Cyril was at pains to point out that not only these mythical monsters, but also death itself was vanquished by baptism, in his phrase: 'Baptism draws death's sting.'[25]

Cyril continued to put the baptism of Jesus in its historical setting as he pointed out that it preceded both his temptations and his ministry, stressing that before his baptism Jesus did not preach the gospel,[26] and after his baptism he was tried for forty days. From this fact, Cyril encourages his catechumens:

'so do you also, who before your baptism dared not close with your adversaries, from the moment of receiving the grace, trust henceforth in the armour of justice, do battle, and if you will, preach the gospel.'[27] They were to expect baptism to be active in transforming their lives and to expect to be strengthened and empowered by the inward and spiritual grace they received.

Cyril warned his candidates against entering the waters of baptism hypocritically, or unworthily, very early in his course of lectures by speaking of Simon Magus who: 'was dipped in the font, but he was not enlightened. While he plunged his body in the water, his heart was not enlightened by the Spirit.'[28] He also referred to the parable of the incorrectly dressed wedding guest, using him as an object lesson of one ill-prepared to receive the grace that was offered freely.[29] He returned to this parable and to this theme later in his course of lectures, constantly putting the onus upon his catechumens to ensure their readiness to receive the sacrament.[30] They were to equip themselves with piety of soul with a good conscience: 'For as the water purifies the body, so the Spirit seals the soul, that having our hearts sprinkled, and our bodies washed with clear water, we may draw near to God.'[31] The preparation for baptism involved confession and exorcism; it involved the forgiveness of others and a true repentance, granted by God.[32] The catechumen had come in faith, being told to: 'Make clean your vessel that you may receive more grace. For though the remission of sins is granted to all alike, the communication of the Holy Spirit is granted in proportion to the faith of each.'[33] Cyril distinguished two effects of baptism, first the remission of sins, which all who sincerely approach the sacrament received; and secondly positive graces, or as he put it, 'the communication of the Holy Spirit'. The second effect would vary, he felt, according to the fervour of faith and the intensity of love for God on the part of the recipient.[34]

Making reference to Holy Saturday night during which the candidates were baptized in the Church of the Resurrection, brilliantly illuminated to symbolize the return of the risen light and their own sacramental enlightenment, Cyril told the candidates 'Then may the gate of paradise be opened to every man of you and every woman. Then, may you enjoy the fragrant, Christ-bearing waters. Then may you receive Christ's name and the power of things divine.'[35] Baptism was

4

to grant them regeneration. He further illustrated the importance of this element of baptismal regeneration in reminding the candidates of the household of Cornelius.[36] After they received the gift of the Spirit, 'Peter "ordered them to be baptized in the name of Jesus Christ" that after the soul had been regenerated by faith, the body also, by means of the water, might share the grace.'[37] With their regeneration in baptism would come the 'illumination' of the candidates and their enlightenment. For this reason Cyril addressed the candidates as candidates for enlightenment,[38] constantly emphasizing the need for sincerity.[39] In his lecture on the credal article 'Crucified and Buried', he referred to the power of salutary baptism being granted by water to those being enlightened.[40] In concluding his lectures he returned to this theme, telling his candidates: 'But when the holy day of Easter dawns, and your love for Christ is enlightened by the water of regeneration you will, God willing, receive the further necessary instructions.'[41]

The illuminatory qualities of baptism were recognized as early as the second century, after which time to enlighten was found as a technical term for baptism. In the second and third centuries its use is not to be found in the popular writings but among the more educated writers who like also to refer to baptism as a rebirth.[42] However, by the fourth century Cyril was able to use this word quite freely in his address to his candidates, who were unlikely to be particularly learned men and women.

Baptism was also the way in which the spiritual adoption of the candidates was shown, and Cyril noted this in his list of the effects of baptism, describing it as the grace of adoption as sons.[43] Referring once again to Jesus' baptism and relating it to that of the candidate, he said that, for them, the voice from heaven accompanying the descent of the Holy Spirit would say: ' "This has now become my Son" . . . To you belongs "has now become" since you do not possess the sonship by nature, but receive it by adoption. He is Son eternally but you receive that grace by advancement.'[44] Cyril made this point when he was distinguishing between the sonship of Jesus, the only begotten Son, and the adoptive sonship of the candidates:

Not as you, who are beginning enlightenment, now become sons of God, for you also become sons, but by adoption through grace, as it is written "But to as many as received him he gave the power of becoming the sons of God; to those who believe in his name: who were born not of blood, not of the will of the flesh, nor of the will of man, but of God".

He made the point that God's intention was that he might show that even before the act of baptism Jesus was God's Son, the only begotten of the Father, and this was plain from his declaration at Jesus' baptism.

Cyril then described baptism as an indissoluble holy seal,[46] and Ysebaert points out that this seal was above all a mark of ownership by which the Lord recognized his own and which repelled the evil spirits. Cyril developed this phrase later when he said: 'come forward for the mystical seal, that you may be recognizable by the Lord.'[47] He advised his candidates that if they were counted worthy of the grace of baptism:

> your soul will be enlightened, and you will possess a power you did not possess before. You will receive arms that cause terror to evil spirits, and if you do not cast your arms away but keep the seal upon your soul, the evil spirit will not approach; he will cower away in fear, for by the spirit of God devils are cast out.[48]

This seal did not itself confer the Holy Spirit, but the seal was received through the operation of the Spirit.[49] Later Cyril saw it as a type of circumcision when he told the candidates that like Abraham, consequent upon their faith: 'we receive the spiritual seal, being circumcised by the Holy Spirit through the laver of baptism.'[50] Both the water of baptism and the operation of the Spirit were necessary to gain entrance to the kingdom of heaven. 'Neither does he who is baptized, but has not been deemed worthy of the Spirit, possess perfect grace; nor will a man who acts virtuously, but does not receive the seal by water, enter into the kingdom of heaven.'[51] In support of this statement he cited the necessity of Cornelius and his family to be baptized.[52]

And it was to the theme of the seal that Cyril returned at the close of his *Procatechesis* when he prayed for the candidates: 'May he fill you with heavenly treasures of the New Covenant and sign you with that seal of the Holy Spirit that no man shall break forever.'[53]

Baptism was the means by which the candidate died to sin and began a new life in Christ. Cyril described it thus: 'For you go down into the water bearing your sins, but the

6

invocation of grace, placing a seal upon your soul, makes you proof against the dragon's maw. Though dead in sins when you went down, you will come up vivified in justice.'[54] Similarly baptism prepared the candidate for the resurrection, Cyril once again linking this with the seal of the Holy Spirit received in baptism: 'For this reason, the Lord, beforehand in His loving kindness has granted us the repentance of the laver of baptism, that, by casting off the chief, nay, rather the whole burden of our sins, and receiving the seal of the Holy Spirit, we may be made heirs of eternal life.'[55] Thus baptism enabled the candidates to share fellowship with the sufferings of Christ,[56] and once again he directed the candidates' attention to Romans 6.2–4.

In this passage listing the effects of baptism, Cyril used a number of titles to convey to his candidates a composite picture of the spiritual effect of the baptismal rite: 'ransom for captives, remission of sins, death of sin, a new spiritual birth, a shining garment, a holy seal inviolable, a Heaven-bound chariot, delights of Paradise, a passport to the kingdom, the grace of the adoption of sons.'[57] The use of the phrase 'a ransom for captives' in connection with baptism seems to belong specifically to Cyril. Lampe[58] listed no other uses of this word in connection with baptism, and we can only assume that Cyril saw baptism in terms of identification of the believer with Christ and so the believer benefited as a result of his baptism from Christ's work of providing himself as a ransom for many.[59] He reaffirmed that baptism brought remission of sins, and then spoke of repentance in terms of the death of sin, suggesting that in the new life upon which the believer embarked at baptism, he had buried the power of sin with his old life.[60] Such a death of sin was followed in baptism by a new spiritual birth, and this term too was quite a familiar one with the early Greek Christian authors, following its use in the New Testament.[61] Cyril then described baptism as a shining garment, using similar terminology to Basil,[62] who quotes Galatians 3.27, although Basil is using the phrase 'to be accounted worthy of clothing'.

Cyril then described the effect of baptism in terms of a heaven-bound chariot. This phrase seems to be a metaphor of Cyril's own. Cyril was using this phrase to remind his candidates in yet another way of the blessings of the new life which would be theirs if they stayed the course. In similar vein came his next metaphor 'the delights of Paradise', taking up an earlier theme when he had referred to baptism as the gate of Paradise, pointing his candidates to the luxurious living in Paradise which baptism would open to them. In this connection he was saying that baptism would restore to them the experience of man's idyllic state before the fall.[63] In similar context he described baptism as a passport to the kingdom using a phrase to describe the way in which baptism granted the candidate admission to the kingdom as its effect. Finally he described baptism in this sentence as the grace of adoption as sons, an area which we have looked at above.[64]

He often referred to baptism in terms of grace or a free gift, using these terms to combine the grace which was mediated through baptism with the grace which enables man to come to God to receive remission of sins, and to receive the gift which God imparted to them.[65] However, he made it plain that this gift was mediated through men,[66] although again he warned them against playing the hypocrite for: 'If you pretend, men will indeed baptize you, but the Spirit will not baptize you, but if you approach with faith, men will minister to you visibly, but the Holy Spirit will bestow upon you what is not visible.'[67] The idea of sacramental grace in the Catechetical Lectures was twofold — of the water and of the Spirit — and these two were inseparable.[68] He pointed out to his candidates that his twofold grace, though freely given, had to be cherished and reverenced once they had received it: 'It rests with God to bestow grace, but with you to accept and cherish it. Do not despise the grace because it is freely given, but rather cherish it with reverence once you have received it.'[69] To reinforce this teaching he reminded his candidates that all their deeds after baptism were recorded, whether they were deeds of almsgiving or fasts, or covetous deeds or theft: 'All these are henceforth recorded, if after baptism you commit the same faults; for what went before is blotted out.'[70] Cyril obviously interpreted the several biblical passages in this classic way, following the tradition of many of the early Fathers in respect of post-baptismal sin.[71]

2. *The Liturgy of Baptism and its Mystagogical Explanation*

The *Mystagogical Catecheses* were significantly shorter than the Catechetical Lectures, and so it may be that the time which Cyril had at his disposal was shorter than the three hours from

6 a.m to 9 a.m. which he had available before baptism. The Mystagogical material was delivered during the five or six days following Easter,[72] and Cyril stated his purpose thus: 'The time being now come to spread for you the board of more perfect instruction, let me explain the significance of what was done for you on that evening of your baptism.'[73] Noting that seeing was more persuasive than hearing, he then proceeded to deal with the component rites of the baptismal liturgy and to explain their meaning, beginning with the first act in the ceremony, the rite of the Renunciation of Satan, and Profession of Allegiance to Christ.

a) *The Rite of Renunciation and Profession.* Cyril dealt with this rite in his first Mystagogical Lecture, for which his text was 1 Peter 5.8–11. He related this passage to the drama in which his audience so recently had been involved. The rite had taken place in the vestibule of the baptistry.[74] The candidates entered the vestibule, and stood facing the west, listening for the command to stretch forth their hand and to address to Satan the words of renunciation. Then, turning east, they addressed to God their belief in him.

Using the dramatic framework suggested by the reading and the rite, Cyril described to his candidates the dramatic pursuit of Satan to enslave men, fear giving way to strength based on faith, and the support of the brotherhood, which enabled the candidate to meet Satan in a face-to-face encounter, and to break his power and enslavement, strengthened in this endeavour by God's power. The candidates thus began this pilgrimage under the biblical admonition to vigilance, and were plunged into the struggle and glory of salvation-history, and into a new birth, as in the darkness they closed with the adversary who was in pursuit of the candidates right up to the very font of baptism itself.[75] However, the calmness of the candidates was not shattered, as Riley points out:

> They are able to stand, to stretch forth their hand in rejection, because 'strong in faith,' derived from the consciousness that they are not alone in the struggle, but that in the history of the chosen people in Egypt and now, on this evening, the struggle will end in victory, for God will give them the strength to do what must be done, even to the point of overcoming Satan, whose devouring power becomes the power of death itself. And this victory will be gained in Christ.[76]

Cyril used the tyrant Pharaoh as a type in this situation, seeing Pharaoh's pursuit of the Israelites into the Red Sea after the Passover as typical of Satan's pursuit of the candidates right up to the waters of the baptistery; leading to his destruction as far as the candidate was concerned, and his disappearance in the baptismal waters which Cyril described as the saving waters.[77] The candidate had thought of Satan as though actually present, and had faced the west with arms outstretched to emphasize rejection of Satan, and declared: 'I renounce you, Satan, and all your works, and all your pomp, and your service.'[78] He explained the significance of the west in this manner: 'Because the west is the region of visible darkness, Satan, who is himself darkness, has his empire in darkness – that is the significance of your looking steadily towards the west while you renounce that gloomy prince of night,'[79] and it was from the west which the candidates turned. He explained that their turning was irrevocable, and to turn back to the things renounced would not merely return the candidate to the pre-baptismal *status quo* but to a position far worse than before because of the annoyance and exasperation produced in the tyrant by the duplicity of the candidate:

> For if you should succumb to such practices after renouncing Satan and transferring your allegiance to Christ, you will find the usurper more cruel than ever. For if formerly treating you as a familiar, he abated the rigours of your slavery, now he will be furiously exasperated against you. So you will lose Christ and taste Satan's tyranny.[80]

He used the familiar image of turning from slavery to freedom which was also used by Chrysostom and Theodore.[81] To emphasize the danger of turning back to slavery and Satan, Cyril took as a type the story of Lot's wife from Genesis 19.15–26, and described her transformation into a pillar of salt as 'a monumental warning and memorial of her wicked choice (her turning back).'[82] Cyril continued, reminding the candidates that they had then turned to face east:

> When you renounce Satan, trampling under foot every covenant with him, then you annul that ancient 'league with Hell,' and God's Paradise opens before you, that Eden, planted in the east, from which for his transgression our first father was banished.

Symbolic of this is your facing about from the west to the east, the place of light. It was at this point that you were told to say: 'I believe in the Father and in the Son, and in the Holy Spirit, and in one baptism of repentance.' But these subjects have been treated at large, as God's grace allowed, in the previous discourses.[83]

Cyril also used here the imagery of light and darkness, and of the severing of the pact with hell and entry into Paradise, which he had used in the *Procatechesis*.[84] For Cyril, the significance of the darkness in the region of the sunset and sunrise in the east was combined with the biblical symbol of the Garden of Paradise planted in the east, from which Adam was exiled for his transgressions.'[85] So, for Cyril, turning was a symbol of the repentance which brought the candidate back to the east, the symbolic location of Paradise, from which man had first been exiled.

As we have seen, Cyril described Satan as the wicked and cruel tyrant[86] and he described his domain in words from Hebrews 2.14–15, in terms of a power which held man in bondage as it held them enslaved, living in fear of death, over which they had no control. Satan was a clever and ruthless serpent who brought Adam and Eve to their apostasy and fall. The words of renunciation are thus designed to sever and finally break the ancient pact with Satan and with hell.[87] He defined the pomps of Satan in terms of the spectacles offered by the pagan city, as he attacked 'the craze for the theatre, the horseraces in the circus, the wild-beast hunts and all such vanity'[88] and included in his condemnation any items associated with idol worship, and polluted by the invocation of unclean spirits.[89] The works of Satan he defined as the cult of idolatry and that which attracted people towards divinations, amulets, omens, and sorcerers and these were to be decisively shunned by the neophytes folowing their renunciation of Satan.[90] But, for Cyril, the act of renunciation and commitment, although personal to each candidate, could only be made because of the neophyte's common bond of flesh and blood with Christ.[91] Riley puts this: 'In other words, the power of the salvific act of Christ, united in the blood of common humanity with the candidate, lends him the power to break the ancient covenant with hell and death.'[92] However, this act of renunciation and commitment was of a contractual nature, and perpetually recorded in God's books.[93]

b) *The Rite of Baptism*. Cyril's second *Mystagogical Catechesis* was based on Romans 6.3–14, and was mainly concerned with the rites of baptism which took place in the inner chamber. As he began, Cyril made it quite plain that these *Catecheses* were given daily during Easter week as introductions for the neophytes into the mysteries which they had so recently experienced.[94] In the inner chamber they divested themselves of their garments and stood there 'naked in the sight of all.'[95] Once they had removed their clothing the candidates were anointed with exorcized oil from the topmost hairs of their head right down to their feet.[96] After this anointing the candidates were led to the baptismal pool. After making an individual confession of faith in answer to the interrogation of the celebrant, the candidate plunged three times into the water, and emerged from it three times.[97]

Cyril began his explanation with an interpretation of the nakedness of the candidates,[98] employing a Pauline image, speaking of the neophytes 'having stripped off the old man wih his deeds'[99] in which the Pauline metaphor was that of a person removing his clothing. With this clothing, symbolically the old self was peeled off as well, and with it the evil deeds which emanated from the old self. Cyril stated this explicitly in his Mystagogical explanation of this part of the baptismal rite: 'immediately then on entering you removed your tunics. This was a figure of the "stripping off of the old man with his deeds"' (Col. 3.9).[100] Then Cyril moved on to the dimension of mortality and immortality, considering the old man from the standpoint of salvation-history. Cyril associated the candidate once again directly with Christ himself; as he told the neophytes that in their nakedness they were: 'In this also imitating Christ, who was naked on the cross, by His nakedness "throwing off the cosmic powers and authorities like a garment and publicly upon the cross leading them in his triumphal procession"' (quoting Col. 2.15).[101]

Riley points out that this association between the nakedness of the candidates and the nakedness of Christ upon the cross was peculiar to Cyril of the four fathers whom he is studying, and suggests that this was due to the unique dramatic advantage in the location of his lecture.[102] Whilst this reason for the connection between the two ideas is possible, I am not convinced that this is any stronger a reason for such a vivid association than simply to suggest that it is due to Cyril's own particular style of preaching, and the example which he happened to select to illustrate his point. He had already used the imagery from Colossians of putting off the old man, and it would be natural for a preacher like Cyril to use this image of the nakedness of Christ and the triumphant result of his humiliation described earlier in Colossians as a link to the next point in which he wanted to instruct his neophytes, contrasting the Second Adam in his nakedness with the first Adam, 'who was naked in the garden, and was not ashamed.'[103]

In the Pauline teaching, the discussion concerned the power of the law which would do nothing for the sinner but condemn him to death. It was this death sentence for man which God carried out once and for all on his own Son in order to abrogate it forever, to cancel the debt of humanity by 'nailing it to the cross.'[104] The humiliation of Jesus on the cross was then transformed into the triumph of the Son of God. Man's enemies were divested of their power of corruption and stripped of their power. The stripping away of Christ's garments signified the stripping away of these evil powers, and the nakedness, meant to be a humiliation, became thereby the final sign of victory. So too in the candidate who imitated Christ's humiliation in being himself stripped of his clothes, in his case before baptism, the old clothes, symbol of the mortality, corruption, and consequent vices and sins of the old man were stripped away, and their evil effects rendered powerless in and with Christ. Cyril confirmed this point to his neophytes thus:

> For as the forces of the enemy made their lair in our members, you may no longer wear the old garment. I do not, of course, refer to this visible garment, but to "the old man which, deluded by its lusts, is sinking towards death" (Eph. 4.22). May the soul that has once put off that old self never again put it on, but say with the Bride of Christ in the Canticle of Canticles: "I have put off my garment; how shall I put it on?" (Cant. 5.3).[105]

Similarly the nakedness which the neophytes had experienced also signalled their return to primeval innocence. Picturing the baptismal pool as a symbol of the garden of paradise, he explained to the candidates who had stood naked before each other at that pool: 'Marvellous! You were naked in the sight of all and were not ashamed! Truly you bore the image of the first formed Adam, who was naked in the garden and "was not ashamed"' (Gen. 2.25).[106]

Moving to the anointing before baptism, Cyril's explanation of this was based on a comprehensive drawing from metaphors which spoke of anointing for healing, for combat, and to produce a state of union with Christ. In terms of healing and exorcism Cyril seemed for a brief moment to be speaking of a ritual which had at least an echo in the pagan purification rites, just as the ceremony of disrobing had done. As with that ceremony, he gave it its own very Christian interpretation, which underscored the whole idea of the renunciation of Satan. He described the exorcized oil with which the ritual was performed as having the effect of dispersing 'every concentration of the cosmic forces arrayed against us'[107] but, with his next breath, he described it as on a par with the breathing of the saints and the invocation of the name of God insofar as it 'received, through prayer and the invocation of God, power so great as not only to burn and purge away the traces of sin but also to put to rout all the invisible forces of the evil one.'[108] Piédagnel noted in connection with the above phrase:

> The insufflation, which consists of a breathing upon the face of the catechumens, was one of the rites of exorcism preparatory to baptism... The "saints" are without doubt the priests who prepare them for baptism.[109]

He also referred to the use of 'breathed upon' in *Procatechesis* 9 where Cyril implied that this was an alternative to 'exorcized' within the rites of exorcism preparatory to baptism.[110] It was an exterior sign, for the candidates' benefit, of the inward work of spiritual cleansing which was being wrought within them during their catechumenate as part of an integrated programme of instruction, moral assistance, spiritual advice, and prayer. Thus, while the oil was not seen in any magical connection, with prayer it had symbolic value, and here was described as removing the 'traces of sins'. That which remained from the ravages of evil in the soul, its marks and traces, was burned away in a final pre-baptismal ceremony of purification and healing.

However, it was no good cleansing the soul to leave a spiritual vacuum, and so in the brief but concise paragraph, Cyril pointed out that the oil not only would preserve the candidate from attack by Satan, and from all hostile influence, but would also have the effect of incorporating the candidate into the life of Christ. He drew his symbolism from the use in the ceremony of olive oil, which he explained with reference to Romans 11.17–24. It was through their act of faith in Jesus Christ that the neophytes to whom Cyril was speaking had received a share in the life of Christ, being made partakers of the good olive tree, Jesus Christ.'[111] Cyril's mystagogy develops from the symbolism of the prolific olive tree in its production of oil and in its fertility. He adds material from Paul and brings a christological unity to his explanation of the prebaptismal anointing of the body.[112]

Following the final exorcism and anointing the candidates were led to the pool itself, and Cyril's explanation in his next paragraph formed an interesting comment on Romans 6.3–14, for he used the image of Christ being carried from the Cross to the Sepulchre, and in this image he certainly had a topographical advantage. He capitalized upon the fact that his lectures were held in the Rotunda of the resurrection, built upon the assumed site of the sepulchre itself. So he was able to press home the meaning of baptism as a participation in the sufferings, death, burial and resurrection of Jesus, and in particular the interpretation of the act of baptism as being buried with Christ.[113] The imagery vividly continued Cyril's concept of the mystical association of the candidate with Christ. Although Cyril touched on other aspects of baptism, his chief concern was to link the liturgical ceremony which the neophytes had experienced with the real historical event of the burial and resurrection of Christ, for this was the central plank in his mystagogical platform. He made this plain at the very beginning of his explanation, stressing the presence of the sepulchre in front of his audience.[114] Thus the stage was set for a mystagogical comparison between the actions of the candidate and those of Christ. Before the act of baptism, the candidate was required again to affirm his personal faith in God, the Father, the Son, and the Holy Spirit, and then underwent triple immersion-emersion, which Cyril explained as 'therein mystically signifying Christ's three days burial.'[115] As the candidate plunged beneath the water and came up three times, Cyril interpreted this aspect of the ceremony which the neophytes had undergone as a symbol of the three days and three nights which Christ had spent in the tomb, explaining that the nights were symbolized by the time when the head was under water, and the days symbolized by the time when the head was above the water. This interpretation also used the natural symbolism of light and darkness, and Cyril borrowed a biblical expression from Matthew, 'three days and nights in the depths of the earth' which Christ used in describing the sign of Jonah, who 'spent three days and nights in the big fish.'[116] Cyril made the choice of the explanation of the symbolism rather than the more popular Trinitarian explanation, to further the christological symbolism of the baptismal act.

Although we would expect Cyril to continue this symbolism to make the seemingly obvious parallel between coming out of the pool and resurrection, he was more concerned to explain how the candidate was actually conformed sacramentally to the death, burial, and resurrection of Christ. Cyril was well aware of the obvious interpretation, as we can see from other references to it,[117] but it is not his main concern here. His main concern here is to teach the neophytes' relationship to the sufferings of Christ, and just how the efficacy of the cross is sacramentally present in the baptismal rite.

> Let no one imagine, then, that baptism wins only the grace of remission of sins plus adoption, as John's baptism conferred only the remission of sins. No; we know full well that baptism not only washes away our sins and procures for us the gift of the Holy Spirit, but is also the antitype of the passion of Christ. That is why Paul just now proclaimed: 'Do you not know that all we who have been baptized into Christ Jesus have been baptized into his death? For through baptism we were buried along with him'. Perhaps this was directed against those who supposed that baptism procures only the remission of sins and the adoption of sons and does not, beyond this, really make us imitatively partakers of the sufferings of Christ.[118]

Although the neophytes' baptism had been only an imitative figure of Christ's real sufferings and death, Cyril taught them that it still made their salvation a reality. By their baptism they shared in the fellowship of Christ's pain, by which he vouchsafed their salvation.[119] In pursuing this argument, Cyril was crossing and recrossing the thin line between mystagogy and theology, for it is difficult to see an exact parallel between the explicit details of Christ's passion and the liturgical practice of the baptismal rite. However, we must remember that Cyril was delivering these lectures to neo-phytes with a minimal theological background. If we are mindful of this it is no surprise to find that occasionally he contradicted himself, and occasionally he was carried away with the enthusiasm of his own oratory, led on by the circumstances surrounding his lectures. The position became a little clearer in his final exposition of this relationship:

> To teach us, then, that all that Christ endured 'for us and for our salvation', he suffered in actual fact and not in mere seeming, and that we have fellowship in his passion. Paul cried aloud in unequivocal language: 'For if we have become one planting with him by the likeness of his death, we shall be one with him by the likeness of his resurrection also' (Rom. 6.5). 'One planting' is apt, for since the true vine was planted here, we, by partaking in the baptism of his death, have become 'one planting' with him. Mark closely the words of the apostle: he did not say: 'for if we have become one planting by his death,' but 'the likeness of his death'. For in the case of Christ, death was real, his soul being really separated from his body. His burial, too, was real, for his sacred body was wrapped in clean linen. In his case it all really happened. But in your case there was only a likeness of death and suffering, whereas of salvation there was no likeness but the reality.[120]

His reference to the vine provided a further example of his topographical references and he carefully used this term to describe the cross of Jesus, planted in Jerusalem where his lectures were being delivered, and drawing on Jesus's words from John 15.1–8, he used a further likeness to baptism as a symbol showing once again that the Christian was united to the cross of Jesus.

Cyril also used the symbol of the new birth of the neophyte: 'In the same moment you were dying and being born and that saving water was at once your grace and your mother.'[121] Just as baptism had brought the candidate to participate in the sufferings and death of Christ, so it also brought him to participate at the same time in the resurrection of Christ, and the new life which that promised. Thus the water was at one and the same time womb and tomb.[122] Cyril did not develop this point any further, but contented himself with pressing home to the neophytes that their baptism had conformed them to the death and resurrection of Christ.

c) *The Post-Baptismal Rites.* Cyril dealt with the rites following baptism in his third *Mystagogical Catechesis*, which was based on 1 John 2.20–28. This post-baptismal rite involved chrismation with the purpose of setting the candidates apart, just as Christ at his baptism had been set apart for God's service. He began by reminding the neophytes that the meaning of the word Christ was 'the anointed one'. Hence as the candidates by their baptism had been made 'partakers of Christ,'[123] they might properly be called God's anointed ones. This anointing had come with their reception of the Holy Ghost. As he explained, again using the mystagogical image of the association of the candidate with Christ:

> He bathed in the river Jordan and, after imparting the fragrance of his godhead to the waters, came up from them. Him the Holy Spirit visited in essential presence, like resting upon like. Similarly for you, after you had ascended from the sacred streams there was anointing with chrism, the antitype of that with which Christ was anointed, that is of the Holy Spirit.[124]

To achieve this point, Cyril developed his previous imagery to fit the current interpretation; no longer merely is the baptismal font the 'pool', as it was earlier,[125] but it has the added connotation of flowing water, becoming 'pool of sacred streams', to match the symbolism which has changed from the pool as tomb to the pool as symbol of the waters of the River Jordan. The 'type' is the coming of the Holy Spirit upon Jesus and its messianic implications, the 'antitype' to this salvific event being the chrismation of the neophyte. Cyril confirmed this mimesis theology which he had applied to this ceremony in this passage from the next paragraph:

> As Christ was really crucified and buried and rose again and you at baptism are privileged to be crucified, buried and raised along with him in a likeness, so also with the chrism. Christ was anointed with a mystical oil of gladness; that is with the Holy Spirit called 'oil of gladness'; because he is the cause of spiritual gladness; so you, being anointed with ointment have become partakers and followers of Christ.[126]

His final phrase referred back to the passage from Psalm 45.7 which Cyril had quoted earlier in this section.

Next he warned his audience against regarding the ointment as simple ointment, for after the invocation and its dedication to its sacramental use it became

> the gracious gift of Christ and the Holy Spirit, producing the advent (presence?) of his deity. With this ointment your forehead and sense organs are sacramentally anointed, in such wise that while your body is anointed with the visible oil, your soul is sanctified by the holy, quickening spirit.[127]

Cyril drew a parallel between the invocation over the bread and the invocation over the ointment, but as Riley pointed out we must avoid applying the framework of later 'transubstantiation' theology to this context.[128] Cyril's main interest here was not to explain the oil and to discuss any possible changes in its nature and substance, but rather to discuss its dynamic use in conjunction with the operation of the Holy Spirit. So, for Cyril, with the use of the sanctified ointment, the neophyte himself was sanctified as the Holy Spirit worked through the act of anointing within the sacrament of initiation. This change, wrought in the neophyte, brought about the neophyte's participation in the Anointed One himself, in the Messiah Christ.

In marked contrast to Jesus' practice when washing his disciples' feet in the Upper Room,[129] the neophytes whom Cyril addressed had been anointed on forehead, ears, nostrils, and breast. As the biblical basis for the first anointing, Cyril used 2 Corinthians 3.18 and explained that man's fall from Paradise had brought with it a sense of shame, darkening man's countenance, so that it could no longer reflect his intimate gaze of union with God. Man's sense of shame tainted his relations both with God and with his partner, and in this act of anointing on the forehead, man's sense of shame before God was removed as the gift of God's Spirit, which it represented, was restored. Once again the neophyte might fulfil his purpose, and 'so you may reflect as in a glass the splendour of the Lord.'[130]From the context of the passage which Cyril chose to illustrate this truth to the neophytes, we may conclude that he understood this effect of the Spirit to be not one single act but a process and a progress 'from glory to glory' as the neophyte developed upon his spiritual pilgrimage. Already this sense of shame before God had been removed in the neophytes' innocent nakedness before their baptism; perhaps evidence that Cyril's idea of God's work in the total sacrament of initiation took precedence over his idea of God's activity in any particular section of the sacrament.

The anointing of the ears was explained by Cyril in two verses from scripture.[132] The first dealt with the communication of the divine message to the Servant of YHWH, and Cyril used this to illustrate the need for neophytes' ears to be awakened to receive the spiritual message which God sought to communicate with them. The second passage came from a quotation of the Lord regarding the preaching of the kingdom and thus implied the transmission of the truths revealed by God. Thus the coming of the Spirit, symbolized by the anointing of the ears, brought with it the spiritual awareness that made the neophytes learn and transmit the message of the kingdom.

The anointing of the nostrils made the neophytes aware that through the sweet smelling fragrance of the oil they were participating in Christ himself.

Finally the anointing of the breast was used by Cyril to teach the neophytes that they had put on 'the breastplate of righteousness'[133] and was symbolic of the whole armour of God which Paul described in his passage and which had its roots in the Isaianic passage[134] describing the virtues and characteristics of the coming Messiah King. So the Christian after his baptism and because of his incorporation into Christ was similarly armed for the fight secure in the knowledge that 'I can do all things in the Christ who strengthens me.'[135]

Thus each separate element in the act of anointing was explained by Cyril in terms of the equipment of the new Christian as an apostolic instrument. He was sent out, renewed in fellowship with God. As Riley concluded: 'God's kingdom, restored in Christ, and communicated to the neophytes through the anointing of the Spirit of Christ, must now manifest itself in a dynamic way, interacting with the forces in the world opposed to it, until it reaches its full growth and maturity.'[136] Coupled with this anointing, the neophytes were now called 'Christians', having been initiated into Christianity by the rites which culminated in their Chrismation.[137]

Cyril then drew parallels with the anointing of Aaron and of Solomon in the Old Testament, and reminded his hearers that these happened in a figure, but to the new Christians they happened in truth because of their anointing by the Holy Ghost. He then used the analogy of Christ's holiness as the First-fruit so that his holiness could be passed on to the whole as the yeast passed on its life to the dough.[138]

It remained, however, the duty of the new Christian to lead a good life, unspotted by sin and unsullied by temptations, as Cyril reminded them: 'Anointed then with this holy oil, keep it in you unsullied, without blame making progress through good work and becoming well-pleasing to "the trail blazer of our salvation" Christ Jesus, to whom be glory for ever and ever, Amen.'[139]

Much of the remainder of the *Mystagogical Catecheses* were devoted to the Eucharist and the Lord's Prayer, but when referring to a passage which he ascribed to Solomon,[140] Cyril referred to the new post-baptismal garments of the neophytes thus:

> Now that you have put off your old garments and put on those which are spiritually white, you must go clad in white all your days. I do not, of course, mean that your ordinary clothes must always be white, but that you must be clad in those true, spiritual garments which are white and shining. Then you will be able to say with the blessed Isaiah: 'Let my soul rejoice in the Lord; for he has dressed me in the garments of salvation, and with the robe of gladness he has clothed me' (Isa. 61.10 *LXX*)[141]

The white garment had connotations of purity and of joy, and had a distinct eschatological significance. The life of the Christian was to reflect the purity and joy of the coming kingdom of Christ. This formed a further extension of the idea of the Christian being one with the resurrected Christ following his baptism. As Cyril pointed out, it referred back and provided the antithesis for the removal of the garments before baptism, and although he did not make plain whether the new baptismal robe was donned, he was still quite clear that the white robe was an expressive symbol of the event of rising with Christ. As he used the phrase 'having put on Christ' as a link sentence between his second and this *Mystagogical Catecheses*, it may well be that the baptismal robe was donned by the neophytes immediately following their emergence from the waters of baptism. Cyril's explanation also had distinct eschatological connotations, symbolizing the robe of gladness and the sign of the consummation of life. Thus the life of the Christian, because of its association with the resurrection of Jesus, should reflect the purity and joy of the coming kingdom. It went beyond the imagery of the garment in the

Procatechesis, which Cyril saw in terms of readiness for baptism, but saw rather the life of the neophyte at one with Christ, living under the sign of the *eschaton* (last things) to which the risen life, symbolized by the baptismal garment, tended in the Christian.

We move some 300 miles north to Antioch, and to the place where the followers of Jesus were first called Christians, to consider the material provided by John Chrysostom.

2

John Chrysostom and the Church at Antioch

John Chrysostom was born about AD 347 in Antioch, just a year or two before Cyril gave his lectures to his candidates in Jerusalem. John Chrysostom spent much of his life in Antioch, where he trained as an orator. His reputation as an orator followed him into the Church after his baptism as an adult Christian in 370. Shortly afterwards he abandoned the world to take up the study of scripture as both monk and hermit. Over-enthusiastic fasting and the rigours of his enforced solitude undermined his health, and forced him to return to Antioch where, in 386, he was ordained to the priesthood. He served the church under Bishop Flavian as an exegete, preacher, and moralist until 397, when he was elevated to the patriarchate of Constantinople. This was an unhappy appointment, for although Chrysostom was spiritually an acceptable candidate, he lacked the worldly wisdom to avoid making powerful enemies among the hierarchy and at court. This resulted in his deposition in 403, his exile in 404, and his death on 14 September 407.

The catechetical material which has been discovered and collated, much of it only in this century, comes from the time of his priesthood in Antioch under Bishop Flavian. It seems highly likely that the material which we have was originally from two different Lenten periods, as will appear below. So in Antioch the catechetical lecturer was not the bishop, as he seems to have been in Jerusalem, but the task was delegated to the one who was probably the most able candidate for the job. The character of the lectures too is more a pastoral than a definitive exposition of the faith, and he seems less concerned with denouncing heretics than with combating the temptations of the hippodrome. For the purpose of this study, reference will be made only to the following material[1] of an

23

overtly catechetical nature:

a) Two lectures edited by Abbé Montfaucon.[2]

b) However the first Montfaucon lecture has now been reunited with the remainder of the series of four lectures, following the discovery and publication of lectures 2, 3 and 4 by A. Papadopoulos-Kerameus in 1909 in an obscure Russian series from the then University of St Petersburg, since reprinted in Leipzig.[3]

c) The *Stavronikita* series, discovered and published by Antoine Wenger in 1955.[4]

This latter series is similar to the other two series in that it has a mystagogical content, and explains the ritual leading up to the bath of regeneration. It is also different from them in that it includes five post-baptismal lectures delivered during Easter week. The structure varies accordingly, and the pre-baptismal lectures are reduced to two, one at the beginning of the period of instruction and the other at the end. The third Instruction was given on Holy Saturday night after the candidate had been baptized and communicated, and this instruction is also included as *P-K* 4. The last five lectures are designed to impart moral instruction to the newly-illumined, and to give them what Harkins describes as 'a concrete initiation into the Christian way of life.'[5] The moral aspect of Christian living predominates in these lectures, and Chrysostom's teaching reflects his own experience and his own mentality: 'hence he leads the catechumens along the path of asceticism and progress in virtue rather than into speculative consideration on the articles of faith. For him there was no purpose in receiving baptism if one had not first purified the eyes of the soul for the reception of the divine illumination.'[6]

1. *The Theology of Baptism and its Catechetical Explanation*

Chrysostom in his homilies, particularly those given to baptismal candidates, normally used simple and vivid imagery. From his first homily in the Montfaucon series we find a list of titles of baptism with supporting texts so that he could build up a composite dramatic picture of baptism for the candidate, featuring not only the act of baptism but the spiritual effects which they might expect it to have:

This cleansing is called the bath of regeneration. He saves us, says

St Paul through the bath of regeneration and renewal by the Holy Spirit. It is also called an enlightenment, and again it is St Paul who calls it this. But call to mind the days gone by, in which, after you had been enlightened, you endured a great conflict of sufferings. And again: For it is impossible for those who were once enlightened, and who have tasted the heavenly gift and then have fallen away, to be renewed again to repentance. It is also called baptism. For all you who have been baptized into Christ, have put on Christ. It is called a burial. For you were buried, says St Paul, with him by means of baptism into death. It is called a circumcision. In him, too you have been circumcised with a circumcision not wrought by hand but through putting off the body of sinful flesh. It is called a cross. For our old self has been crucified with him, in order that the old body of sin may be destroyed.[7]

These titles make a useful framework to begin our consideration of the theology of baptism evident from these homilies.

Describing it first as the bath of regeneration, he supported this by reference to Titus 3.5, and went on to develop this idea in the next few paragraphs.[8] First he contrasted the efficacy of the 'bath of the Jews' with the 'bath of grace.'[9] He taught his candidates that their forthcoming baptism would completely transform their lives, and make their spiritual rebirth evident:

> And why, someone will say, if the bath takes away all our sins, is it not called the bath of the remission of sins, or the bath of cleansing, rather than the bath of regeneration? The reason is that it does not simply remit our sins, nor does it simply cleanse us of our faults, but it does this just as if we were born anew. For it does create us anew and it fashions us again, not moulding us from earth, but creating us from a different element, the nature of water.[10]

Although the baptism of John the Baptist was superior to that of the Jews, it was much less than the sacrament his candidates were to receive, and it served to link the 'bath of the Jews' with the 'bath of grace'. John's baptism did not give the Holy Spirit, nor did it provide forgiveness through grace. It enjoined penance following repentance but could not forgive sins. Then he explained that the baptism of the Jews was abrogated by the institution of the sacrament of baptism by the Lord.

> Where there is the dignity of adoption, there is also the removal of evil and the granting of all good things. On that account the

Jewish baptism ceases and ours begins; what occurred at the Pasch now occurs in baptism. After he had celebrated both Paschs, he abrogated the old and gave a beginning to the new; here again, after he fulfilled the baptism of the Jews, he opens the doors of the Church's baptism at the same time.[11]

However, the 'bath of grace' accomplished the regeneration of its recipients without the conception, gestation, and labour periods of a human birth, and when addressing the neophytes following their baptism, Chrysostom commented: 'See how many children this spiritual mother has brought forth suddenly and in a single night! But we must not be surprised. Spiritual child-bearing is such that it needs neither time nor a period of months.'[12] In this process of regeneration, it was plain that the baptized has the Church for his spiritual mother, and Christ for his father. The regeneration of the Christian came from Christ's uniting to himself his bride.[13]

In the *Stavronikita* series, much of his imagery is matrimonial and so there is little surprise when he pointed out to his listeners that no man would ever have poured out his blood for the woman who was going to be his bride:

> But the kindly Master imitating his own goodness, has accepted this great and marvellous sacrifice because of his solicitude for her, that by his own blood he might sanctify her; that, having cleansed her by the bath of baptism, he might present her to himself a Church in all her glory. To this end he poured forth his blood and endured the cross, that through this he might freely give sanctification to us too, and might cleanse us through the bath of regeneration, and might present to himself those who before were in dishonour and unable to speak with confidence, but now are glorious, without spot or wrinkle, or any such thing.[14]

He also reminded the baptized that Christ has made them a new creation as the grace of God entered their souls, moulded them anew, and made them different from what they were.[15] In this he was alluding to what he had said to the candidates when describing the baptismal rites: 'Instead of the man who descended into the water, a different man comes forth, one who has wiped away all the filth of his sins, who has put off the old garment of sin and has put on the royal robe.'[16] So extensive was the transformation effected by the bath of regeneration that the person who was baptized was different, literally 'one person instead of another', as his will was made over into the possession of God.

> It did not change their substance, but made over their will, no longer permitting the tribunal of the mind's eyes to entertain an erroneous notion, but by dissipating the mist which was blinding their eyes, God's grace made them see the ugly deformity of evil and virtue's shining beauty as they truly are.[17]

However fine this may sound, Chrysostom makes it plain that he is speaking 'in theory' and that in spite of the spiritual event of baptism, the will can still sometimes be opposed to God, and so he exhorts his audience:

> I exhort you, therefore, both you who have previously been initiated and you who have just now enjoyed the Master's generosity, let us all listen to the exhortation of the apostle, who tells us: The former things have passed away; behold, they are all made new. Let us forget the whole past and, like citizens in a new world, let us reform our lives, and let us consider in our every word and deed the dignity of him who dwells within us.[18]

For even new creatures, regenerated through baptism, have to make an effort after baptism, as he pointed out in the Montfaucon series, where he refers to faith as a matter of trust;

> He has commanded you, too, to do this as far as you can in the things which have been entrusted to you – to increase the sanctity which you have received, to render more shining your justice after the bath, and to make your grace more lustrous, just as Paul did, who, by his subsequent toils and zeal and eagerness, increased all the blessings he had received.[19]

Chrysostom further illustrates the aspect of baptismal regeneration by using the analogy of the smelting furnace which not only cleansed the gold placed in it, but made it new too. Whilst other baptisms could not remove the stain of sin, the bath of regeneration could return a life shining even more brightly than the old:

> This bath does not merely cleanse the vessel but melts the whole thing down again. Even if a vessel has been wiped off and carefully cleansed, it still has the marks of what it is and still bears the traces of the stain. But when it is thrown into the smelting furnace and is renewed by the flames, it puts aside all dross and, when it comes from the furnace, it gives forth the same sheen as newly-moulded vessels. When a man takes and melts down a gold

27

statue which has become filthy with the filth of years and smoke and dirt and rust, he returns it to us all-clean and shining. So, too, God takes this nature of ours when it is rusted with the rust of sin, when our faults have covered it with abundant soot, and when it has destroyed the beauty he put into it in the beginning, and he smelts it anew. He plunges it into the waters as into the smelting furnace and lets the grace of the Spirit fall on it instead of the flames. He then brings us forth from the furnace, renewed like newly-moulded vessels, to rival the rays of the sun with out brightness. He has broken the old man to pieces but has produced a new man who shines brighter than the old.[20]

He was then reminded of the analogy in the Psalms and Jeremiah[21] of the potter's vessel, and used this analogy to teach the catechumens that, once their nature was renewed, even if they were to slip and fall prey to temptation, the vessel was of raw clay, not of fired terracotta, and so it could be restored to its former state by God through sincere repentance. 'It is possible for God not only to correct us through the bath of regeneration, since we are clay, but also after we have received the working of the Spirit and then have slipped, he can lead us back through sincere repentance to our former state.'[22] After baptism Chrysostom specifically excluded the remission of sins by a new baptism but realistically he offered the baptizands a subsequent remission of sins after the bath of regeneration. He was less clear on the details of the manner of this subsequent remission of sins, but suggested that confession to God, repentance, tears, prayers, and almsgiving were means which could win the Christian pardon for sins.[23]

The next name he gave to describe baptism is 'an enlightenment', the point at which Cyril began his lectures, but unfortunately, the preacher in Chrysostom took over, and he was sidetracked from his syllabus after quoting Hebrews 10.32 and Hebrews 6.4–6 in support of his statement. He was sidetracked by the constraint which he felt to warn his hearers against the evils of the sins of speech and particularly the habit of swearing. Perhaps this tells us something about the differences in emphasis placed upon morality and philosophy by Chrysostom and Cyril. When preaching to a congregation of newly baptized and established Christians during Easter Week he cited the example of Paul who was 'baptized and illumined by the light of truth,'[24] and exhorted his congregation to 'be eager to make brighter by good deeds the light within us – I mean the grace of the Spirit – so that it is never quenched, we shall enjoy the title of newly baptized for all time.'[25] Illumination for Chrysostom was that which after baptism led the Christian towards a virtuous lifestyle, as he made plain in his instructions to the neophytes:

> Did you see how he urges us to let the light within us shine forth not by garments but by deeds? After he said: Let your light shine, he added: in order that they may see your good works. This light does not stop with the bodily senses but illumines the soul and understanding of those who see it; after it dispels the darkness of evil, it draws those who find it to shine with their own light and to imitate the life of virtue.[26]

Although Chrysostom was in no doubt that illumination and enlightenment came through baptism, he tends to associate illumination rather more closely with the baptismal robe, and the witness of the quality of life of the Christian after baptism, than with the baptism itself.[27] However he did link light with justification in the context of faith in Christ:

> By this he showed in brief that those who, by their faith in Christ, had put off like an old cloak the burden of their sins, those who had been set free from their error and been illumined by the light of justification, had put on this new and shining cloak, this royal robe. This is why he said: If any man is in Christ, he is a new creature: the former things have passed away; behold, they are all made new.[28]

But primarily light and illumination was provided for the Christian, Chrysostom felt, so that light might attract others to Christ, rather than the Christian be especially enlightened in rational terms.

His third descriptive name was 'baptism' and for this he cited Galatians 3.27.

On the other side of the coin to his description of the mystic cleansing of the rite as a bath of regeneration, came his next title, in which he described it as a burial, and in support of this he cited Romans 6.4. This tied in with a statement in *Stavronikita* 2 that 'baptism is a burial and a resurrection.'[29] It was also linked with his final definition in a section of the *Papadopoulos-Kerameus* series which was headed by the editor 'Baptism is a Cross, Death and Resurrection.'[30] In this passage Chrysostom dealt in more detail with the surrounding verses from Romans 6, and continued his explanation of the titles promised in *Montfaucon* I. He amplified his teaching on Romans 6 in his commentary on Romans.[31] Romans 6 recalled to his mind the incident involving Jesus and the mother of the sons of Zebedee in which Jesus referred to his cross and passion as a baptism:

> How, then, did Christ answer? Can you drink of the cup of which I am about to drink, and be baptized with the baptism with which I am baptized? You see that he called the cross a baptism. How is this clear? Can you drink, he says, of the cup of which I am about to drink? He calls his passion a cup and on this account he says: Father, if it is possible, let this cup pass away from me. Did you see how he called the cross a baptism and the passion a cup?[32]

He then proceeded to remind his listeners of Paul's words in Romans 6 and stressed the immediate nature of baptism as death, burial, and resurrection: 'For in baptism there are both burial and resurrection together at the same time. He who is baptized puts off the old man, takes the new, and rises up, just as Christ has arisen through the glory of the Father. Do you see how, again, St Paul calls baptism a resurrection'[33] But such an immediate transformation needed to issue in a radical alteration in the baptizand's moral behaviour, for death to sin had to be a once and for all thing which meant that the baptized 'have nothing to do with the passion of the flesh and the affairs of the world.'[34] Chrysostom then counselled his congregation of those baptized:

> For your old self, he says, has been crucified and buried through baptism. Therefore, get for yourself none of the things that are on earth, and be not active in the affairs of the present life. For your life is hidden now and unseen by those who do not believe, but the time will come when it will be seen. But now is not your time. Since you have died once and for all, refuse to mind the things that are on earth. The greatness of your virtue is plainly seen especially when you have prevailed over the arrogance of the flesh and act toward the good things of the world just as if you were dead to this life.[35]

Those who were dead to sin and Satan's power had nothing to fear in the combat with Satan, which Chrysostom graphically described in terms of their post-baptismal life. He taught them that they were equipped for their struggle against Satan, and he used that element of the service which involved the candidate in shedding his clothes as the basis of the metaphor in which the Christian stripped for the combat against Satan, the opponent in the boxing bout and the fight.[36] Also from the elements of the rite, Chrysostom took the profession, in opposition to the renunciation, for it was the positive side of the contract which the baptized was making with Christ. In this he was in parallel with Cyril and Theodore. The verbal act of renunciation and confession for Chrysostom supplanted and made void the previous contract which man had with Satan, and this new profession was seen as coming into force at this point in the baptismal rite:

> We confessed his sovereignty; we rejected the domination of the devil. This was the signature, this the agreement, this the contract.
> See to it that we do not again become debtors to the old contract. Christ came once; he found the certificate of our ancestral indebtedness which Adam wrote and signed. Adam contracted the debt; by our subsequent sins we increased the amount owed. In this contract are written a curse, and sin, and death, and the condemnation of the law. Christ took all these away and pardoned them.[37]

So with the life that the Christian left behind and buried in baptism, he left also his bondage to Satan, and began to live his resurrected life in the power and commitment to Christ.

In his list of the titles of baptism, Chrysostom next referred to it as a circumcision, citing Colossians 2.11 to support his statement. However, he did not develop this title further in these lectures, but in two series of expository sermons there appear passages relating baptism and circumcision.[38] These make it plain that he saw baptism as the physical sign of the new covenant between Christ and his Church.

As we have seen, Chrysostom was very easily deflected from his declared outline, perhaps evidence that he preached from brief notes rather than a fully prepared text. His list of the names of baptism was not inclusive, and we shall now consider other descriptions of baptism which emanate from elsewhere. Probably Chrysostom's most frequently used descriptive term for baptism was 'the gift', and often he used this term to imply the act of baptism without actually using the term baptism. His preference for 'the gift' carries us into the very heart of his baptismal theology and indicates strongly his understanding of the saving work of Christ, of which baptism was a symbol, as an act of grace, completely unmerited and unearned by man, even though, as recipients of the gift, the baptized had their own responsibility to continue to live a life worthy of those in receipt of such a gift of God. Such a lavish gift had to be received worthily, and he scathingly contrasted those baptized on their deathbeds with his congregation in terms of their reception of the gracious gift of God:

> Even if the grace is the same for you and for those who are initiated on their deathbeds, neither the choice nor the preparations are the same. They receive baptism in their beds, but you receive it in the bosom of the common mother of us all, the Church; they receive baptism amidst laments and tears, but you are baptized with rejoicing and gladness; they are groaning, while you are giving thanks; filled with an abundance of spiritual pleasure. So in your case everything befits the gift, while in their case everything is opposed to it. For the dying man weeps and laments as he is baptized, his children stand about in tears, his wife mars her cheeks with her nails, his friends are downcast, his servants' eyes well with tears, and the whole house gives the appearance of a gloomy winter's day.[39]

The first theological point that this conception of baptism as gift led him to emphasize was that, although baptism was administered by human hands, it was really the act of God himself. He interpreted Jesus' baptism by John in the Jordan as a baptism by each member of the Trinity, by the Word which led Jesus into the water, by the Father as he spoke the words, 'This is my beloved Son', and by the manifestation of the Holy Spirit which descended upon him in the form of a dove. Similarly, for the candidates, baptism was given in the name of the Father, and of the Son, and of the Holy Spirit:

> For this reason, when the priest is baptizing he does not say, 'I baptize so-and-so', but, 'So-and-so is baptized in the name of the Father and of the Son and of the Holy Spirit'. In this way he shows that it is not he who baptizes but whose names have been invoked, the Father, the Son and the Holy Spirit.'[40]

Similarly, it was part of the grace of God for the believers to be equal before God. God gave the gifts in accordance with his gracious will alone, with no relation to merit or desert, so that the spiritual gifts with the baptized received gave no right either to boast about superiority, or to wallow in inferiority:

> all these gifts are given to all of you in common, so that the rich man may not look down on the poor man, nor the poor man consider that he has any less than the rich man; for in Christ Jesus there is neither male nor female, there is no Scythian, nor barbarian, no Jew, no Greek; not only is there no difference of age or nature, but even every difference of honour is cancelled out; there is one esteem for all, one gift, one brotherhood, binding us together, the same grace — so then, when you have all been led into (the Church) then must you all together bend your knee and not stand erect; you must stretch your hands to heaven and thank God for this gift.[41]

Thus Chrysostom interpreted Paul's words in Galatians 3.28 to suggest that even differences in honour were cancelled out in Christ, through the gracious gift of baptism. By baptism the believer received the forgiveness of his sins, and also was allowed the privacy of confessing his sins in a private encounter with God: 'But this is ... the case in baptism. God forgives our sins and does not force us to make a parade of them in the presence of others. He seeks one thing only: that he who benefits by the forgiveness may learn the greatness of the gift.'[42] The consideration of the gracious goodness of God should always be part of the Christian's countenance. He told the catechumens beginning their course of proximate instruction for baptism to prepare beforehand to abstain from evil deeds, and to do good.[43] Such a gracious invitation from the Master to those who would never be able to earn such a gift for themselves, so affected the lives and lifestyle of those who benefit from it that Chrysostom reminded that same group of catechumens after their baptism: 'Since we have benefited from so great a gift, let us show abundant zeal, and let us remember the contract we have made with him.'[44]

In a subsequent lecture he linked the gift of the Holy Spirit with the baptismal act, describing the newly baptized as those 'who have just been judged worthy of the gift of the Spirit.'[45] However, he was quite prepared to admit that even rhetoric could not fully express the grace of God evident through baptism, as he indicated when addressing the neophytes following their baptism: 'If there is joy in heaven over one sinner who repents, much more fitting is it for us to exult and rejoice over so large a throng, and to glorify God in his kindness for this gift of his which defies description.'[46] Later Chrysostom indicated the need to guard such a valuable gift[47] by maintaining a life of integrity and virtue and a life free from the stain of post-baptismal sin, and he suggested that one of the purposes of maintaining a guard upon the gift of baptismal regeneration symbolized by the baptismal robe was to display the greatness of the gift to others.[48]

At other times Chrysostom referred to the same concept of God's undeserved gift given in baptism in terms of the grace of baptism. On these occasions he had in mind God's gracious act in granting grace to catechumens before their baptism:

> In this knowledge, then, my beloved, make yourselves ready to receive this grace with joy and gladness of the spirit, that you may enjoy the abundant benefits of this gift. May all of us together, by making our conduct worthy of the grace, deserve to receive eternal and ineffable gifts by the grace and love of our Lord Jesus Christ.[49]

Once again, in the light of such grace on God's part, the least the candidates could do was to respond to the grace of God by seeking to live a life worthy of such grace. However, Chrysostom was aware that this would not be easy, and he reminded his audience that the cure for sins could be a wound for them:

> For the bath can do away with sins previously committed; but there is no small fear nor insignificant danger that we may fall again into the same sins, and then the cure becomes a wound for us. For those who sin after baptism the punishment is proportioned to the greatness of the grace we received in it.[50]

He insisted that there must be a genuine desire and sincere intention for repentance shown in the exorcisms and at baptism. For Chrysostom there was no such thing as faith without works, and there had to be a desire to accomplish in the outward and visible life what God had already accomplished in the inward and spiritual realm at baptism. As we saw above,[51] Chrysostom took the picture of gold fired in the furnace to illustrate the regenerative aspect of baptism.[52] In the *Stavronikita* series he used a similar concept to encourage the catechumens to enjoy the title of newly-baptized for all time.[53]

An allied concept to that of baptismal grace was that of 'the kindness' of baptism, an expression which Chrysostom used in

Stavronikita 1 and *Montfaucon* 2. In the former this was within the context of his analogy of baptism with a marriage, contrasting the wealth of the bridegroom with the poverty of the bride.

> Let me give you, too, a glimpse of the bridegroom's exceeding wealth and of the ineffable kindness which he shows to his bride. Let me point out to her the sordid past from which she is escaping and the glorious future she is about to enjoy. And if you wish, let us first strip from her her garb and see the condition in which she is. Despite her plight, the bridegroom still allows her to come to him. This clearly shows us the boundless kindness of our common Master. He does not have her come to him as his bride because he has longed for her comeliness, or her beauty, or the bloom of her body. On the contrary, the bride he has brought into the nuptial chamber is deformed and ugly, thoroughly and shamefully sordid, and, practically, wallowing in the very mire of her sins.[54]

He highlighted the ineffable kindness of the bridegroom by sparing no blushes in his description of the bride – deformed, ugly, thoroughly and shamefully sordid, and practically wallowing in the very mire of her sins. Although the text is damaged here, there cannot be much doubt as to Chrysostom's meaning on the basis of the context of what he was saying. He developed his analogy making it quite plain to his candidates that they were the doomed bride in terms of the reception and acceptance of the bride by the bridegroom:

> But when the good master saw his bride in such a plight and swept down into what I might call the very abyss of wickedness, naked and unseemly, he considered neither her ugliness, nor her utter poverty, nor the enormity of her evils, but he manifested his own surpassing kindness and received her into his presence.[55]

He pointed out that the bridegroom was demonstrating his kindness by requiring no accounting for the bride's offences, nor did he exact judgement, but only urged her to accept his exhortation and remonstrance, and encouraged her to forget the past. He took up this theme again in *Montfaucon* 2 describing God's forgiveness of sins and God's discretion in that act of forgiveness of not forcing man to make public his sins as an act of kindness to man: 'When he shows us his kindness, he is satisfied to have us alone as witnesses.'[56] Thus in baptism God's kindness was plainly demonstrated for all to see, both in receiving the candidates, and graciously and kindly granting them forgiveness of their sins and newness of life.

As we have just seen, Chrysostom used the analogy of baptism as a spiritual marriage, a union between Christ and the candidate;[57] and this was one of his favourite pictures. He began the *Stavronikita* series by telling his catechumens:

> This is a time for joy and gladness of the spirit. Behold, the days of our longing and love, the days of your spiritual marriage, are close at hand. To call what takes place today a marriage would be no blunder; not only could we call it a marriage but even a marvellous and most unusual kind of military enlistment. Nor does any contradiction exist between marriage and military service.[58]

Harkins in his notes points out the differences between fourth-century matrimonial practice and that of the twentieth century.[59] No wedding of course, would be complete without the bridal gown and the wedding breakfast, and in this analogy the same was true, as Chrysostom exhorted his candidates to maintain after baptism the lifestyle which they had begun at their spiritual marriage:

> This is why, in my fear of the enemy's tricks, I am continually exhorting you to keep the marriage robe in its integrity, that with it you may enter forever into this spiritual marriage. And what takes place here is a spiritual marriage. Just as in marriage between man and woman the bridal feast is prolonged for seven days see how we too extend for the same number of days your bridal feast, setting before you the table of the mysteries, filled with good things beyond number. And why did I say seven days? If you are willing to live soberly and keep vigilant, this banquet is prolonged for you through all time, provided that you keep your bridal robe inviolate and radiant.
>
> For in this way you will draw the bridegroom to a fuller love and you yourselves will shine forth with increasing radiance and lustre as time goes on, because grace increases more and more with the good deeds we do.[60]

Providing the neophyte was prepared to conduct himself soberly and to remain vigilant against the tricks of the enemy there was no reason why he might not keep the bridal robe bright for all times. Wenger points out in this note: 'Still as I have said many times already, sobriety of spirit is the most important condition of all'.[61]

Chrysostom employed this analogy of a spiritual marriage in the *Papadopoulos-Kerameus* series, using in his third address in this series, probably given on Holy Thursday, material very similar to that which he developed later in *Stavronikita* 1. Speaking of the profession of the candidate to the bridegroom he said:

> Therefore, remember these words. They are your contract with the bridegroom. It is necessary, before a marriage, to complete an account of the gifts and the dowry; you too must do so before this marriage. He found you naked and a beggar, behaving in an unseemly manner, but he did not run away; you were the one who had to choose. Instead of a dowry, contribute these words, and Christ will consider that the wealth you bring is great – if you will keep and observe these words through all your life. For Christ finds his wealth in the salvation of our souls.[62]

However, in *Montfaucon* 2, the analogy seemed to change to that used by Cyril of the wedding guest who refused to dress appropriately for the wedding.[63] Chrysostom suggested that the candidate had been invited to a spiritual wedding and a royal banquet: 'But you have been invited to a spiritual wedding and a royal banquet; consider, then, what sort of a wedding garment you should buy, because he who has invited you gives you the garment as a gift, so that you cannot offer poverty as an excuse.'[64] Still, however, the emphasis was upon the gracious benevolence of the host, who not only invited those who were poor and ill-clad, but made arrangements for their clothing.

Following on from his spiritual marriage analogy, it was natural that he should see some form of kinship between those who are spiritually married to Christ through baptism. In the homily addressed to the neophytes after baptism he spoke in these terms:

> My dearly beloved brothers – if I may call you my brothers – it is true that I share with you the same birth, but by my later negligence I destroyed the true perfection of our kinship. Nonetheless, let me call you brothers because of my great love, and let me urge you to show a great zeal to match the great honour bestowed on you.[65]

Similarly he addressed them in this manner in anticipation at the beginning of *Montfaucon* 1.

Chrysostom reminded his audience of the honour and dignity of baptism:

Should you not see to it that you deserve such reverence, inasmuch as you are about to acquit so great a dignity? And this is a great dignity. It coextends with the present life and the life you will live together hereafter. What is this dignity? Henceforth through the kindness of God, you will be called a Christian and one of the faithful. There is not one dignity here, but two. Soon you will put on Christ. You must act and deliberate in all things with the knowledge that he is everywhere with you.[66]

Once this dignity was conferred upon the neophytes, God intended it to be permanent. Chrysostom told them that nobody could take away the gifts and the dignity that God has bestowed upon them unless they themselves permitted it. He contrasted the earthly king, who had power to take away any honour he gave, with God:

> For whenever someone obtains some dignity from an earthly king, to take it away does not lie in the will of him who received, but the one who offers the honour also has the power to take it away; when he wishes, he strips the recipient of his honour, releases him from his office, and immediately makes him a private citizen again. In the case of our king, it is altogether different. Once the dignity has been given to us through his kindness – I mean such honours as sonship by adoption, sanctity, the grace of the Spirit – no one will ever be able to take these things away from us, unless we grow lax. What do I mean, 'take away'? If he sees that we are well disposed, he supplements what he has already bestowed on us and, according to the great honour which is ours, he will increase the gifts he has given.[67]

On the contrary, the honour and the dignity which God gave could grow, and the gifts develop as they had done with Paul, Chrysostom pointed out.[68]

John Chrysostom's somewhat rambling style makes analysis of his baptismal teaching difficult, but I have attempted above to draw out the highlights of his baptismal theology as it is to be found in his catechetical material. From that we move on to consider his explanation of the liturgy of baptism.

2. *The Liturgy of Baptism and its Mystagogical Explanation*[69]

a) *The Rite of Renunciation and Profession*: The rite began for the candidates on Good Friday afternoon at three o'clock,[70] when they were led into the church by the priests.[71] The candidates were instructed to kneel down and stretch out their hands towards heaven.[72] Then the bishop himself[73] approached each kneeling candidate individually,[74] and prepared each candidate to recite his personal act of renunciation of Satan and then his profession of adherence to Christ.[75] Answering the question of the bishop, the candidate said: 'I renounce you, Satan, your pomps, your service, and your works,'[76] and then made his profession of allegiance to Christ, as he said: 'And I enter your service, O Christ.'[77] Following this commitment, the candidate was anointed on the forehead 'with the spiritual unguent,'[78] which was a mixture of olive oil and unguent.[79] The anointing was made in the sign of the cross with the apersonal formula: 'So-and-so is anointed in the name of the Father, of the Son and of the Holy Spirit.'[80]

Chrysostom saw this liturgy as a drama to be interpreted from the standpoint of salvation-history, and added a number of descriptive phrases to help build up the dramatic effect, and to heighten the candidates' emotional appreciation of the rite. he described the act of renunciation and profession as awesome and frightening.[81] He suggested the presence of angels at the scene who inscribed the words from the tongues of candidates in the heavenly books.[82] He described the candidates as quivering with fear at the thought of renouncing Satan,[83] whom he vividly describes as a roaring lion,[84] enraged and frenzied, as the candidates are signed with the mark of the cross.[85] He imagined the candidates being led into the arena by the priests as athletes of Christ to engage in the combat with Satan.[86] His chief biblical vehicle for conveying the drama of salvation-history to his audience was to use the Exodus as a type, just as Cyril had done.[87] The miracle of the Exodus story was repeated on a greater scale:

> The Jews saw miracles. Now you shall see greater and much more brilliant ones than those seen when the Jews went forth from Egypt. You did not see the Pharaoh and his armies drowned, but you did see the drowning of the devil and his armies. The Jews passed through the sea; you have passed through the sea of death. They were delivered from the Egyptians: you are set free from the demon. They put aside their servitude to barbarians; you have set aside the far more hazardous servitude to sin.[88]

Earlier in this homily he spoke of the power of the blood of Christ, delivering the new people of God, just as the blood of the paschal lamb had delivered the Jewish people from the angel of death. So the blood of Christ strengthened and protected those who had to make the frightening renunciation of Satan:

> Today, will the devil not check himself all the more if he sees, not the blood of the type smeared on the doors, but the blood of the truth smeared on the mouths of the faithful, since these mouths have become doors of a temple which holds Christ? If the angel stood in awe when he saw the type, much more likely is it that the devil will flee when he sees the truth.[89]

Having set this act of renunciation and profession in its context of salvation-history, Chrysostom used the bodily movements of the candidates to develop his teaching further and he explained these elements as participation in the act of conversion. Chrysostom's candidates made the act of renunciation and profession in a kneeling position. He saw in the gesture of kneeling the fact that the baptizand was in bondage to Satan:

> Those who endure captivity of the body show by their posture their dejection at the disaster which has overcome them. So, too, when the devil's captives are about to be set free from his domination and to come under the yoke of goodness, they first remind themselves of their prior condition by their external attitude. They do this that they may be able to know from what evil they are being delivered and to what good they are hurrying, and that this very knowledge may be the foundation for greater gratitude and may make their souls even more than well disposed.[90]

This posture of kneeling was not only a sign of slavery to Satan, but it was also a sign of confessing the absolute rule of Christ, and he cited Philippians 2.10 to support his argument. Thus, at the same time, the posture of kneeling suggests the transfer of the Christian from enslavement to Satan to the Lordship of Christ. The fact that all were kneeling reminded Chrysostom of oneness with Christ. He interpreted this in terms of Galatians 3.28,[91] applying Paul's commentary on baptism, and making a sociological point of the equality and fraternity which came as a direct result of acknowledging Christ as Lord. The arms outstretched to heaven further strengthened the meaning of the kneeling posture in connection with the conversion of the candidate from servitude to Satan to obedience to Christ. The outstretched arms reminded the candidates from what evil they had been delivered and to what good they would dedicate themselves,[92] and were a sign of thankfulness to God for the gift of faith.[93]

Chrysostom does not specifically mention the direction the candidates faced for the renunciation and the direction they faced for the profession, but he drew the same symbol as Cyril out of the time-scale of these acts:

> Tomorrow, on Friday at the ninth hour, you must have certain questions asked of you and you must present your contracts to the Master. Nor do I make mention to you of that day and that hour without some purpose. A mystical lesson can be learned from them. For on Friday at the ninth hour the thief entered paradise; the darkness, which lasted from the sixth to the ninth hour, was dissolved; and the Light, perceived by body and mind, was taken up as a sacrifice for the whole world. For at that hour Christ said: Father, into thy hands I commend my spirit. Then the sun we see looked on the Sun of Justice shining from the cross and turned back its own rays.
>
> Therefore, when you are about to be led (into the church) at the ninth hour, do you also recall to mind the great number of your virtuous deeds and count those gifts which await you; you will no longer be on earth, but your soul will raise itself up and lay hold of heaven itself.[94]

The symbolism of the messiahship of Christ as Sun of Justice and the re-entry into paradise appear in the framework of the symbolism of light. His mystagogy was more directly christological, owing to the different circumstances of his liturgy, different gestures, and a different time for the rite.

It was the piety of Chrysostom which brought to bear most vividly the mystical relationship between the candidate and Christ in the act of renouncing Satan. Chrysostom began his interpretation of the rite by recalling for the candidates that they were at the foot of the cross, reminding them that the ceremony took place at the time of Christ's death upon the cross, and through the power of that death they were enabled to break the power of Satan which held them banned from Paradise. By this identification of the candidate with Christ, Chrysostom portrayed Christ as the strong ally of the Christian, who had made the candidate superior to the demon,[95] and used the picture of Christ in comparison to the olympic judge; whereas the judge was impartial, Christ did not stand aloof, but was entirely on the side of the combatant.[96] It was Christ who had given the candidate the armour for the battle, specifically prepared for the kind of combat in which the candidates were involved.[97] He used Paul's pictre of Christ ransoming slaves from Satan[98] to bring out the relationship between the acts of renunciation and commitment and the historical act of Jesus on the cross. It was the power of that act of Jesus which enabled the candidates to make effective by their statement the salvation already won for them in Christ.[99] Chrysostom summed this up in a passage suggested by Colossians 2.14:

> Christ came once; he found the certificate of our ancestral indebtedness which Adam wrote and signed. Adam contracted the debt; by our subsequent sins we increased the amount owed. In this contract was written a curse, and sin, and death, and the condemnation of the law. Christ took all these away and pardoned them. St Paul cries out and says: The decree of our sins which was against us, he has taken it completely away, nailing it to the cross. He did not say 'erasing the decree', nor did he say 'blotting it out', but nailing it to the cross, so that no trace of it might remain. This is why he did not erase it, but tore it to pieces. The nails of the cross tore up the decree and destroyed it utterly, so that it would not hold good for the future.
>
> Nor did he destroy the note of our debt in some secret corner but in full view of the world, from a lofty stage. Let the angels see it, he says, let the archangels and the powers above behold; let the wicked demons and the devil himself see. It was these wicked ones who made us liable to our creditors for our debts, but now the contract is destroyed, so that they may not hereafter assail us.[100]

Chrysostom elaborated his image of the contract to stress that commitment to Christ was entirely voluntary. It was neither a forced mastership, nor did Christ demand the service of any who were not grateful to him:

> But Christ does not deal in this way; he paid the price for all of us, his precious blood. You have been bought with a price, says St Paul. And even so, he does not force those to serve him who are unwilling to do do. Unless you are grateful, he says and are willing of yourself and of your own accord to be enrolled under me as your Master, I do not force or compel you.[101]

As we have seen above, he linked the profession with the concept of the engagement of the candidate with the Bridegroom, and the dowry contributed by the baptizand to respond to the Bridegroom's gift of salvation.[102] This response was not only to be simply a verbal one, but to be an intelligent commitment made with the heart:

> Keep strong and unshaken your contract with the Master, which you wrote not with ink nor on paper, but with faith and in confession. Be zealous to remain all the days of your life in the same brilliance. If we shall be willing constantly to contribute our fair share, it is possible not only to remain in this shining brightness, but even to make this spiritual robe of ours more brilliant, since Paul too, after the grace of baptism, appeared all the more bright and shining as the grace within him bloomed forth with each passing day.[103]

Thus Chrysostom strongly revealed the candidate's union with the power of Christ and the contractual nature of the act of renunciation and commitment.

Hence it was not surprising that Chrysostom interpreted the concluding anointing as a sign of belonging to Christ, and the sign of the cross upon the forehead, placed there by Christ himself to indicate that the candidate belonged to Christ as a result of his contract with the Master.[104] Not only did the anointing imply ownership but it signified the candidate's appointment and equipment for his life's task. Following his fondness for athletic metaphors, Chrysostom saw the anointing with the cross as a sign that the candidate had been chosen as a combatant in the spiritual arena, playing in the game on the side of Christ.[105] As a result of this, a struggle was announced in which the candidate had to be involved: 'Henceforth from that day there is strife and counterstrife with him, and on this account the priest leads you into the spiritual arena as athletes of Christ by virtue of this anointing.'[106] However, Chrysostom went far beyond the notion of merely an external talisman for protection and exorcism, for it again linked the candidate with Christ: 'Through his contract with Christ, sign for which is this sealing, the candidate joins in the struggle which his cross represents, and through the power of that cross he is protected in reliving that struggle in his own life.'[107] He taught that the seal of the cross on the candidate's forehead radiated a power for the combat which guaranteed the confounding of the adversaries of the baptizand: 'Therefore the priest anoints you on the forehead and puts on you the sign (of the cross), in order that the enemy may turn away his eyes. For he does not dare to look you in the face when he sees the lightning flash which leaps forth from it and blinds his

43

eyes.'[108] Thus this anointing was a spiritual weapon to accompany the candidate in the struggle. Chrysostom summed up this mystagogy of the anointing as a sign of his appointment to the task of living the Christian life, and the protection it implies in pursuing this task, in these terms:

> When you are going to cross the threshold of a doorway, first speak these words: 'I renounce thee, Satan, thy pomp and service, and I enter into thy service, O Christ'. And never go forth without saying these words. This will be your staff, this will be your armour, this will be your impregnable tower. And after you speak these words, make the sign of the cross on your forehead. In this way no man will be able to hurt you, nor will the devil himself be able to do so, when he sees you appear with these weapons to protect on every side.[109]

Thus he interpreted the anointing as a sign of the Christian's mystical union with the struggle of Christ under the victorious and protective power of his cross.

b) *The Baptismal Rite*: Following the rite of renunciation and profession, the candidate then underwent the second anointing immediately before the rite of baptism on Holy Saturday night. He had his robe stripped off him by the bishop[110] in full darkness of night,[111] and then the bishop prepared the candidate's whole body to be anointed with the 'olive oil of the spirit.'[112] Chrysostom's choice of the verb 'to prepare' indicates that others actually performed the anointing, which was understandable, given the large numbers of candidates and the extent of the anointing. Following the anointing, the bishop led the candidate down into the flowing water,[113] where he placed his right hand on the candidate's head, pushed it down into the water and lifted it out three times, saying: 'So-and-so is baptized in the name of the Father, and of the Son, and of the Holy Spirit.'[114] Once again the formula was apersonal to deflect attention away from the minister and towards the God whose agent he was.

As Riley has pointed out,[115] *Stavronikita* 2 contains two paragraphs which in condensed form reveal practically the entire mystagogical dynamic which was at work in these explanations:

> Next after this, in the full darkness of the night, he strips off your robe and, as if he were going to lead you into heaven itself by the ritual, he causes your whole body to be anointed with that olive

oil of the spirit, so that all your limbs may be fortified and unconquered by the darts which the adversary aims at you.

After this anointing the priest makes you go down into the sacred waters, burying the old man and at the same time raising up the new, who is renewed in the image of his Creator. It is at this moment that, through the words and the hand of the priest, the Holy Spirit descends upon you. Instead of the man who descended into the water, a different man comes forth, one who has wiped away all the filth of his sins, who has put off the old garment of sin and has put on the royal robe.

That you may also learn from this that the substance of the Father, Son, and Holy Spirit is one, baptism is conferred in the following manner. When the priest says, 'So-and-so is baptized in the name of the Father, and of the Son, and of the Holy Spirit', he puts your head down into the water three times and three times he lifts it up again, preparing you by this mystic rite to receive the descent of the Spirit. For it is not only the priest who touches the head, but also the right hand of Christ, and this is shown by the very words of the one baptizing. He does not say, 'I baptize so-and-so', but 'So-and-so is baptized', showing that he is only the minister of grace and merely offers his hand because he has been ordained to this end by the Spirit. The one fulfilling all things is the Father and the Son and the Holy Spirit, the undivided Trinity, It is faith in this Trinity which gives the grace of remission of sin; it is this confession which gives to us the gift of filial adoption.'[116]

Chrysostom's central thought was the Pauline theology of Adam and Christ, the old man and the new man. In this light the candidate whose clothes were removed, was anointed, and entered the baptismal pool, and the neophyte who emerged, put on new clothes, and was anointed, are two 'different' men, because in the baptistry a new birth, a new creation has taken place.

Chrysostom developed his thought to recognize first the old man and the deeds he would leave behind in the baptismal grave. He used the same Pauline metaphor as Cyril did to interpret the removal of garments before baptism:

Baptism is a burial and a resurrection. For the old man is buried with his sin and the new man is resurrected, being renewed according to the image of his Creator. We put off the old garment, which has been made filthy with the abundance of our sins; we put on the new one, which is free from every stain. What am I saying? We put on Christ himself. For all you, says St Paul, who have been baptized into Christ, have put on Christ.[117]

As we saw above, he returned to his metaphor to describe the man emerging from the baptismal pool cleansed of sin and wearing 'the royal robe'.[118] He expanded his mystagogy by using, once again as Cyril had done, the image of the marriage banquet, although he used it to urge the candidates to come to baptism wearing a garment suitable for a wedding feast. Thus the habit of evil deeds, symbolized in the filthy garment, had to be overcome, or else the new garment could become soiled as well.[119] Similarly he used the invitation of the bridegroom to the bride as we have seen above.[120]

However, Chrysostom could not resist the implications of mystagogical stripping off of the old clothes which were for him the symbol of the veil and seductive display in terms of dress and jewellery, and he pointed out that unnecessary luxury in terms of dress and adornment was a sin against social justice: 'That you may wear a single ruby, countless poor are starved and crushed.'[121] Not only this but such a display signified vanity, and was likely to lead another to envy and even to theft. In place of such unnecessary luxury should come good works, through which the soul would become attractive and shine. Chrysostom particularly directed his remarks to the female candidates for baptism, suggesting they sought to adorn themselves with almsgiving and modesty which were more becoming those born anew in Christ:

> Adorn your face, therefore, with modesty, piety, almsgiving, benevolence, love, kindness towards your husband, reasonableness, mildness and forbearance. These are the pigments of virtue; by these you draw not men but angels to you as your lovers; for these you have God himself to praise you. When God shall approve of you, he will win over your husband to you in every way; for if wisdom illumines the face of a man, much more does virtue make the face of a woman shine forth.[122]

Cosmetics also failed to meet Chrysostom's approval. These he saw as an insult to the Creator, since the need to paint the face implies defective workmanship on the part of the Creator.[123] Christ sought 'the beauty which came from within,' and he advised his female candidates most strongly to strip off such habits, as well as stripping off clothing before baptism, so that such behaviour would be a sign of the return of good deeds.[124]

The nakedness of the candidates at baptism reminded

Chrysostom of the primeval innocence of Adam and Eve, who in the garden had been naked and unashamed, and he wrote in most descriptive terms of this:

> After stripping you of your robe, the priest himself leads you down into the flowing waters. But why naked? He reminds you of your former nakedness, when you were in Paradise and you were not ashamed. For Holy Writ says: Adam and Eve were naked and were not ashamed, until they took up the garment of sin, a garment heavy with abundant shame.
> Do not, then, feel shame here, for the bath is much better than the garden of Paradise. There can be no serpent here, but Christ is here initiating you into the regeneration that comes from the water and the Spirit. You cannot see here beautiful trees and fruits, but you can see spiritual favours.[125]

Thus from the imagery it was evident that the candidate at baptism was re-entering that state of innocence and bliss that Adam and Eve enjoyed before the fall, evidence of the new creation in Christ.[126]

Much of Chrysostom's explanation of the baptismal act was inseparably linked with his earlier teaching which we have examined in section 1, and there is no need to duplicate it here.

c) *The Post-Baptismal Rites.* Upon their emergence from the font the neophytes were embraced, greeted, and kissed by all present. Other than this kiss, Chrysostom did not make any specific mention of post-baptismal ceremonies, nor of any post-baptismal anointing.[127] The emergence from the pool was described by Chrysostom thus:

> As soon as they came forth from those sacred waters, all who are present embrace them, greet them, kiss them, rejoice with them, and congratulate them, because those who were heretofore slaves and captives have suddenly become free men and sons and have been invited to the royal table. For straightaway after they come up from the waters, they are led to the awesome table heavy laden with countless flavours where they taste of the Master's body and blood, and become a dwelling place for the Holy Spirit. Since they have put on Christ himself, wherever they go they are like angels on earth, rivalling the brilliance of the rays of the sun.[128]

Chrysostom obliquely referred to both their new light and their new robe in the last sentence, and it was plain that he was too overwhelmed at the prospect of the royal table to bother to spell out the liturgical details of dress and illumination. He wanted to leave his candidates contemplating their welcome into the fellowship of God's people.

Our consideration of Chrysostom completed, we now move some twenty-five miles out of the city of Antioch to consider the writing of Theodore of Mopsuestia.

3
Theodore and the Church at Mopsuestia

Among his list of the works of Theodore of Mopsuestia, Ebedjesu[1] refers to two works '*Of the sacraments*' and '*Of the faith*', which were first edited by A. Mingana.[2] Theodore presented the faith of the Church to his catechumens in sixteen homilies; the first ten homilies explained the articles of the faith as expounded by the Nicene Creed, whilst the other six explain the Lord's Prayer (11), the liturgy of baptism (12–14), and the Eucharist (15–16). These then form the scope for our study of Theodore's catechetical material.

There seems to be no real reason to doubt Theodore's authorship of these homilies. Although Quasten[3] favours Antioch as the location of these lectures, Lietzmann[4] supposed that these instructions come from the time when Theodore occupied the episcopal see of Mopsuestia, i.e. from 392–428. These homilies seem to have become something of a manual of instruction for the Syriac Church after Theodore's death, and since as bishop he gained a wide reputation for his learning and orthodoxy, on balance, I agree with Riley that this latter location and date are more likely.[5] For the purposes of this study, I shall assume Mopsuestia as the location and that Theodore was lecturing there as the bishop. For the purpose of ordering the material we shall classify the material from the lectures on the Nicene Creed as providing the theology of baptism, and the material from the lectures on the sacraments as providing the liturgical and mystagogical explanation of baptism.

1. *The Theology of Baptism and its Catechetical Explanation*
For Theodore the credal declaration which his candidates were to make was an integral part of the total baptismal rite,

49

and that he saw it as essential is evident from one of his earliest lectures in the series on the Nicene Creed:

> Now which is the faith and which are the promises through which we have our part in mysteries in the hope of these heavenly gifts in which we will delight? These are found in the profession of faith which we make before Christ our Lord at the time of our baptism. If it were possible to comprehend their power by hearing only, our words would have been useless, because their mere recitation would have made them understood by those who heard them.[6]

He was not looking to his candidates merely to repeat back the words of the profession of faith parrot-fashion, but he wanted to guide them to make the words of their lips reinforce the experience of their lives. So he suggested that the profession of faith contained much hidden power, and so the catechumens had to be taught the sense and the meaning hidden within it.

Unlike Chrysostom, Theodore was able to stick to his theme rather than be readily sidetracked from it as was his friend. The next four lectures dealt with the fatherhood of God and the divinity of the Son and there was scant reference to baptism in them. However, when Theodore taught about the incarnation and the humanity of the Son, he stressed the important place of the baptism of Jesus by John the Baptist. Jesus, he said, 'was baptized so that he might be given an emblem to the grace of our baptism and he showed effectively in himself the economy of the gospel to all men.'[7] He stressed the fact that Christians were baptized following the example of Jesus in his submission to John's baptism of repentance in the river Jordan. The only reasons for Jesus' baptism were obedience to the command of the Father and his identification with sinful men. He stressed both these aspects when he made the point that, during his earthly life, Jesus was subject to the Law: 'He practised in a right will all (things dealing with) the justification of the law, and then received baptism, from which he gave the New Testament as in a symbol.'[8] In this he was developing Hebrews 4.15 to stress Jesus' identification with man during his earthly life. However, Theodore was also applying to John's baptism – strictly speaking a baptism of repentance only – the effects of Christian baptism outlined in the New Testament supremely by Paul,[9] for this was the only baptism which could be said to be a symbol of the message of the New Testament. Theodore confirmed this point and developed it further as he taught that: he was also baptized so that he might perform the economy of the gospel according to order, and in this (economy) he died and abolished death.[10]

Tonneau's translation, however, makes it plain that Christ's saving death and resurrection was part of the meaning of Jesus' baptism by John as Theodore understood and taught it. It prefigures the death of Christ upon the cross, and was the symbol of the life, and of the good news about the availability of that life, which Jesus had come to bring. Through his baptism by John, Jesus was, according to Theodore, setting forth in the microcosm of the baptismal act the macrocosm of his whole ministry. He summed up: 'He was baptized so that he might give a symbol to our own baptism. In it he was freed from all the obligations of the law.'[11] However, Tonneau used a different word order in his translation to convey a different sense. Mingana coupled the idea of the 'economy of the gospel' with the choice of the disciples and the teaching of Jesus, but Tonneau links the phrase with Jesus' baptism: 'He therefore made his way to baptism in order to give a model of our baptism to us, and from there he detaches himself from all the conduct conformed to the law and accomplishes all the life of the gospel.'[12]

Theodore developed his argument to teach that in baptism candidates demonstrated a symbol of the world to come and expressed the hope of the life which he hoped to share with Christ as the resurrection from the dead.[13] Theodore taught that the Christian's life was lived in the hope of the future resurrection and this future resurrection was attained only as the candidates lived according to the commandments of Christ.

> It is with justice, therefore, that he paid the debt of the law, received baptism, and showed the new economy of the gospel, which is the symbol of the world to come, so that we also who believed in Christ and became worthy of baptism, through which we received the symbol of the world to come, should live according to his commandments.[14]

Urging his candidates to live a life in accordance with the dominical commandments of love for God, for neighbour, and for fellow Christian, he quoted Romans 6.17 and explained their obligations to them further:

> In this he shows that through baptism we have received the

teaching of the new economy which is the symbol of the world to come, and as much as possible we strive to live according to it, while remote from all sin, and not according to law. Indeed we are baptized as men who die with him and will rise symbolically with him, because 'so many of us as were buried into Jesus were baptized into his death and were buried with him by baptism into death; that like as Jesus Christ was raised from the dead in the glory of his Father, even so, we should walk in newness of life.'[15] After having received the grace of baptism we become strangers to all observance of the law and we are as in another life: You are become dead to the law by the body of Jesus Christ.[16] He said this because you have attained new life in the baptismal birth and have become part of the body of Christ our Lord; and we hope to have communion with him now that we are freed from the life of this world and dead to the world and to the law, because the law has power in this world and we become strangers to all this world according to the symbol of baptism.[17]

In one sense there was a contradiction here with his earlier teaching when he had dealt with the sense of Romans 7.4. He had explained this using the perfect tense, indicating completed action in the past, when speaking of the attainment of new life and of becoming part of the body of Christ. If salvation were a completed past event implied in 'you have become dead to the law by the body of Jesus Christ', then how could the new life which was implied be conditional on the works of this life? This produces just another variant of the faith/works controversy which is seen in the New Testament by some, but within our context here we cannot stress too much this change of tense, because, as Riley points out, the very nature of catechetical homilies precludes them from being presented in the 'closed, ordered form of the theological treatise.'[18] In any case Theodore went on to qualify what he had said:

And in order that we may possess these future good things in a firm faith without doubt, he gave us even in this world the first fruits of the Spirit which we received as the earnest, of which the blessed Paul said: 'In whom ye believed, and ye were sealed with that Holy Spirit (of promise) which is the earnest of our inheritance.'[19] The economy of the grace of Christ our Lord, for which we receive baptism, is like unto this.[20]

The fact that the Christian received the Holy Spirit at baptism, just as Christ himself had done, enabled him to think of his life with Christ in a firm faith without any doubt.

He developed this point when he dealt with the phrase 'And in the Holy Spirit' from the credal statement later on in the course of lectures. He taught his candidates:

It is in this name that we are baptized and expect that the communion of the ineffable divine benefits will accrue to us through baptism. We would not have named at baptism a being that was not the cause of the benefits that we are expecting to possess. We name (him) because we know that he has the power to grant us the heavenly and imperishable benefits in the hope of which we receive the gift of baptism. In the same way as (the Book) said, 'In the name of Jesus of Nazareth rise up and walk,' and showed that it was Christ who was the cause of the cure of the lame man, in this same way where it ordered, 'Baptism in the name of the Father, and of the Son, and of the Holy Ghost,' it clearly showed that these names which are pronounced at baptism are the cause of all the benefits which we are expecting to possess. It is not to no purpose that it says, 'in the name of the Father, and of the Son, and of the Holy Ghost,' but in order that from their names we may derive our hope of enjoying the future good things.[21]

He developed this idea, too, to explain to his candidates that the divine nature was called by the threefold name of Father, Son, and Holy Ghost:

(Our Lord) said here also, 'In the name of the Father, and of the Son, and of the Holy Ghost,' in order that his disciples might learn from him that all the nations were looking for this name as the cause of all their good things, because the nature which is called 'Father, and Son, and Holy Ghost' and in which we are baptized, is truly the Lord who is able to give us the heavenly good things which we are expecting and in the hope of which we draw nigh unto the grace of baptism.[22]

He further linked the threefold name with baptism to stress the confidence which the Christian may put upon the promises of God in baptism.

As he ordered us to name the Father in the act of our discipleship and our baptism, because he is the divine nature which is eternal and cause of everything and because he is able to vouchsafe unto us the benefits involved in the promise of baptism and as he ordered us to name the Son because he was an identical nature and is able to vouchsafe unto us the same benefits, it is likewise evident that he names the Holy Spirit side-by-side with the

53

Father and the Son for this very reason, that is to say because he is of the same nature as that which is eternal and cause of everything to which is truly due the name of Lord and God.[23]

The triune God could not be false to his promise where he guaranteed the benefits of baptism, so the Christian's hope of eternal benefits rested upon a sure and certain foundation, even though it remained a 'hope'.

Theodore firmly understood that baptism was indissolubly linked with the trinitarian formula, and he used the place of the Spirit in the baptismal formula, based on Matthew 28.19, to justify the place of the Spirit in the Trinity;[24] later describing the Spirit in terms of, 'One who by the mention of his name frees us from death and corruption through baptism, and renews us according to the teaching of our Lord.'[25] He further supported this with reference to the Pauline epistles[26] and explained to his candidates:

> We have been called to the hope of these (benefits), and we were born of baptism by the power of the Holy Spirit, and as a symbol and earnest of the future things we received the first fruits of the Spirit, through whom we were reborn and by whom we obtained the gifts of being one body of Christ.[27]

Using Ephesians 4.4–6, and applying it personally to the candidate, he explained once again that they believed in only one nature in the godhead and that this fact made possible Paul's declaration of 'one faith'. Similarly, he taught, Paul had said 'one baptism' because he was aware that 'those names which are pronounced at baptism had only one power, one will, and one act through which the grace of our second birth was accomplished.'[28] Mingana suggested in his footnote that the phrase 'grace of our second birth' was used to mean the spiritual birth of the candidates through baptism to newness of life in Christ. In Theodore's recapitulation at the beginning of the tenth lecture, he summed up his argument in regard to the Holy Spirit thus: 'I know that you remember that we spoke to your love concerning the Holy Spirit, when we showed the greatness of his glory from the fact that in the initiation of baptism he is believed in side-by-side with the Father and the Son.'[29]

Later in that lecture Theodore dealt with the fact that even those from a polytheistic background, as many of the Gentiles had been in the days of the early Church, had been taught that Father, Son, and Holy Spirit were in fact one divine nature. He stressed the need for a correct understanding of the position and cited this as part of the rationale behind the lectures:

> This is the reason why our Lord caused baptism to follow catechumenate, so that baptism should be the end of catechumenate. It was necessary for those who had rejected false gods and learnt that divine nature was one, eternal, and cause of everything, which is Father, Son and Holy Spirit, to receive through these names the gift of baptism which is bestowed for the sake of a wonderful happiness and is the earnest of the future and ineffable benefits. Faith is professed at baptism by the mention of these names, because those who mention them designate one divine nature which is eternal, cause of everything, and able to create all things from nothing while always caring and providing for them. We also rightly expect to be renewed and to receive the freedom of truth through these names of Father, Son, and Holy Spirit, which are pronounced at baptism.[30]

Baptism also incorporated the candidate into the great body of the Christian Church, making the baptized a member of what Theodore was later to describe as a new and great city. Commenting on Ephesians 3.10–11, he taught:

> He shows here that in this manifold wisdom of God the invisible powers were astonished that he assembled together all men to the worship of God, and made them as one body of Christ at the second birth from the holy baptism, and prepared them to hope that they will participate with him in the future good things of the next world. He calls this Church the body of Christ because it received communion with him through the regeneration of baptism, symbolically in this world but truly and effectively in the next.[31]

He continued:

> We symbolize this state in baptism, since we die in Christ in baptism and rise again according to the testimony of the blessed Paul. This is the reason why each one of us declares: 'I will believe and be baptized in the name of the Father, and of the Son, and of the Holy Spirit through one holy Catholic Church.' (The catechumen) shows by his words: I am not preparing for baptism for the sake of little things but for the sake of great and wonderful things and heavenly benefits, as I am expecting that through baptism I shall be made a member of the Church, which is the congregation of the faithful, who through baptism became worthy

to be called the body of Christ our Lord and received an ineffable holiness and the hope of the future immortality and immutability.[32]

Theodore concluded his study of the Creed by reminding the candidates he had been addressing that the Church Fathers at Nicaea

> taught us the profession of faith (which is to be made) at baptism in order to show that all this is in accordance with the sequence of the teaching of our Lord who said: 'Go ye, teach and baptize in the name of the Father, and of the Son, and of the Holy Spirit.' Thus they (the catechumens) are taught and thus they perform the (sacrament of) baptism in the name of the Father, and of the Son, and of the Holy Spirit.
>
> Those who are about to be baptized in the hope of ineffable benefits ought not to name another nature beside the one from which all benefits are bestowed on all created being. This is the reason why they added to this the profession of faith concerning the future benefits in the hope of which we draw nigh unto the grace of baptism, as by necessity we have to know what kind of benefits are granted to this discipleship, and also that the Father, the Son and the Holy Spirit are one divine nature, and also that at the second birth from the holy baptism we receive the faith in the heavenly and imperishable benefits that the divine nature, which is eternal and cause of everything, is able to bestow upon us.[33]

This provided his candidates with a fitting and memorable summary of the contents of his last two lectures in relation to the effect of his words upon their baptism, and the effect of the Spirit's work in their lives as they prepared to profess their faith in Christ not only with their lips but with their lives.

2. *The Liturgy of Baptism and its Mystagogical Explanation*

a) *The Rite of Renunciation and Profession.* This rite for Theodore's candidates also began the ceremonies closely connected with the baptismal rite. They were made to stand barefoot on a sack-cloth made of goat's hair and their outer garment was removed. They stretched forth their hands towards God imploring his help and assistance[34] and then knelt down upon the sackcloth, body erect, arms still stretched out imploringly to God with their gaze fixed towards heaven.[35] They were then approached by ministers appointed for the service and addressed with a message which was an elaboration of the message of the angel to Cornelius from Acts 10.4:

God has looked upon your tribulation which you were previously undergoing and had mercy upon you because you were for a long time captives of the tyrant and served a cruel servitude to him. He saw the number and nature of the calamities which you have endured, and this moved him to deliver you from that servitude and from the great number of your ancient tribulations, and to bring you to freedom and to grant you to participate in the ineffable heavenly benefits, which immediately after you have received, you become undoubtedly free from all calamities. It is now time for you to learn the things through which you will surely receive deliverance from your ancient tribulations and enjoy the good things that have been shown to you.[36]

Deacons then approached the candidates and prepared them for the solemn formula of renunciation and profession of commitment. The candidate said: 'I abjure Satan and all his angels, and all his service, and all his deception, and all his worldly glamour; and I engage myself and believe, and am baptized in the name of the Father, and of the Son, and of the Holy Spirit.'[37] Following this the bishop, who had changed from his previous garments and was now clad in a supple and radiant linen robe, approached the candidates and signed them on the forehead with the oil of anointing and said, once again in apersonal terms: 'So-and-so is signed in the name of the Father, and of the Son, and of the Holy Spirit.'[38] During this time the sponsors were standing behind the candidates and, following the anointing, they spread a prayer shawl of linen upon the head of the candidate, raised him from his kneeling position and caused him to stand erect.[39]

When explaining this feature of the rite, Theodore was at pains to give a detailed explanation of the formula of re-nunciation itself.[40] However, he did explain the reasons behind the bodily position which the candidates were required to adopt:

> First you genuflect, while the rest of your body is erect, and in the posture of one who prays you stretch out your arms towards God. As we have all of us fallen into sin and been driven to the dust by the sentence of death, it behoves us to 'bow our knees in the name of Jesus Christ,' as the blessed Paul said, 'and to confess that Jesus Christ is the Lord to the glory of God His father.'[41]
>
> In this confession we show the things that accrue to us from the divine nature through the economy of Christ our Lord, whom (God) raised up to heaven and showed as Lord of all and head of

our salvation. Because all these things have to be performed by us all who 'are fallen to the earth' according to the words of blessed Paul, it is with justice that you, who through the sacrament become partakers of the ineffable benefits to which you have been called by your faith in Christ, bow your knees and make manifest your ancient fall, and worship God the cause of all those benefits.[42]

Thus the candidates prayed for deliverance from the fall and received the assurance that their prayers had been heard and their applications answered. The candidates knelt symbolizing man's servitude to Satan as a result of the ancient fall. He was using the same mystagogy of the dynamic of conversion as was used by Chrysostom.[43] But to this Theodore added his own personal touch in referring to the conversion of St Paul on the road to Damascus. He then proceeded to show the repentance that took place, teaching the candidates that it was through faith in Christ that the point of turning again came. Theodore emphasized not the turning but the falling and rising, stressing that Paul and his companions who had fallen to the ground were enabled to get up only through the power of Jesus. Thus it was significant that the candidates following their anointing were not left to rise unaided, but were helped to their feet by their godparents. The candidate stood as a sign that the ancient fall and captivity expressed by the kneeling had been overcome and as a symbol that the gesture of kneeling, expressing the candidates' acknowledgement of the lordship of Christ, had been accepted:

> By your rising from your genuflexion you show that you have cast away your ancient fall, that you have no more communion with earth and earthly things, that your adoration and prayer to God has been accepted, that you have received the stamp which is the sign of your election to the ineffable military service, that you have been called to heaven, and that you ought henceforth to direct your course to its life and citizenship while spurning all earthly things.[44]

During the act of renunciation and commitment the gaze of the candidates had been directed to heaven, and their hand outstretched towards heaven in what Theodore described as 'the posture of one who prays.'[45] In this posture their attitude of mind and spirit ought to be one of prayer, imploring God to grant deliverance from the ancient fall, and to grant their participation in the heavenly benefits.[46] Theodore summed up:

> These engagements and promises you make in the posture which we have described above, while your knee is bowed to the ground, both as a sign of adoration from you to God, and as a manifestation of your ancient fall to the ground; the rest of the body is erect and looks upward towards heaven, and your hands are outstretched in the guise of one who prays so that you may be seen to worship the God who is in heaven, from whom you expect to rise from your ancient fall. This is the reason why you have, through the promises and engagements which we have already described, directed your course towards him and have promised to him that you will make yourself worthy of the expected gift. After you have looked towards him with outstretched hands, asked grace from him, risen from your fall and rejoiced in (future) benefits, you will necessarily receive the first-fruits of the sacrament which we believe to be the earnest of the good and ineffable things found in heaven.[47]

It was the candidates' heavenward gaze that Theodore explained in terms of light and darkness using the story of the conversion of St Paul. The candidates' upturned eyes sought the light of the world in Jesus Christ. This was reinforced by his explanation of the bishop's robe of clean and radiant linen which was worn for the anointing which followed: 'the joyful appearance of which denotes the joy of the world to which you will move in the future, and the shining colour of which designates your own radiance in the life to come, while its cleanness indicates the ease and happiness of the next world.'[48] Theodore explained that the sign of the cross with which the candidate had been anointed on the forehead was to be compared with the mark of ownership, so that the candidate might have the confidence to address God with an open face, showing him the stamp by which they were seen to be members of the household and soldiers of Christ our Lord.

Theodore also used a mystagogy based on the natural symbol of light and darkness. He was not able to be as explicit as his colleagues because of the differences in the images which he used. In the two biblical images which he used of the conversion of Cornelius and the conversion of St Paul, the conversion experience was described in terms of the passage from darkness to light.[49] These two conversions described in Acts indicated for Theodore various features of the rite of

Initiation. The times – the ninth hour for Cornelius and midday for Paul – encompassed the time of the crucifixion, the appearance of Jesus in the symbolism of brilliant light, the falling to the ground and rising, the turning from darkness to light, from the dominion of Satan through the act of confession of faith in Jesus, the forgiveness of sins in baptism: these linked these two stories indelibly for Theodore with the rite of Initiation in which his candidates were to share.

Theodore's description of the candidate's frame of mind as he knelt in the rite of renunciation and profession indicated an interpretation which implied an almost face-to-face encounter between the candidate and Satan:

> It is in place here to explain to you the power of these words, in order that you may know the force of the engagements, promises and words of asseveration through which you receive the happiness of this great gift. Because the devil, to whom you had listened, was for you the cause of numerous and great calamities – as he has begun his work from the time of the Father of your race – you promise to abjure him, since facts themselves and your own experience had made you feel his injuries. This is the reason why you say, 'I abjure you, Satan.' Formerly, even if you wished it, you did not dare make use of these words, because you were afraid of his servitude, but as you have by a divine decree received deliverance from him, you proclaim and abjure him with confidence and by your own words, and this is the reason why you say, 'I abjure Satan.' In this you imply both your present separation from him, and the former association that you had with him.
>
> You rightly said, 'I abjure Satan,' but you can hardly realize that, after formerly having felt the injury which he inflicted upon you in his relation to you, you could be in a position to be delivered from him.'[50]

The candidate was united with Christ in the act of renunciation and profession. It was by 'divine decree' that the candidate, having received deliverance from Satan, was able to declare: 'I abjure Satan.'[51] This he said was the 'great and wonderful grace, which was manifest through Christ, and which freed us from the Tyrant and delivered us from his servitude and granted us this wonderful participation in his benefits.'[52]

However, from the final anointing came Theodore's innovation in his implication that this produced in the candidate the firstfruits of the final victory which Christ would ultimately win over Satan in universal terms. To establish this emphasis he drew attention to several features which surrounded the ceremony of the sealing, or final anointing, and put them into the context of the life to come. He pointed out that the bishop exchanged his ordinary garments for a linen robe, symbolizing by its joyful appearance the joy of the life to come, by its shining whiteness the radiance of the life to come, and by its suppleness the ease and happiness of movement in the world of the future. He explained the bestowal of the prayer shawl by the sponsor upon the head of the candidate, following anointing, as the emblem of freedom, commenting that it was slaves and exiles who stood bareheaded, but free men spread linen on their heads as an adornment both at home and in the market place. Theodore made a link between the anointing and the freedom sybolized by the prayer shawl:

> ...it is through this signing that you are known to have been chosen for the service of heaven. This is the reason why immediately you rise up, you spread on your head linen, which is a mark of freedom, and this signifies that you have been chosen for the heavenly service, and been freed from communion with earthly things, while obtaining the freedom which is in heaven. If a slave is not allowed in this world to do military service to a king, how much more ought the person who has been detailed for the service of heaven to be remote from servitude. All of us, therefore, who have received communion with heavenly things are freemen of that 'free Jerusalem which is above, and which is mother of us all', as the blessed Paul said.'[53]

Within the context of the ceremony, and realizing the symbolism which Theodore applied both to the bishop's robe and to rising and receiving the prayer shawl in connection with both freedom and the world to come, it is much easier to appreciate Theodore's particular interpretation of the anointing itself:

> ...you who have been chosen for the kingdom of heaven... are first stamped on your forehead, that part of your head which is higher than the rest of your body, which is placed above all your body and above your face, and with which we usually draw near to one another and look at one another when we speak. You are stamped on that place so that you may be seen to possess great confidence 'because now we see through a glass darkly, but then face to face, and with an open face we shall behold as in a glass the glory of the Lord, and shall be changed into the same image from glory to glory, even as by the spirit of the Lord', as the blessed Paul said.

We are rightly stamped in a place that is higher than our face, so that from far we may frighten the demons, who will not then be able to come near us and injure us, and so that we may be known to possess so much confidence with God that we look at him with open face, and display before him the stamp by which we are seen to be members of the household and soldiers of Christ our Lord.[54]

This concept of confidence which Theodore used twice in this passage has a particular remarkable usage here, as van Unnik points out. His thesis is that in the Peshitta, the original of 'confidence' is sometimes transliterated and at other times is replaced by an indigenous metaphor meaning literally 'the uncovering or revealing of the face.'[55] Normally, Theodore used 'confidence' – in eight out of nine passages – with a strictly religious meaning to express a particular aspect of the relation between God and man, and to describe one of the specific elements of the new life of the Christian.[56] This confidence became the share of the Christians by their profession of faith at baptism.[57] Jesus Christ, as man, possessed confidence and by this he was able to conquer death and to grant immunity from death to all mankind.[58] Jesus, Theodore taught, 'had such a confidence he became a messenger on behalf of all human race so that the rest of mankind might participate with him in his great change.'[59] In this context, van Unnik reminds us, confidence is not only confidence that he would conquer death, but also, and foremost, in Jesus' perfect union with the Godhead.[60] Through the work of Jesus and as a result of his gracious gift man attained confidence before God and friendship and fellowship with the hosts that were invisible and true to God.[61] Thus not only would Christians, through the gracious work of Christ, have free intercourse with God in the future, but it was already enjoyed here where the sacraments were proleptic eschatology and where the firstfruits of the Spirit were present.[62] Such confidence was awe-inspiring for Christians and their natural feeling would be fear before such an awe-inspiring divine presence, but fear was done away with by grace.[63] Van Unnik summarized his effort to elucidate the meaning of confidence thus:

'Confidence' is an expression for the new life of Christians; the 'freedom of the children of God' who, by the work of Jesus Christ, are no longer separated from the almighty, holy and eternal God, and who, as citizens of God's world, converse with him as their Father. It is a gift of the Holy Spirit, which is enjoyed here in the sacraments and prayer. It is remarkable that, though this new life has its ethical implications, the term translated 'confidence' is practically restricted to the sphere of the relation between God and man and is not applied to inter-human relationships, such as the preaching of the gospel.[64]

He proceeds to consider further the use of the concept of confidence in the passage which he looked at above in the context of the pre-baptismal anointing on the candidate's forehead. Theodore called this anointing 'the firstfruits of the sacrament' and afterwards the candidates received 'the remaining part of the sacrament and were invested with the complete armour of the Spirit.' Theodore concentrated more attention on this anointing than on the other two, viz. of the whole body and the post-baptismal anointing on the forehead. He described it by the use of two similes when he said, 'the sign with which you are signed means that you have been stamped as a lamb of Christ and as a soldier of the heavenly King.' He stressed the positive side of anointing implying allegiance to Christ and the heavenly kingdom rather than the negative aspect of anointing involving only the expulsion of demons. Van Unnik finds the combination of the two different Pauline texts[65] of great interest, because thay are linked by the words 'face' and 'mirror', and illustrated the proleptic eschatology of Theodore's idea of the sacraments, that the sacraments 'by symbols give a share in the heavenly world of what once will be shared in reality.'[66] The nearest parallel to this explanation of the anointing came in Cyril, when in discussing the final anointing in *Cat. Myst.* 3.4 he linked it to the baptismal seal which made the receiver free from shame and allowed him to see the glory of God with an uncovered face; while in Theodore it gives confidence, which was the opposite of shame, so that the candidate might see the glory of God with an uncovered face.[67] Theodore used the concept of the uncovered face to symbolize man's freedom from shame and from the awe which a creature naturally feels before the holiness of God. Van Unnik suggests that the uncovered face is an indispensable element in the train of thought. Theodore made much of the fact that the seal was given on the forehead. This was connected with the fact that the candidates for baptism stood bareheaded, so that their confidence before

God did not need to be stressed so much, as it was implied by their uncovered face and bare head. However, this confidence was no subjective feeling, but a confidence which was a share in the confidence of Jesus himself, and it was this share which made the anointing before baptism 'the passport for free entrance into the presence of Almighty God.'

b) *The Baptismal Rite*. From the 'firstfruits of baptism' we move to a consideration of the baptismal rite as such, which Theodore referred to as 'the remaining part of the sacrament.'[68] Upon arrival at the baptistry, the candidates took off all their garments and were anointed on their whole body with the oil of anointing. The bishop began this anointing, clad in the same shining apparel which he had put on for the first anointing which we have just considered, and 'others appointed for the service' continued the anointing on the entire body.[69] Theodore reported that the bishop had already consecrated the baptismal waters by the invocation of the Holy Spirit, although he gave no indication of when this might have been done. The candidate descended into the baptismal water following the anointing of the whole body, and there the bishop extended his hand and placed it on the candidate's head. He said, 'So-and-so is baptized in the name of the Father'; then, at the end of this phrase, he exerted pressure on the candidate's head, and the candidate, hearing these words and following the leading pressure of the bishop's hand, bowed down his head and immersed himself in the water. Then the candidate raised his head back up out of the water. The bishop said, 'and of the Son', and in the same way, following the pressure of the bishop's hand as he said the phrase, the candidate bowed down his head a second time and immersed himself in the water. After his head emerged from the water, the candidate heard the bishop say the third phrase, 'and of the Holy Spirit', and for the third time following the pressure of the bishop's hand, the candidate, bowing his head, submerged and raised his head back out of the water. Then the candidate left the pool.[70]

Theodore explained the removal of the garments before baptism in terms of the dimension of immortality/mortality. He based his interpretation on the story of Adam and Eve, in that God needed to make clothes for them only after they had sinned. The clothes which the candidates stripped off were the symbol of the primeval aprons. Adam had become mortal by breaking God's commandment, and he had realized the need of a covering when he lost his trust in God, and became 'self-conscious'. The apron which he received from God, was 'a sign of mortality and a reproving mark of that (divine) decree by which you were brought low to the necessity of a covering.'[71] Since baptism brought the candidate new birth and immortality, so he removed the clothing which since Adam had been the symbol of his mortality. Similarly, Theodore saw the nakedness of the candidate preparing to receive baptism as a symbol of Adam's former state – naked and unashamed[72] – although he did not present the mystagogy of the baptistry as a symbol of paradise.

Theodore's explanation of the pre-baptismal anointing is a somewhat original approach:

> After you have taken off your garments, you are rightly anointed all over your body with the oil of anointing, a mark and sign that you will be receiving the covering of immortaltity, which through baptism you are about to put on. After you have taken off the covering which involves the sign of mortality, you receive through your anointing the sign of the covering of immortality, which you expect to receive through baptism. And you are anointed all over your body as a sign that, unlike the covering used as a garment, which does not cover all the parts of the body, because although it may cover all the external limbs, it by no means covers the internal ones, all our nature will put on immortality at the time of the resurrection, and all that is seen in us, whether internal or external, will undoubtedly be changed into incorruptibility according to the working of the Holy Spirit which shall then be with us.[73]

Basically, it was his own application of the concept of exorcism and healing at this point in the rite. It formed a unity with his interpretation of the removal of the garments, and this anointing becomes the sign of the immortality to come. Thus the oil healed the corruption of mortality, becoming a healing covering of the entire body. In sign, it demonstrated itself more effective in making the candidate immortal than the garments were in making him mortal, not only covering more of the external limbs than the garments could, but reaching internal limbs that the garments could not reach, symbolically elaborating the penetrating quality of oil.

He summarized the effect of the baptismal rite as a whole in these terms:

In the same way the sentence 'In the name of the Father and of the Son and of the Holy Spirit' reveals the giver of the benefits of baptism which are: second birth, renewal, immortality, incorruptibility, impassibility, immutability, deliverance from death and servitude to all evils, happiness of freedom, and participation in the ineffable good things which we are expecting. The person who is baptized is baptized for these things.[74]

To explain the means by which these benefits were achieved, Theodore also chose the Pauline recounting of the death and resurrection of Christ as his principal vehicle. 'It is indeed evident to us, according to the words of the Apostle, that when we perform either baptism or the Eucharist, we perform them in rememberance of the death and resurrection of Christ, in order that the hope of the latter may be strengthened in us.'[75] Quoting Romans 6.3–4, he explained, in his principal statement on baptism, 'he (Paul) clearly taught here that we are baptized so that we might imitate in ourselves the death and resurrection of our Lord, and that we might receive from our remembrance of the happenings which took place the confirmation of our hope in future things.'[76] This emphasis on the baptismal act as a sign of future realities was also a hallmark of Theodore's thinking, and his mystagogical programme reflected this emphasis:

> As we have a firm belief that things that have already happened will happen to us, so (the thing that happened at the resurrection of our Lord) we believe that they will happen to us. We perform, therefore, this ineffable sacrament, which contains the incomprehensible signs of the economy of Christ our Lord, as we believe that the things implied in it will happen to us.[77]

Theodore taught that the sacrament represented the saving work of Christ but at the same time looked forward to and represented the full realization of the candidate's salvation at the neophyte's final resurrection from the dead. So the sacramental action, for him, contained not only symbols of the passion, death, and resurrection of Christ, and the candidate's participation in these, but also it was a symbol of the candidate's participation in the fulfilment to come which this resurrection of Christ implied.[78]

He related the candidate's baptism to the death and resurrection of Christ in terms of the candidate's immersion and emergence from the pool:

Because Christ our Lord abolished the power of death by his own resurrection, (the Apostle) said, 'As many of us as were baptized into Jesus Christ, were baptized into his death.' As if one were saying 'We know that death has been abolished a long time ago by Christ our Lord, and we draw nigh unto him, and are baptized with such a faith because we desire to participate in his death, in the hope of participating also in the future resurrection from the dead, in the way in which he himself arose.'[79]

This reality is exemplified for the candidates by the liturgical actions of the baptismal act which Theodore described in first person singular terms – a reminder perhaps of the fact that baptism is often evocative of one's own baptism:

> This is the reason why, when at my baptism I plunge my head, I receive the death of Christ our Lord, and desire to have his burial, and because of this I firmly believe in the resurrection of our Lord; and when I rise from the water, I think I have symbolically risen a long time ago.[80]

Although Theodore's central mystagogical statement of the act of immersion and emergence from the water was brief, this was probably because, like Chrysostom, Theodore took it for granted that this was the meaning of the liturgical action. However, he analysed the notion of entering the water as sign of corruption and death in a later passage in connection with a symbol of the baptismal pool as a forge, where mortal nature is tempered and changed into immortal.

> It behoves you, therefore, to think that you are going into the water as into a furnace, where you will be renewed and re-fashioned in order that you may move to a higher nature, after having cast away your old mortality and fully assumed an immortal and incorruptible nature. These things dealing with birth happen to you in the water, because you were fashioned at the beginning from earth and water, and having fallen later into sin you assumed a thorough corruption through the sentence of death.[81]

Using both the natural symbolism of earth and water, its biblical counterpart, and the symbol of the furnace, Theodore explained how plunging into the water exemplified the corruption of death, and how man, made in water, returned to the water, and was dissolved in it, waiting to be remade. Then he added the symbol of the potter's vessel, drawing from Jeremiah 18.1–6, suggesting that the candidate's nature was marred, and so, like a clay vessel, had to be immersed in the water so that it might be refashioned:

> The potters are also in the habit, when the vessels which they fashion are damaged, to refashion them again with water so that they may be remade and reconstructed and given the wanted form. This is the reason why God ordered also the prophet Jeremiah to repair to a potter; and he went and saw him working on a vessel which, because it was marred, he cast in the water, remade, and brought to its former state; and then God said to him, 'O house of Israel, cannot I do with you as this potter? said the Lord.' Because we also were made of earth and clay – as it is said, 'for thou art also made of clay like me', and 'forgive them that dwell in a house of clay because we are also made of the same clay.' When we fell and sin corrupted us, we received a complete dissolution from the (divine) sentence of death, but afterwards our Maker and our Lord refashioned us and remade us by his ineffable power, because he abolished death by resurrection and granted to all of us the hope of resurrection from the dead, and a world higher than the present, where we shall not only dwell but also become immortal and incorruptible.[82]

Theodore related immersion in the baptismal pool to both creation and redemption, in terms of parallels with both Adam and Christ. His main point was to stress that baptism was a sign of resurrection, and, as Riley points out,

> his emphasis is not on how the crucifixion and death are symbolized in the baptismal act, but rather how this act is a symbol of the resurrection, related indeed in a backward glance to Christ's actual resurrection, but more especially as symbol of the baptized's participation now in the eschatological reality which is to come.[83]

Theodore saw the sacramental action of immersion principally as a sign of participation in the future rather than an imitation of the past historical events of Christ's death and resurrection, as can be seen from his use of Romans 6.5, which Cyril had used to illustrate his teaching that the sacrament was an imitation of the crucifixion of Christ:

> Since, however, all this is done in symbols and signs in order to show that we do not make use of vain signs only, but of realities in which we believe and ardently desire, (Paul) said: 'For if we have been planted together in the likeness of his death, we shall be also (in the likeness) of his resurrection.' In using the future tense he confirms the present event by the future reality, and from the

greatness of the coming reality, he demonstrates the credibility of the greatness of its symbols, and the symbol of the coming reality in baptism. The working of the Holy Spirit is that it is in hope of the future things that you receive the grace of baptism, and that you draw nigh unto the gift of baptism in order to die and to rise with Christ, so that you may be born again to the new life, and thus, after having been led by these symbols to the participation in the realities, you will perform the symbol of that true second birth.[84]

Theodore concentrated his attention on the second part of the text and upon the notion of baptism as a sign of future resurrection, stressing the Pauline usage of the future tense to make his point that, while the historical resurrection of Christ was present in the act of baptism, the baptismal act also looked forward to the future accomplishment of this resurrection for the baptized in the eschaton. It was this notion of baptism as a sign of the future which led Theodore to other Pauline texts than his contemporaries and he suggested an interpretation of the emergence from the water of the body of the candidate which made it similar to the risen body of Christ:

> We believe in one godhead and are baptized, and through it we become one body, according to the working on us of the Holy Spirit, in baptism, which makes us children of God and one body of Christ our Lord, whom we consider our head as he is from our nature and was the first to rise from the dead, and as it is through him that we received participation in benefits . . . And we become one body of Christ, because we consider Christ our Lord in the flesh as our head, since he was assumed from us and was the first to rise from the dead, and thus he confirmed for us our participation in the resurrection from which we expect our body to be similar to his body. Indeed, 'our conversation is in heaven from whence also we look for our Saviour, our Lord Jesus Christ, who shall change our vile body that it may be fashioned like unto his glorious body . . .' This will take place in reality in heaven, but we perform its symbols and its signs in baptism.[85]

He grounded his mystagogy by using the Pauline mystagogy of the headship of Christ from 1 Corinthians 11.3, and he quoted Colossians 2.19 to strengthen this notion: 'We are also called the body of Christ our Lord, Christ our Lord being our head, as the blessed Paul said: "Christ is the head from which all the body is joined together and increases with the increase of God". [86] Although he used the same Adam-Christ theology as Cyril, he concentrated more on the resurrection, and that as a sign of the candidate's participation in the coming eschaton, and he summarized thus:

> You have fulfilled by your baptism in water the rite of burial, and you have received the sign of the resurrection by your rising out of the waters ... you are no more part of Adam who was mutable and burdened and made wretched by sin, but of Christ, who was completely freed from sin through the resurrection while even before it he never drew nigh to it. It was congruous that (this sinless state) should have had its beginning in him before his resurrection and that at his resurrection he should fully receive an immutable nature. In this way he confirmed to us the resurrection from the dead and our participation in incorruptibility. [87]

This difference in emphasis meant that other aspects of the baptismal ceremony received a different approach from Theodore, and the triple immersion and the invocation of the Trinity are examples of this. He used the healing of the lame man at the Gate Beautiful in Acts 3.6 to justify a trinitarian formula for baptism, emphasizing that in that name the saving power was given, just as the lame man had been restored in the name of Christ:

> When, therefore, (the priest) utters these words, 'In the name of the Father and of the Son and of the Holy Spirit,' he reveals to you the cause of the things that take place. In as much as the one who said, 'In the name of Jesus of Nazareth rise up and walk,' alluded to Christ as the cause of what would take place and to the fact that it would be he who would give (to the lame man) the power of rising and walking, so also the (priest) who says, 'In the name of the Father and of the Son and of the Holy Spirit,' refers to them as the cause of the benefits conferred upon us in baptism ... The priest does not say, 'In the name of the Father, and in the Name of the Son, and in the Name of the Holy Spirit,' because every one of them has a separate name that does not fit that of the other.' [88]

Linked with Theodore's future application of baptism was his teaching about the second birth, as the Christian following baptism was risen with Christ. Christ died physically, the candidate died spiritually in baptismal death; Christ rose physically, the candidate rose spiritually in baptismal resurrection. Not content with linking the past to the present,

Theodore proceeded to develop the future implications of the baptismal act, portraying baptism as a sign of hope in the future:

> And we become one body of Christ, because we consider Christ our Lord in the flesh as our head, and thus he confirmed for us our participation in the resurrection from which we expect our body to be similar to his body. Indeed, 'our conversation is in heaven, from which we look for our Lord Jesus Christ, who will change our vile body that it may be fashioned like unto his glorious body'.
> We do share by imitation in baptism in the resurrection of Christ, but we also really participate in the heavenly life to come, and this real participation in this coming risen life is mediated by the sacrament. This will take place in reality in heaven, but we perform its symbol and signs in baptism.[89]

Far from being an empty symbol of the eschaton the sacrament was a real participation in a relationship to the future in a hope which contains the whole potency of this future. Thus, although the 'true' second birth would be a feature of the eschaton, baptism was also a second birth, because by virtue of the symbols a real participation in this future second birth had actually been established:

> You should now proceed towards baptism in which the symbols of this second birth are performed, because you will in reality receive the true second birth only after you have risen from the dead and obtained the favour to be in the state of which you were deprived by death. All these things will happen to you in reality at the time appointed for your birth at the resurrection; as to now you have for them the word of Christ our Lord, and in the expectation of them taking place you rightly receive their symbols and signs through this awe-inspiring sacrament, so that you may not question your participation in future things.[90]

Theodore's mystagogical explanation of the baptismal act in terms of the imagery of the second birth built upon the relationship of baptism to the future flowering of the potencies contained within it. Second birth would be accomplished only in the last days, but baptism might be interpreted in terms of this image, because it looked back to the actual resurrection of Christ, and because it contained within it a real relationship in hope that the candidate would achieve ultimately this glorious resurrection.

71

The act of baptism looked forward to the future resurrection of the baptized, of which the past resurrection of Jesus is the model. When Theodore spoke of baptism containing 'the symbol of the birth which we expect,'[91] he meant that the symbol denoted and contained actually in hope the future resurrection, as opposed to the meaning of Cyril and Chrysostom who understood baptism to contain the salvific events of the earthly crucifixion, death, and resurrection of Jesus by imitation. By shifting his emphasis to the future, Theodore set himself a more awesome task, and he had to represent in image the rising of Jesus from the tomb, and then he had to add the images of second birth in so far as they fitted into a plausible relationship to the liturgical ceremony, as we saw, for example, in his water-creation-womb metaphors. As a result he had to sever himself from the liturgy, and pursued instead this metaphorical image of second birth:

> This is the reason why, when at my baptism I plunge my head, I receive the death of Christ our Lord, and desire to have his burial, and because of this I firmly believe in the resurrection of our Lord; and when I rise from the water I think I have symbolically risen a long time ago.
>
> Since, however, all this is done in symbols and signs, in order to show that we do not make use of vain signs only, but of realities in which we believe, and which we ardently desire, Paul said, 'for if we have been planted together in the likeness of his death we shall be also (in the likeness) of his resurrection.'
>
> In using the future tense, he confirms the present event by the future reality, and from the greatness of the coming reality he demonstrates the credibility of the greatness of its symbols, and the symbol of the coming realities is baptism. The working of the Holy Spirit is that it is in the hope of the future things that you receive the grace of baptism, and that you draw nigh unto the gift of baptism in order to die and to rise with Christ so that you may be born again to the new life, and thus, after having been led by these symbols to the participation in the realities, you will perform the symbol of that true second birth.[92]

This led him to draw a different emphasis from others in his application of the Jesus – Nicodemus dialogue in John 3.1–8:

> You draw nigh, therefore, unto the holy baptism which contains the symbol of the birth which we expect. This is the reason why our Lord called it second birth, when he said to Nicodemus,

'Except a man be born again, he cannot see the kingdom of God.' In this he showed that those who will enter the kingdom of God must have a second birth. Nicodemus, however, thought that they will be born according to a carnal birth from a woman, and said, 'How can a man be born when he is old? Can he enter the second time into his mother's womb and be born?' He said this because he believed we shall be born in a way similar to our first birth.[93]

Theodore added the interpretation that there was here a question of two ways to receive the second birth, one in baptism and one 'at the resurrection,' which Jesus did not describe to Nicodemus because this mystery at that moment would have been beyond Nicodemus' capacity to understand. Theodore explained that this second way of receiving the second birth was directly related to the first way, 'so that by means of its symbols they may move to the happiness of the reality itself.' So he could conclude that Jesus 'called baptism a second birth because it contains the symbol of this second birth.'[94] He proceeded to sum up his introductory section and his exposition of the connection between the symbols of baptism and resurrection under the image of the second birth:

> The power of holy baptism consists in this: it implants in you the hope of future benefits, enables you to participate in the things which we expect, and by means of the symbols and signs of the future good things it informs you with the gift of the Holy Spirit, the firstfruits of whom you receive when you are baptized.[95]

Theodore saw the baptistry as a womb for the sacramental birth of the candidates, relating 'the water of second birth,'[96] to the shelter of the unborn child in the womb. He developed this concept particularly by returning a second time to the encounter between Jesus and Nicodemus in a passage which Riley cites as a 'key example of the manner in which Theodore proceeds as mystagogue,'[97] blending Scripture and his own theological orientation with the natural imagery of human conception, birth, and growth to explain the act of baptism to his candidates.

> Our Lord, also, when Nicodemus asked him whether a man 'Can enter the second time into his mother's womb, and be born', answered, 'Except a man be born of water and of the Spirit, he cannot enter into the Kingdom of God.' He shows in this that as in a carnal birth the womb of the mother received the human seed, and the divine hand fashions it according to an ancient

decree, so also in baptism, the water of which becomes womb to the one who is being born, and the grace of the Spirit fashions it into the second birth, the one who is being baptized, and changes him completely into a new man. And inasmuch as the seed that falls into the womb of the mother has neither life, nor soul, nor feeling, but after it has been fashioned by the divine hand, it results in a living man, endowed with soul and feeling, and in a human nature capable of all human acts, so also here the one who is baptized falls into the water as into a womb, like a seed which bears no resemblance of any kind to the mark of an immortal nature, but after he has been baptized and has received the divine and spiritual grace, he will undoubtedly undergo a complete change: he will be fashioned from a mortal into an immortal, from a corruptible into an incorruptible, and from a mutable into an immutable nature; he will be changed completely into a new man according to the power of the one who fashions him.[98]

In this new life of the neophyte there was the potential for all the faculties for an immortal and incorruptible nature to be fully developed upon the divine decree at the time when he was no more a natural but a spiritual man, when the Holy Spirit had rendered the body incorruptible and the soul immutable at the resurrection of the body. To stress this point, he drew the parallel between carnal birth and what happened in baptism, but consistent with his future application of baptism, he suggested that the faculties of immortal and incorruptible activity, although possessed by the baptized, could not be used until God decreed it, at the resurrection.[99]

His analogy of the waters as a womb is followed by a picture of them as a furnace in which the candidate was to be renewed and refashioned in order that he might move to a higher nature, after having shed his old mortality and fully assumed an immortal and incorruptible nature. He illustrated this point with reference to Old Testament passages[100] which referred to man in the prophetic image of the potter's clay, to draw out the image of regeneration as we have seen above.[101] The parallel is as before, and the tension between present potential and ultimate reality is present in this image too, and its particular aptness is strengthened by the Genesis image of the creation of man.[102] Theodore spelt out this in his conclusion to this section:

We perform the symbols and signs of these things in water and are renewed and reconstructed according to the working of the Spirit on it. We who draw nigh unto baptism receive, therefore, these benefits from the sacrament in symbol, while in the next world we shall all of us receive renewal of our nature in reality. As an earthen vessel, which is being remade and refashioned in water, will remain in its softer nature and be clay as long as it has not come in contact with fire, but when it has been thrown on fire and.baked on it, it will undoubtedly be remade and refashioned, so also we, who are in a mortal nature, rightly receive the grace of the Holy Spirit, which hardens us more than any fire can do.[103]

Theodore emphasized that the reconstruction of the immortal nature of the neophyte had actually taken place in the baptismal water, and that nature was hardened by the fire of the Holy Spirit, but he was careful to point out that this refashioning, though real in baptism, was a reality always in hope. This emphasis recurred in his explanation of the priestly garments worn both for the first anointing and for the baptismal act: 'It is in this apparel that he performs the gift of baptism, because it behoves him to perform all the sacraments while wearing it, as it denotes the renovation found in the next world, to which you will be transferred through this same sacrament.'[104]

c) *The Post-Baptismal Rites.* Upon emergence from the baptistry the neophyte put on a shining white garment[105] and was signed upon the forehead by the bishop who said, 'So-and-so is signed in the name of the Father and of the Son and of the Holy Spirit.'[106] He does not allow much detail in his treatment of this part of the baptismal rite, and his entire mystagogy of this post-baptismal anointing is to be found in two paragraphs:

After you have received the grace of baptism and worn a white garment that shines, the priest draws nigh unto you on your forehead, and says: 'So-and-so is signed in the Name of the Father and of the Son and of the Holy Spirit.' When Jesus came out of the water he received the grace of the Holy Spirit who descended like a dove and lighted on him, and this is the reason why he is said to have been anointed: 'The Spirit of the Lord is upon me, because of which the Lord has anointed me'; and: 'Jesus of Nazareth whom God has anointed with the Holy Spirit and with power'; texts which show that the Holy Spirit is never separated from him, like the anointment with oil which has a durable effect on the men who are anointed, and is not separated from them. It is right, therefore, that when (the priest) signs you he says, 'So-and-so is signed in the name of the Father and of the Son and of the Holy Spirit,' so that it may be an indication to you that it is in the name of the Father and of the Son and of the Holy Spirit that the Holy Spirit descended on you also, and you were anointed and received grace; and he will be and remain with you, as it is through him that you possess the firstfruits. Indeed, at present you only receive symbolically the happiness of the future benefits, but at the time of the resurrection you will receive all the grace from which you will become immortal, incorruptible, impassible, and immutable; even your body will then remain for ever and will not perish, while your soul will be exempt from all inclination, however slight, towards evil.[107]

This scant treatment is probably due to the fact that he had devoted a lot of time to the prebaptismal anointing, also on the forehead, and did not wish to become over-repetitive.

From his references to Scripture it is plain to see that Theodore associated this post-baptismal anointing with the communication of the Holy Spirit, and he told the candidates that the anointing with its formula was a sign 'that the Holy Spirit descended on you also.' The anointing of the neophytes was linked with the effect in Christ's life following his own baptism in the Jordan when the Holy Spirit had descended upon him in the form of a dove. This event in Jesus' life and its relationship to the candidate's post-baptismal anointing was interpreted by Theodore in the light of the future resurrection, although not neglecting reference to the past salvific event in the Jordan. Thus the liturgical anointing, in typological terms, was the type, related in retrospect to the anointing of Jesus with the Spirit, and the future benefits of the resurrected body would be the antitype. Thus the liturgical anointing itself communicated to the neophyte a possession of the Holy Spirit, looking to future revelation but already begun in the present. It had a durable effect on the spiritual life of the candidate, equipping him for ministry in the Church and the world just as it had equipped Christ for his messianic ministry. Theodore explained the robe in terms of a symbol of the union of the neophyte with the risen Christ and here, as we would expect, he related his interpretation of the shining garment to the resurrection of Jesus as a sign of the eschatological fulfilment of the promise implied by the garment of freedom and radiance. He drew attention to the radiance of the garment as he had already done when describing the bishop's garment at the pre-baptismal anointing at baptism, which also inspired the candidates as a sign of the world to come. Although Theodore also interpreted the garment as a symbol of purity of life, this was from a unique basis, and it also fitted in with the eschatological emphasis which he taught. The robe was needed only because immortality and incorruptibility had been received only symbolically and sacramentally, rather than in reality:

> When you have received the resurrection in reality and put on immortality and incorruptibility, such a garment will be wholly unnecessary, but since you do not possess such things in reality, and have only received them sacramentally and symbolically, you are in need of garments. Of these you wear those which denote happiness, which you have now received symbolically, but which you will one day possess in reality.[108]

This then became the counterpart of stripping off the garments before baptism, where the logical conclusion of Theodore's teaching would be that after baptism no clothing should be worn.[109] Theodore stressed the temporary need of present clothing, which would be rendered unnecessary when man returned to his paradisal condition. This robe took on the aspect of a future-looking symbol. Theodore developed this through his choice of words, letting the light and radiance of the future world shine through the radiance of the garments of those who belong to that new world by their birth into it, whether bishop or neophyte! He saw the garment as a sign of happiness and joy, but he did not spell out, as Cyril and Chrysostom did, its symbolism of the purity of Christian action in the Christian who wore it. It was a vital intermediate step before the resurrection was actualized in the eschaton, and as such this expectation would transform the life of the Christian and produce a bias towards purity in his life, but his emphasis on the world to come precluded any emphasis on other factors for Theodore.

This eschatological emphasis characterized both the catechesis and mystagogy of Theodore, and gave it its own particular flavour when compared to that of Cyril and Chrysostom, as we shall see when we compare them.

4

A Comparison of the Catechetical and Mystagogical Explanation of Baptism of Cyril of Jerusalem, John Chrysostom and Theodore of Mopsuestia

The material which we are comparing has in common the fact that all three are Lenten lectures given to those enrolled for baptism in the fourth century, but one is almost tempted to say that there the similarity ends! The material differed because of the homiletic style of those giving the lectures, and because of the different needs of the situations in which they were teaching. For example, the community-based church in Mopsuestia had a different emphasis from the more cosmopolitan situation of Antioch, and the tourist/pilgrim centre of Jerusalem. Cyril of Jerusalem made ample use of the advantages of the natural visual aids arising from his situation, whilst John Chrysostom's oratorical style was inimitable. Chrysostom refrained from using the Creed in his syllabus, whilst Theodore taught both the explanation of the Creed, an explanation of the ceremonies, and the Lord's Prayer before baptism, with no evidence of post-baptismal teaching. Cyril taught the explanation of the Creed before baptism, adopting the practice of that church in not revealing details of the mysteries or of the Lord's Prayer to the unbaptized, as was also the case in Milan. Chrysostom made reference to leaving the instruction on faith to 'your teacher,'[1] and frequently referred to 'teachers' in the plural,[2] mentioning also a thirty day period of instruction[3] which he likened to 'the practice and bodily exercises in some wrestling school'. Thus we gather that he was not alone in his task of giving instruction to candidates, but rather he was one of a team which included Bishop Flavian, other clergy, and possibly even visiting bishops as well.[4] In this different situation, in which all the burden of lecturing apparently did not fall upon Chrysostom, quite plainly his lectures would have had both a different purpose and character from those of Cyril and Theodore, even if we were to discount the differences in personalities. Nevertheless, some attempt will be made to compare the three sets of material on the basis of what they said.

1. *The Theology of Baptism and its Catechetical Explanation*

Cyril, Chrysostom and Theodore all spoke of the baptism of Jesus himself by John, and all taught that the baptism of John which Jesus underwent was inferior to the Christian baptism which he instituted. It was inferior because it was only a mark of repentance, and it was abrogated and replaced by the baptism instituted by Christ. Cyril and Chrysostom indicated this strongly,[5] but Theodore saw in Jesus' submission to the baptism of John in the Jordan his obedience to the command of the Father and his identification with sinful man, and he did not reduce the significance of John's baptism by an unfavourable comparison with that of Jesus. Rather he was more concerned to stress the identification of Jesus with the candidate in baptism, and as a result was theologically anachronistic in applying to the baptism of repentance administered by John in the Jordan the effects of Christian baptism.[6]

Cyril's interpretation of the descent of the Holy Spirit at the baptism of Jesus was that it demonstrated the dignity of the one who was baptized.[7] Chrysostom used this feature of Jesus' own baptism to point out that not only was the Holy Spirit bestowed upon the candidates in baptism, but that the baptism of Jesus was a baptism by each member of the Trinity.[8] He used this to explain the threefold baptism of the candidates[9] and also the apersonal formula, stressing that both John and the celebrant were but agents of the godhead. Theodore interpreted the Holy Spirit in this way, but added the concept of the Holy Spirit as the guarantee to the Christian of his hope in the future.[10] He developed this to identify not just the Spirit, but also the Father and the Son equally as guarantors of the future eternal benefits for which the Christian's hope rested upon a sure and certain foundation.

Cyril however added a salvific motif to his description of Jesus' baptism as he described Jesus' baptism in terms of his conquest of the dragon in the waters,[11] but this he applied to Jesus' conquest of death and sin, citing Luke 19.18–19, to allow him to use this passage in the context of Jesus' birth rather than in the more Pauline context of Jesus' death and resurrection. This seems to be an idea peculiar to Cyril, and it was not used by Chrysostom or Theodore. Cyril put the baptism of Jesus into its historical context, and pointed out that it preceded both his temptation and his ministry, and he reminded his audience that, following baptism, they could expect temptation, which they would be enabled to overcome only by the power of the Holy Spirit.[12] Chrysostom suggested to his audience that they received the Holy Spirit at baptism, describing the neophytes he was addressing as 'those who have just been judged worthy of the gift of the Spirit.'[13]

An important pre-requisite of baptism was sincerity of intention, and Cyril warned his candidates against hypocrisy. He constantly put the onus on his candidates to ensure their own readiness to receive baptism, by equipping themselves with both piety of soul and with a good conscience,[14] and making thorough preparation through confession and daily exorcism. Chrysostom also stressed that in spite of the spiritual event of baptism, the will could still sometimes be opposed to God,[15] and although this came from a post-baptismal lecture, he also referred to the role of daily exorcism prior to baptism, and he used the image of gold refined in the furnace to emphasize the need for a genuine desire and sincere intention both during the exorcisms and during baptism. Chrysostom also saw baptism in terms of a spiritual marriage, and he referred to the same passage as Cyril above,[16] but stressed the gracious benevolence of the host who made suitable clothing available to those who would accept his generosity.[17] According to Cyril, there were two effects of baptism, the first being the remission of sins, which all who approached the sacrament received, and the second the communication of the Holy Spirit, positive graces, which he felt would vary according to the fervour of faith and intensity of love for God on the part of the recipient.[18]

He described his candidates as those about to be enlightened, and in this connection he made the most of the advantages which lecturing in Jerusalem gave him. The candidates' baptism would take place in the Church of the Resurrection, brilliantly illuminated during the Easter Vigil to symbolize the return of the risen light and their own sacramental enlightenment,[19] but enlightenment came only to those who were baptized from right motives.[20] Baptism was to grant regeneration to the candidates, and he cited the parable of the sheep and the goats and the account of the conversion of Cornelius; and with regeneration would come the enlightenment of the candidates. Chrysostom also referred to enlightenment as one of the effects of baptism, quoting Hebrews 10.32 and Hebrews 6.4–6 in support of his statement, and later citing the example of Paul who was 'baptized and illumined by the light of truth.'[21] Illumination and enlightenment were seen by Chrysostom as that which *after* baptism led the Christian towards a virtuous lifestyle, and as such these qualities were more closely analogous to the baptismal robe, and the evidence of the spiritual quality of the post-baptismal life of the candidate.[22]

The spiritual adoption of the candidates at baptism to their new role as sons of God was accomplished by the grace of God,[23] and Chrysostom refined Cyril's viewpoint that this happened at the moment of baptism to suggest that this adoptive relationship was mediated through the imposition of the hands of the bishop as he pronounced the baptismal formula.[24] Cyril's rationale for the idea of spiritual adoption came from the voice of God acknowledging Christ at his baptism, but for the candidates, Cyril pointed out, the voice from heaven proclaimed 'This has now become my Son.'[25] He was careful to distinguish between the sonship of Jesus, and the adoptive sonship of the candidates, accomplished by the free grace of God. This adoption was closely linked for Cyril with the concept of the seal which asserted the Lord's ownership of the candidate, and which not only served for purposes of recognition but also as a means of protection against the evil spirits.[26] The protective seal was received through the operation of the Holy Spirit and was analogous to a spiritual circumcision.[27] The relationship between baptism and circumcision was mentioned by Chrysostom in his list of the titles of baptism, citing Colossians 2.11 in support of his statement,[28] but we must look outside the lectures to his expository sermons for clarification of his idea. He concurred that circumcision was performed upon the Christian by the Spirit,[29] and he directly compared baptism and circumcision in his comparison between the Old Covenant and the New Covenant in Christ.[30] Cyril further stressed the need for inward sincerity when he pointed out that both the water of baptism and the operation of the Spirit were necessary to the kingdom of heaven. In the absence of either component, the rite was incomplete,[31] and Cyril stressed this by reversing his image and applying the seal to the water rather than to the Spirit.

Cyril also described baptism in terms of the means by which the candidates died to sin and began a new life in Christ, free from past sins and justified by grace,[32] and were made heirs of eternal life in Christ.[33] He built up this picture by listing a number of titles to convey a composite picture of the spiritual effects of the baptismal rite, bringing the candidates ransom from captivity, the remission of their sins, and both the death and burial of the power of sin in their lives. This was matched by a new spiritual birth, following the Pauline pattern from Romans 6.2–5, and the regeneration of the soul of the candidate was marked by the shining baptismal garment which he donned. This began his journey to eternal life – a heaven-bound chariot – to sample the delights of paradise, with a passport to the kingdom demonstrating his new status as an adopted son of the Father.[34] Chrysostom also saw baptism in terms of a burial and a resurrection,[35] describing it as a bath of regeneration,[36] and as a cross, a death, and a resurrection,[37] a theme which he developed in his exposition of Romans 6.[38] He also stressed the immediate nature of the baptismal death, burial, resurrection, and rebirth of the candidate,[39] but this also presupposed a radical transformation in the baptizand's moral behaviour,[40] in short, transforming him into one person instead of another, and making the baptized a new creature.[41] Chrysostom illustrated this by using the analogy of the smelting furnace, which not only cleansed the gold placed in it, but made it new too;[42] but when he developed this analogy into that of the potter's vessel, he pointed out that the vessel was made of raw clay, not of fired terracotta, and so following inadvertent sin it could be restored to its pristine baptismal state by God through sincere repentance.[43] In this respect he is probably more realistic than Cyril, although his realism was probably inspired by his own sense of unworthiness and failure as his discourse was broken off by his own tears;[44] and although he was adamant that there was no second baptism, he suggested that confession to God, sincere repentance and tears, prayers and almsgiving could all help the Christian to win pardon for subsequent sins, but·it was still far better never to have sinned at all. His own list of the benefits and gifts of baptism contained ten gifts: freedom, holiness, justice, sonship, heirs, brotherhood, joint-heirs, members, temples and instruments of the Spirit. Five out of the ten gifts which he listed were based upon the new relationship into which the baptized entered through their baptism and as a result of their adoptive sonship, and Chrysostom had a high sense of the fraternity which should exist among the followers of Christ, although he suggested that this relationship can be marred by later negligence and failure.[45] Earlier he had pictured the candidates as the bride making a marriage contract with Christ the Bridegroom,[46] and such a common relationship to Christ in itself would involve those who had made their profession to Christ in a relationship to each other, after he had transformed them into new creatures. Theodore interpreted this picture of baptism as burial and resurrection in terms of a symbol of the life to come and of an expression of the candidates' hope of the life which they hoped to share with Christ at the resurrection of the dead.[47] This was in keeping with his teaching that the Christian's life was lived in the hope of the resurrection which was only attained if the Christian lived in accordance with the commandment of Christ. So, following baptism, the Christian's life was one of constant effort to live up to the hope of resurrection-life with Christ, a stranger to the law, remote from sin, freed from the life of this world, and dead to the world.[48] Although there is an apparent contradiction here between the actual time of possession of the Christian's new life – at baptism, or at the resurrection – he interpreted the candidates' sealing with the Holy Spirit at baptism as the guarantee of their future inheritance, given that they 'may possess these future good things in a firm faith without doubt'.[49]

Both Cyril and Chrysostom described baptism in terms of

the gracious gift of God, completely unmerited and unearned by man. Cyril combined the idea of sacramental grace, mediated through baptism, and prevenient grace which enabled man to come to God to receive remission of sins, and to receive the gift which God imparted to man.[50] The idea of sacramental grace in the *Catechetical Lectures* was twofold, being conveyed by water and the Spirit, and these two components were inseparable for the sacrament to be valid.[51] Although grace was freely given and mediated in baptism, Cyril was quite adamant that it had to be cherished and reverenced once it had been received by the candidate, and used this to stress once again the candidate's responsibility for his life after baptism, with all his deeds, both good and bad, being recorded by God.[52] Chrysostom used similar terms to describe baptism as the symbol of the saving work of Christ, completely undeserved by man, but laying upon the candidate the obligation to live a life worthy of such a lavish gift of God. Similarly it had to be received worthily, and Chrysostom attacked those who postponed baptism to their deathbeds, to avoid post-baptismal sin, in scathing terms, pointing out that although the grace was the same, the circumstances of the gift being bestowed were utterly inappropriate.[53]

Chrysostom saw the grace of God as the means of making all Christians equal before God, and the spiritual gifts which the believers received were given entirely in accordance with God's gracious will alone.[54] In the light of the grace which God showed by his great goodness to Christians, the least they could do was to respond to that grace by seeking to live a life worthy of such grace. He too stressed the danger of post-baptismal sin,[55] although, of God's grace, the Christian was granted privacy of confession for his sins.[56] So the Christian throughout his life must consider the grace of God which he had received, and from which he had benefited.

We see, then, that the three catechists delivered their own material, using their own imagery, and stressing their own particular emphasis. For Cyril, lecturing in the pilgrim/tourist centre of Jerusalem, this was to stress the need for absolute sincerity before baptism, and this he emphasized by teaching the severe punishment which would be meted out in respect of any sin after baptism. Although Chrysostom also stressed the need for genuineness and sincerity, his emphasis was upon the gracious act of God in Christ, and in describing the new life with its new relationships which God had made possible in Christ. Theodore saw things on a broader canvas, and although his references to baptism in the credal material are scant, he saw baptism as the means by which God made the Christian part of his plan for his world, and the means by which the Christian was assured of his participation in a future life with Christ. Having seen such variations in that which we are regarding as catechetical material, we are not surprised to find similar variations in their treatment of liturgical themes.

2. *The Liturgy of Baptism and its Mystagogical Explanation*

a) *The Rite of Renunciation and Profession*: The first area of liturgical explanation which we shall consider is the treatment which Cyril, Theodore, and Chrysostom gave to the rite of renunciation and profession. Although each worked within the different liturgical framework of his own situation, the basic meaning of this for the candidates was explained by all of them with a substantial unity of interpretation. Cyril had the gesture of turning, which he explained in terms of repentance, as the candidates turned from slavery in bondage to Satan to freedom in unity with Christ.[57] However, although Chrysostom and Theodore had liturgical frameworks which used the gesture of kneeling, rather than turning, they were able to demonstrate the same meaning in a different way. For them the bondage of man's natural state brought him to his knees in degradation, and reminded them of the fall of Adam, which had begun the various forms of man's degradation and enslavement.[58] But they were able to apply a double meaning to the posture of kneeling, to show that it expressed the candidate's return to the adoration and acknowledgement of Christ as Lord of the Universe. They contrasted the humiliation of man kneeling before a despotic master, with man's free kneeling in reverent answer to the possibility of the restoration of his lost fulfilment by choosing to accept the freedom of the call of the gospel. Chrysostom took this one step further in explaining the kneeling posture of the candidates as an expresson of the equality of all men before God.[59] Cyril developed his mystagogy to include the story of Lot's wife and the effects of her turning back to look at Sodom.[60] Theodore, on the other hand, turned to the New Testament and to the descriptions of the conversion of Saul and Cornelius, where kneeling played a role in the actions prior to baptism. He spelt out the meaning of the eventual rising from the knees; firstly as the reversal of slavery, and of the fall which was its cause; secondly as the sign that the adoration of Christ as Lord is accepted; and thirdly that the candidates' prayers for deliverance are answered.[61] Similarly the hand gestures, although different liturgically, were interpreted by Cyril as a natural sign of the baptizand's rejection of Satan,[62] whilst Chrysostom saw the outstretched arms towards heaven as a sign of deliverance from evil, as a sign of the baptizand's willingness to strive for good deeds, and as an act of gratitude for the gift of faith.[63] Theodore, on the other hand, saw this same gesture as a reminder of the helplessness that the fall into slavery had brought, and as a prayer for deliverance from this, as well as a sign of adoration of God.[64]

Cyril's candidates turned from West to East, and in his liturgy there was the factor that the renunciation and profession had taken place at a night vigil, so he could build upon the natural symbolism of the East as the place of light, and the West as the place of darkness. Although those being baptized in Antioch and Mopsuestia did not apparently make this gesture, still their mystagogues used this element in their teaching. Cyril used the natural darkness of the midnight hour, developing the idea of the West as a sign of the darkness of Satanic works and of hell, and reminded his baptizands that the East was not only the realm of light, but also the place where the Garden of Eden was planted.[65] Prompted by the temporal feature that the rite of renunciation and profession took place on Good Friday at three o'clock in the afternoon in Antioch, Chrysostom explained the darkness in terms of the darkness of the crucifixion. Thus the kneeling candidate found himself looking towards both the Messiah and Paradise. The imagery which he created was more biblically based: as, in mystical symbolism, the glorious Messiah appeared shining from the cross, the natural sun turned back its rays before the splendour of 'this Sun of Justice'. From the crucifixion he also drew the picture of Paradise, and, on the basis of the acceptance of the penitent thief and his admission to Paradise, Chrysostom assured his candidates that the token of their adoration and commitment would also be accepted.[66] Theodore arrived at the same point by a different route, using rather the conversion accounts in Acts of Cornelius and Saul, which occurred at the ninth and sixth hours respectively.[67] So the mystagogues developed a mystagogy for the bodily actions of the candidates within the liturgy which underscored in both breadth and depth the act of renunciation and commitment, and thus enabled the candidates to grasp the significance of the renunciation of Satan and profession of allegiance to Christ in the fullest possible way.

Although the bodily actions were important, and underscored the significance of the act, they could not replace the importance of the words themselves with which the candidate professed his personal allegiance to Christ. In explaining the significance of the formula, the fathers rested solidly on the fact of the indispensable importance of the spoken word of a human being in revealing his state of mind and heart, and the Semitic concept that the word, once spoken, had a life of its own. Through the spoken word the interior act of conversion was made visible and publicly declared. Thus it was the candidate who dramatically confronted Satan, and the candidate was encouraged to think of Satan as virtually present, literally breathing down his neck![68] In his renunciation of Satan and his rejection of the service of Satan, the candidate was summing up in his rejection all that he had come to know about his own impediments to faith through exorcism and vowing finally to reject them. Theodore and Chrysostom raised the act to a personal plane by increasing the awareness of the candidate to the strength of the network of evil which ensnared and enslaved him, but at the same time stressing the personal terror which the candidates felt at renouncing such a cruel tyrant.[69] All three mystagogues used the imagery of the legal contract, and pictured the verbal act of renunciation as applying to a previous contract which Scripture described man as having made with Satan as enslaving tyrant, with death, and with hell. This was dissolved at the point of renunciation and a new contract established in union with Christ. This idea, although present in all three fathers, was probably most highly developed by Chrysostom,[70] who also stressed the binding nature of the new covenant made with Christ. This contract was recorded in a heavenly book by God himself – a testimony to its binding and eternal nature[71]. Chrysostom based his mystagogical teaching on Pauline teaching. The price of invalidating the old contract was paid by Christ with his blood on the cross; but although the candidate found the price already paid, his acceptance of the contract was voluntary, and was a non-compulsory gift, with an emphasis upon the freedom from coercion on the part of Christ who had already paid the cost of the contract in full. Chrysostom moved from here to a bridal metaphor, emphasizing the personal relationship of love involved in the verbal assent to the contract. For him, the profession became not merely a verbal assent, but the personal response of love made by the bride to the Bridegroom's gift of himself.[72] Thus the act of commitment to Christ became the dowry which the bride happily brought to the Bridegroom. As the candidates made their act of renunciation and profession, their fear and awe in confronting Satan was overcome by the fact that they were united with the struggle and the victory of Christ in liberating them from Satan. Cyril and Theodore both encouraged their candidates by emphasizing the bond which existed between Christ and the candidate at this vital moment.[73] Chrysostom extended his mystagogy to embrace the idea of the candidate's struggle in terms of a metaphor of the struggle at the Olympic games, where Christ as the Olympic judge decided for the candidate, and by referring the struggle of the candidate to the struggle of Christ on the cross, using once again the temporal analogy from the time of celebration of his liturgical rite.[74]

Theodore and Chrysostom described in detail the interpretation of the act of anointing which followed this rite. Probably this is a further indication that for Theodore as well as for Chrysostom the rite of renunciation and profession came as a separate rite, possibly one or two days before the rite of baptism. Cyril, whose service was a corporate one, does not from his situation, mention this anointing, nor would it have been necessary when the rite of baptism followed in a matter of minutes. Chrysostom and Theodore based their mystagogy on two elements in this ceremony. The first was the signing of the candidate's forehead with the sign of the cross, and the second the use of oil to trace that sign on to the candidate's forehead. Both found that this ceremony formed an apt conclusion to the rite of renunciation and profession, and a symbolic expression of what had taken place. The sealing symbolized belonging and commitment expressing the candidate's new-found relationship with Christ, Chrysostom chose 2 Corinthians 1.21 to emphasize that the anointing was performed by Christ himself, albeit at the hands of the priest.

Through the anointing. Christ took possession of the candidate.[75] Theodore also interpreted the ceremony in terms of the candidate belonging to Christ, but used Ephesians 2.19 to link the seal of the cross with the name-plate of ownership in a household, once again using a favourite image of heaven as a great city, the household of God.[76]

The seal was also a mark of protection and appointment, and Chrysostom's image here was drawn from the combat arena, as the olive oil reminded him of the olive oil used to rub down the athlete before the combat. Because the seal was made in the sign of the cross, it contained the power of the cross, and thus it protected the candidate from the attack of Satan. The glistening quality of the oil used in tracing the sign of the cross on the forehead helped Chrysostom to see the cross as the power of a brilliant lightning flash which blinded the eyes of the devil.[77] On the other hand, Theodore's mystagogy concentrated on the sign of the cross as a sign of Christ's suffering, death, and victory, using 2 Timothy 2.11–13 to interpret the cross with which the forehead was signed in terms of the call to follow Christ through suffering to glory.[78] His mystagogy, however, rested on the central concept of freedom, which would be complete in the heavenly city, but which through the sacrament was actually present in some way at the moment of anointing, and Theodore sought to explain just what this freedom meant. He did this by featuring the various aspects of the liturgy – the bishop's robe signifying the freedom and joy of heaven, the prayer shawl bestowed by the godparent to confer the status of a free man, and finally through the signation with the cross, he assured the candidate of his status, and that he might freely and with confidence approach God face-to-face in just the same way as the Son of God gazed eternally at his Father.[79]

By comparing the christological approach of Chrysostom and Theodore to this anointing, we discover that they do exhibit a common element in teaching the candidate about his participation in the life of Christ. For Theodore, the interior gift of confidence which the candidate demonstrated before God by virtue of his signation came directly from the candidate's participation in the confidence which the man Jesus possessed in his unity with the godhead, and in which, as the firstfruits of the sacrament, the candidate participated.[80] Chrysostom also spoke of participation in the life of

Christ, but he expressed this in terms of the image of the cross, stamped by God himself on the candidate's forehead, and he linked this idea with the culminating expression of confidence, uttered by Jesus on Good Friday, giving man access to the Holy God: 'Father, into thy hand I commend my Spirit.'[81] In both cases, the candidates were being taught that they were participating in the life of Christ. Theodore used this concept to speak of the citizenship of heaven, and the confidence and freedom which belonging to that city implied. For Chrysostom, the candidate was appointed through his anointing to join in the struggle of Jesus, thus coming to the ultimate victory under the protection of the sign of the cross of Christ.

b) *The Baptismal Rite*: As we move towards the baptismal rite as such, we find that the fathers chose very similar points to emphasize, and although diverse in approach, there seems to have been a basic unity about their teaching. The previous rite of renunciation and profession was linked firmly to this new phase in the rite of initiation. Cyril mentioned the movement of the candidates from the outer chamber to the inner chamber,[82] whilst Chrysostom emphasized the transition by his stress on the time difference,[83] and Theodore described the baptismal rite as 'the remaining part of the sacrament.'[84] Their explanation began with two ceremonies which preceded the baptismal act, the removal of the candidates' garments, and the anointing of the whole body with oil.

Cyril and Chrysostom taught that the removal of clothing before baptism was on the basis of the Pauline metaphor of laying aside the deeds of the old man as one might lay aside old clothing. They added to this the gospel allegory of the wedding feast, and used both as an exhortation to increased effort, so as not to come improperly clad to the feast. Cyril used this image in the *Procatechesis*, and commented that, although a candidate with soiled clothes could get into the catechetical assembly by following the crowd, he had to face the embarrassment of ultimate exposure. Even at that point, however, there was still opportunity for the candidate to mend his ways.[85] Chrysostom applied the allegory in the same way, as an instruction to those who were going to be baptized, and he stressed the imagery of coming to baptism – the wedding feast – to highlight the candidates' need for serious moral purpose.[86] Similarly the imagery of the bridal call with a special emphasis on the clothing of the bride was used by both

Cyril and Chrysostom. For both, soiled clothing represented an unworthy condition for appearing for the marriage, but whilst for Cyril the garments had to be washed, representing conversion from evil deeds, for Chrysostom, the bridegroom himself would take care of this, and would not make this cause for rejecting the bride. Chrysostom went further than Cyril in dealing with the deeds of the old man, and thus for him the implications of clothing were expressed in terms of the reality of Christian conduct. Sins were part of the burden of the old life which had to be laid aside, just as old clothing was discarded, and Chrysostom developed this to include the implications of the clothing which the candidates wore. Jewelled clothing could imply a careless attitude to the poor who had been exploited to make it available. Envy and jealousy could be caused by over-sumptuous dress. He was particularly concerned with the motivation behind the dress and make-up of women.[88] In this area Chrysostom was meeting some of the pastoral realities in the environment of the candidates, and possibly this implies that he had a closer pastoral relationship with the candidates than was possible for Cyril.

The candidates were naked following the removal of their clothing, and this nakedness Cyril and Theodore explained with a similar underlying theme, although with different mystagogies. Cyril's explanation was based on the vivid image of the crucifixion which he described, noting the fact that Christ was stripped on the cross, and thus overcame the power of corruption, a feature emphasized by his use of the Pauline interpretation of the triumph represented by the cross.[89] Theodore chose rather to reflect on the mortality of Adam, represented by the clothing, the sign of his fall, which he wore to cover his shame. The clothes which the candidates removed were symbols of the aprons God made Adam and Eve, and as such were a symbol of sin and ultimate death. By removing these garments the candidates demonstrated their call to immortality, and the reversal of the fall of Adam and all its consequences.[90] Whilst Theodore saw this in terms of Adam, Cyril took this imagery from the new Adam, and it was through Christ that the reversal of the fall had taken place, and so the garments removed represented the history of sin and the power of sin, and consequently the mortality of man. All three Fathers pointed to the picture from Genesis of Adam and Eve, naked and yet unashamed, to explain that it was as a result of the candidates' own restoration to the state of primeval innocence that they also had not been ashamed in their moment of nakedness. Cyril and Chrysostom depicted the baptismal pool as a symbol of paradise, and Theodore's point was the same, although he did not use the term 'paradise' to describe the baptismal pool.[91]

The body anointing which preceded baptism was described in three fundamental ways: in terms of exorcism and healing, in terms of fortifying and protecting, and in terms of union with Christ; and once again a unity of interpretation emerges. Both Cyril and Theodore used the natural symbolism of oil as a healing agent. Cyril explained the image by considering the oil itself, the prayers used in its blessing, and its relationship to the exorcism programme which ran throughout the proximate period of baptismal preparation. This caused his mystagogy to develop from the natural symbolism, with which it began, to the symbolism of sin as corruption, which left its trace in the souls of the candidates and had to be healed by this medicinal oil.[92] From this same natural symbolism of oil as a healing agent, Theodore reverted to his former image of clothing as sign of corruption, and showed how the oil penetrated and covered the body, removing sin and its effects. Thus the oil was seen to replace the clothing, the healing power of immortality set over against the decaying power of corruption and mortality.[93]

The idea of oil fortifying and protecting the candidate comes most strongly from Chrysostom. In a sense his idea was related to that of Theodore which we have just considered, and he used the additional pictures of the athlete, oiled to enhance the suppleness and agility of his muscles, and of the soldier, clad from head to toe in protective armour.[94] Riley summarizes the interpretation of these effects of pre-baptismal anointing thus:

> by removing the traces of sin or 'ethical sickness' by use of this medicinal oil, the candidates' weakness of 'mortality' and 'corruptibility' was removed and in its place comes an invulnerability or 'cloak of immortality' which protects and strengthens him as a soldier or an athlete is strengthened or protected.[95]

The Fathers then related these effects to the power of Christ, and the union of the candidates with Christ. Cyril took the

Pauline image of the cultivated olive oil and the wild olive tree from Romans 11.17ff.; and for his candidates the oil became a direct christological symbol, a sign of richness of the life of Christ shared by the candidate as he was anointed.[96] Chrysostom used 2 Corinthians 1.21 to depict for his candidates Christ anointing them, so that Christ made the candidate an athlete and a soldier of Christ.[97] Theodore described the anointing in terms of the action of the Holy Spirit, who in the sign communicated to the candidates the gift of heavenly immortality now.[98] Once again he interpreted this action in line with his eschatological views.

When teaching their candidates about the nature of the baptismal act, once again we find the same fundamental unity of view, although variously expressed, concerning baptism as a participation in the cross, death and resurrection of Jesus Christ. As a basic framework this was seen by the mystagogues to signify the actions of the candidates in entering the pool, in being immersed in the water, and in leaving the pool. They went on to use their particular liturgical framework to teach how this revealed the candidates' new status as associates of Christ in his death and resurrection. Each mystagogue quoted from the Pauline passage in Romans 6.3ff., but Cyril possessed the especial and unique advantage of being at the very scene of the events of Christ's death and resurrection, and so he was able to present to his candidates the stark comparison between the body of Christ being brought from the cross and buried in the tomb and the movement of the candidate to the pool.[99] He developed this advantage of location to press home his mimesis theology, and his own unique interpretation of the candidates' triple immersion/emersion as a sign of the three days which Christ spent in the tomb.[100] Chrysostom portrayed entry to the pool as burial with Christ, and he linked the candidates with salvation-history as he suggested that the baptistry was reminiscent of the garden of Eden, stressing that, following his death to sin and burial with Christ, the Christian must live a life of detachment from sin.[101] Theodore, on the other hand, recreated the salvation-history of sin and death also by alluding to water and earth as the elements of creation, so the pool was not only the tomb but also a furnace for refashioning the marred and corrupted vessel, and a potter's tank into which the clay pot was cast by the Maker to be refashioned and remade.[102]

Cyril and Chrysostom sought to show that baptism also forgave sins, because it was related to the crucifixion of Christ, which contained the power to forgive the sins of men, although Cyril found it impossible to explain this mystagogically, and had to use the theological image of the vine 'planted in Jerusalem' to explain to his candidates their participation in the sufferings and crucifixion of Christ.[103] Chrysostom also occupied himself with the question of how baptism was the cross, and found the basis for his answer in the word of Jesus to the mother of James and John that the baptism of Jesus' followers is an association in his cross.[104] He linked the baptismal bath with the crucifixion, reminding his audience of neophytes that blood and water had poured forth from the side of Christ,[105] and applying this to his audience through the Pauline statement in Romans 6.5.

Coming out of the pool was seen by the Fathers as a sign of the resurrection, and, although Cyril did not develop this point in the *Mystagogical Catecheses*, he made it strongly in the *Catechetical Lectures*, as we have seen above. Chrysostom links his explanation of the resurrection with the mystagogy which he applied to death, placing it under his pastoral emphasis of death to sin and detachment from it. The baptized, he taught, emerged from the pool possessing the new, resurrected, but hidden life of Christ which would show itself in his Christian conduct before the world.[106] Theodore developed this idea of emergence from the pool as a sign of resurrection more fully than his contemporaries, as we might expect from his basic concept that the sacrament was a participation in the future reality rather than an imitation of the past historical events of salvation. He took the second part of Romans 6.5 to emphasize the baptized's conformity to the risen Christ in the eschaton, and because of this emphasis on future resurrection Theodore chose texts referring to the glorious body of Christ to which the baptized will ultimately be conformed,[107] and he continued this development in his explanation of baptism as new birth.

For all the fathers, their image of baptism as a new birth was rooted deeply in the New Testament, but their task was to apply this image to their baptismal liturgy to show how that liturgy itself could suggest that in some way the candidate is reborn in baptism, and this was an image which derived from the notion of the resurrection. Chrysostom concentrated on the scriptural description of baptism as the 'bath of rebirth', but rather than explaining it, his teaching was more in the nature of a pastoral meditation, and verged upon the mystical. His mystical approach was particularly evident through its application of the bridal metaphor, seeing the baptismal bath as the bridal bath, and describing regeneration in terms of the power of the love of the Bridegroom for his bride.[108] This mystagogy was presented in terms of the blood and water flowing from the open side of Christ into the baptismal pool, endowing it with its power of cleansing and regeneration; and he pictured the baptized begotten from the side of Christ 'asleep' on the cross, just as Eve was begotten from the side of the sleeping Adam. This elaboration was only used by Chrysostom. Theodore seized upon the imagery of new birth as being the most apt to get across his theological pre-occupation with the future. He combined scripture references about the future resurrection with a detailed illustration embracing the whole process of conception and birth in order to demonstrate how baptism was a new birth, a symbol of the real new birth that would take place for the Christian in the eschatological resurrection of the body. He interpreted the Jesus/Nicodemus dialogue in John 3 in terms of two new births, of which he explained baptism as the type and the future resurrection as the antitype.[109]

Thus the image of the baptismal pool as womb emerged, and Cyril graphically stated the paradox of the pool being womb and tomb at the same time, describing the candidates' death to their old selves in the pool and rebirth from it to newness of life in Christ.[110] Chrysostom extended this imagery to remind the neophytes that they were brought forth without the customary pains or time of birth labour.[111] He proceeded to explain the supernatural character of the rebirth of the candidates by using the allusion of the Virgin Birth;[112] while for Theodore it was the invocation of the Holy Spirit upon the waters of the baptismal font that transformed it into the womb of rebirth.[113] He then went on to explain why, in the Jesus/Nicodemus dialogue, Jesus called baptism a second birth, basing his explanation on the distinction between the child in the womb, in one sense born there in his conception, and the actual coming out of the womb and being born, when the child began to be able to use his faculties and sense. On this basis he explained that at the second birth of baptism, just like the child in the womb, the candidate had all the potential faculties but could not use them, but that the second birth of the resurrection in the future eschaton was like the emergence of the child from the womb. The other image within this framework of baptism as rebirth which was used by Chrysostom and Theodore was that of the potter remaking the imperfect clay vessel. Theodore, as by now we would expect, suggested that the object would reach its final restoration only in the last days.[114] Chrysostom demonstrated the pastoral concern which we have come to expect from him, and drew the distinction between the terracotta vessel which once shattered can never be restored, and a clay vessel which could be remade;[115] and Riley pointed out that he alone of the Fathers added 'the realistic pastoral note that God's forgiveness which brings about the regeneration in baptism can extend to post-baptismal falls as well.'[116]

c) *The Post-Baptismal Rites*: The post-baptismal rites of anointing, and the bestowal of the baptismal garment similarly exhibit a unity of basic theme although with a diversity of interpretation. In presenting the anointing, Cyril explained this in terms of the picture of Christ in the Jordan, anointed by the Holy Spirit following his baptism, as he had done in his catechetical material, and developed this in terms of mimesis theology to present the interpretation of the anointing of the different senses under the aspect of the Christian's conformity to Christ and to his mission in the world, and he chose appropriate Scripture texts to reinforce this concept.[117] Theodore, on the other hand, with his eschatological perspective, placed the emphasis upon the anointing as a sign of the coming resurrection, with the presence of the Spirit given as the 'firstfruit' for the purpose of protecting the Christian on his way to incorruptibility, but he did not develop the explanation of the detailed anointing of the senses in terms of mission.[118] Cyril coupled his teaching with a play on the words 'Christ', 'Christian', and 'chrism', which enabled him to present the communication of the Spirit as a closer association with Christ himself, in this way demonstrating how the Holy Spirit was the Spirit of Christ. As a result of his anointing the candidate became another Christ, and Cyril's particular mimesis mystagogy showed his candidates just how this took place.[119] Based upon this anointing, Cyril developed his mystagogy of the ointment, by warning his candidates against regarding the oil as simple ointment,[120] because after the invocation it became the gracious gift of Christ, and the Holy Spirit, and thus linked the Christian with Christ. He concluded his third mystagogical lecture by using the Isaianic picture of the banquet with its anointing of the guests, and emphasizing the eschatological dimension to the rite of anointing, depicting the Spirit as the eschatological gift already anticipated in the foregoing liturgy in which Christ and the Christian were united in the messianic work which led the world to his goal.[121] Although Theodore did not use this image, he returned to his favourite eschatological theme teaching that the firstfruits of the Spirit would flower in incorruptibility and immortality, impassibility, and immutability.[122]

The other aspect of the post-baptismal rites was the baptismal robe, of which the most important mystagogical aspect was the symbolism of union with the risen Christ. As a practicality, some clothing was necessary at this point in the baptismal liturgy, but it also formed a counterpart to the act of removing the garments before entering the pool, and so it became a ritual garment. Cyril and Chrysostom both used the ready-made imagery of Galatians 3.27, teaching that putting on the garment was like putting on Christ. Cyril was content to spell this out literally by stating that this means conformity to the risen body of Christ, using Philippians 3.21.[123] Chrysostom, on the other hand, referred to the robe in each of his lectures to neophytes and built a composite picture featuring the newness of the robe, the radiance of the robe, and its resemblance to a bridal garment to spell out for his audience what conformity to the risen body of Christ meant to them.[124] So the robe became for Chrysostom a central symbol to call to mind all the aspects of baptism. He saw in the radiance of the robe the manifestation in the individual of the indwelling of the Trinity.[125] Theodore seemed to assume the robe was a symbol of union with Christ without actually spelling it out, but he did describe its radiance as a sign of the coming joy of the resurrection at the eschaton.[126] The garment was also seen as a symbol of the forgiveness of sins, and this picture was drawn by Cyril with the assistance of the candidate's recollection of the liturgical procession into the church for the Eucharist.[127] Chrysostom noted that the radiance of the white garment indicated that inner transformation of forgiveness which had taken place in the neophytes. He also added two further images of the robe as the symbol of forgiveness, as a royal robe given to the former beggar, and as a bridal robe thrown over the shame of nakedness.[128] Thirdly, the clean, white robe was described as a symbol of purity of life, and Chrysostom developed this symbolism most thoroughly to stress the need for the neophytes to make an effort to keep their robe spotless, to increase its lustre, and by it to attract others to Christ. Ultimately it became the eschatological banquet robe.[129] Cyril's mystagogy was basically similar, although only in précis form.[130] Theodore saw in the works represented by the wearing of the robe the reflection of the joy of eschatological fulfilment already present in Christian action.[131]

So we see the theme for our study was fixed in the classic fourth-century period by the Fathers, Cyril of Jerusalem, John Chrysostom, and Theodore of Mopsuestia. Although there was a unity of theme, even in the fourth century there were variations of approach to the preparation of the Christian adult for the rite of baptism. Cyril gave a particular emphasis to the relationship between the liturgical actions of baptism and the actual events of the life of Christ, especially the salvific events of the life, death, and resurrection of Jesus, building upon his particular advantage of being at the very place where the death and resurrection of Jesus took place. Chrysostom applied his teaching pastorally to the everyday lives of his candidates in a secular city, amidst the horseracing and other spectacles, constantly challenging them to live out the new life which they had applied to themselves by faith in the death and resurrection of Jesus Christ. Theodore directed his interpretation towards the future, and explained those same events described in the liturgical actions, the life, death, and resurrection of Christ, with reference to the Christian's sure and certain hope through those actions in the resurrection with Christ at the last days, a resurrection and rebirth already begun in symbol.

So from this teaching of the fourth century we now proceed to examine the same theme as we find it expressed in a selected variety of church situations during the twenty years from 1960 to 1980.

5

The Orthodox Church – Direct Heirs of the Fourth Century

It seemed necessary to consider the practice of the Orthodox Church in the twentieth century to provide a bridge between the two areas of study, and in this respect I have been advised that the present day material given to candidates would be contained in Dr Alexander Schmemann's *Of Water and the Spirit*[1] and the service followed would be that of the translation of the *Service Book of the Holy Orthodox Catholic Apostolic Church* by Miss I. F. Hapgood.[2]

Schmemann's book is basically mystagogical, following the footsteps and tradition of Cyril, Theodore and John Chrysostom as he attempts to explain the meaning and symbolism of baptism within the Orthodox Church. In a sense Schmemann has a more difficult task than his forebears as he is attempting to explain a liturgy designed for adults to a church which sees infant baptism as the norm – hence his final section. Hapgood makes a special note of this point in the *Service Book*: 'It will be observed that this rite remains in its ancient form; that is to say, as arranged for adults – the catechumens being all adults in the early Church'.[3] Schmemann points out: 'For centuries now the Church has been practising almost exclusively *infant baptism*. It is all the more significant, then, that liturgically the sacrament has nevertheless preserved the form and the structure it had when the majority of those baptized were adults'.[4] However, although the distinction between catechesis and mystagogy is an artificial division of catechesis, we will examine first those elements of the work which appear to give catechetical explanation of baptism.

1. The Theology of Baptism and its Catechetical Explanation

This is primarily contained in two consecutive sections[5] entitled ' "Form" and "Essence" ' and 'in likeness of Christ's death and resurrection'. As he attempts to explain to his catechumens the place of baptism in the life of the Church, Schmemann has to define his own understanding of baptism because of the effect of centuries of theology which have separated the 'form' of what is done in baptism and the 'essence' of what the Church believes to happen. He feels that a reaffirmation of the early Church's understanding of baptism is vital if baptism is not to be, for so many, an 'incomprehensible means' of an equally 'incomprehensible grace'. He is alarmed at the inability of much post-patristic theology to explain the relationship between baptism and the death and resurrection of Christ, and he suggests that this is because of the breach of the organic connection between baptism and the paschal season. Although he does not want to enter the immersion/sprinkling debate, the common practice of sprinkling candidates detracts from the connection between the water and the tomb, and thus is a further point of division between the form of the sacrament and its essence.

Schmemann points out that baptism was always accepted as the self-evident beginning of the Christian life, but that, from rather early in the Church's history, theologians encountered difficulty in holding together the various aspects of the effects of the baptismal rite, and experienced the utter inadequacy of human words to express the totality of the baptismal mystery. So there appeared a certain distinction between baptism as such, the liturgy and symbols of the form of the baptismal rite, and the various explanations and definitions of baptism. This became particularly pronounced when theology began to be understood as a rational explanation and interpretation of the faith of the Church. Lip-service was still paid to the baptismal 'symbolism' of death and resurrection, but the real emphasis was put on the way in which baptism cleansed the candidate from original sin and bestowed grace upon him, and he cites the fact that in virtually every manual of systematic theology the two essential references in explaining baptism refer to original sin and grace.[6] Baptism was a means of grace, removing from man original sin, liberating him from it and bestowing upon him the grace necessary for his Christian life. Still it was absolutely essential for salvation, but it was no longer presented as being truly *death and resurrection*.

He therefore poses the question: 'What does Tradition mean when it affirms baptism to be in the *likeness* and *after the pattern* of Christ's death and resurrection and why in modern theology does this affirmation seem to have lost its focal position?'.[7] This in turn presents the broader question of the relationship in the sacrament between *form* and *essence* – what is done and what the Church believes to happen. He suggests that it is in the answers to these questions that the post-patristic theology which permeates orthodox manuals and catechisms moved away from the experience of the early Church which played such a large part in the formulation of that early sacramental vision. Thus, the post-patristic theologians in emphasizing questions of sacramental validity have deeply and radically altered both the understanding of the sacraments and their place in the life of both Christian and Church. Once again, Schmemann is guilty of generalization in oversimplifying the case in the cause of writing for a popular audience. Bishop Kallistos points out that he overlooks the emphasis of Eustratios Argenti in *Encheiridion peri Baptismatos*, who stressed the integral connection between baptism and the death and resurrection of Christ. However, this emphasis came from a work written to challenge the validity of the baptism practised in western Churches.[8]

The approach of the early Church was basically to ignore the question of the dichotomy between form and essence. In the early Church the terms 'likeness' and 'pattern' most obviously refer to the *form* of baptism. Yet it was this *form* of baptism which manifested and fulfilled the *essence*, and so the terms 'likeness' both described the form of baptism and revealed and communicated its *essence*. 'Baptism being performed "in the likeness" and "after the pattern" of death and resurrection therefore is death and resurrection'.[9] It was this clarity of vision concerning baptism which allowed the early Church to put to one side the 'why', the 'what', and the 'how' of baptism, and to start instead with the knowledge that to follow Christ one must begin by dying and rising again in him and with him.[10] Because baptism was an event, the distinction between *form* and *essence* was 'an irrelevant abstraction'. For the early Church the experience of the baptismal event, of death and resurrection, in Christ was so self-evident, so direct, that initially she did not explain it but saw it as the source and the condition of all theologies.

However, the time came, although Schmemann, prone to generalize because of the nature of his potential readers, does not specify when this was, when the Church decided that the *essence* of the sacrament would be known and defined apart from its *form*. It then insisted that the *essence* of the sacrament must be known apart from its form as a preliminary condition for understanding the sacraments. This began the progression to an entirely different view of baptism. The *form* was preserved but not for the same reason as in the early Church. In the early tradition, the importance of the *form* had been due to its epiphanic nature, as it revealed, fulfilled, and was the essence, and was seen as the means by which the *essence* was known and explained. In the new approach, however, the form was no longer an epiphany, but merely an external sign. Thus it became the guarantee that a particular *essence* had been duly bestowed and communicated by the Church to the candidate. The *essence* itself had to be capable of independent definition, prior to its communication, so that all might know what was being signified and guaranteed by means of the *form*. The *form* became that which made a sacrament *valid*, but no longer was it the revelation of *that which was made valid* in the sacrament.

Schmemann comments that the controversies raging concerning the form of baptism are centred almost exclusively on the issue of validity, rather than upon the issue of meaning or essence.[11] However, the tragedy is that by applying the dichotomy between *form* and *essence*, the notion of the *essence* of the sacraments has been altered and impoverished. Whilst there is nothing new in defining *essence* as 'grace', indeed it is scriptural to do so; in reality the term 'grace' acquired new connotations and a kind of 'self-sufficiency' it did not have before, precisely because of its identification with what the Church believes to happen rather than with what is done. In the early Church, grace meant above all the victory of Christ himself, and the way in which man was allowed to share in that victory, applying it to himself through baptism. The grace of baptism in the early Church was the event of man dying and rising again, following the pattern set by Christ's death and resurrection. It opened up to the candidate the unique and totally new possibility of walking in newness of life with Christ.

All this was grace: the 'likeness' revealed and experienced as 'reality', the baptismal death manifesting again the destruction of death by Christ, the baptismal resurrection 'making sure' again Christ's resurrection, becoming the very gift of the new life which shone forth from the grace. All this was grace![12]

Schmemann concludes that grace for the early Church was so bound up with their experience of Christ, that they saw no need to define it in itself. Possibly this points the way to the reason for the difficulty which modern scholars have discovered in their search for definitions of grace in the earliest period of the Christian era.[13]

However, gradually the understanding of grace changed, and it became what Schmemann describes as an 'essence in itself'. It was divorced from its form, and was given and received through all kinds of means of grace, and yet remained distinct from each of them. The Church in the west defined grace as a created substance, distinct from God and the world, and whilst the eastern Church denounced 'created grace' as a western heresy, Schmemann points out that it adopted a very similar approach in its own theology, and Ware points out that St Gregory Palamas (c.1296–1359) even used the phrase 'created grace'. So an abstract 'grace' replaced the concrete 'event' as the focus of the theological explanations of the sacrament, and the function of the 'form' of the sacrament was to assure its validity. For this approach, there is no interest in either death or resurrection, and the real purpose of baptism is regarded as the endowment of grace upon the baptizand. And whilst this grace may be the fruit of Christ's death and resurrection, it is no longer an event which must be termed essentially death and resurrection in both its form and its essence.

Schmemann concludes that the sacraments have been transformed by this thinking into mere obligations, which have often lost their meaning even for the faithful. Very few experience them as the joyful source of their lives as Christians. Rather, for so many, they have become an 'incomprehensible means' of an equally 'incomprehensible grace'. In the twentieth century, both faith and piety have ceased to experience them as genuine and true events of that 'newness of life' which is grace.

He appeals for a deeper understanding of what truly happens in baptism, and asks why it happens, and how baptism makes a Christian. The early Church knew, and they knew even before they could express it or explain it. The early Church realized as part of the baptismal mystery, that in baptism we must truly die and truly rise again with Christ. Schmemann suggests that we must return to this principle if we want baptism to recover its original function in the Church. He poses the ultimate questions: 'How do we die in the likeness of Christ's death? How do we rise again in the pattern of his Resurrection? And why is this, and this alone, our entrance into the new life in him and with him?'.[14]

He begins his answer by making the point that Christ's own death was a voluntary death. Jesus was willing to give up his life, of his own free will, and for this reason the Father loved him.[15] His sinless humanity was in no way subject to death, but his free choice to die in obedience to the Father's will makes it a saving death, and the Church needs to recover the true significance of Christ's desire to die, and his willingness to obey the Father's commands.

Schmemann demonstrates that the Christian view of death has changed since the New Testament era in such a way as to obscure the spiritual meaning of death. The majority of Christians see death as a physical event, marking the end of this life, beyond which faith posits another, purely spiritual, endless life, speaking of an immortal soul. Thus death becomes the mode of passage from one to the other. However, this view obscures the fact that Christ at his resurrection destroyed death,[16] and destroys death for those who share his death and resurrection. Christians no longer know what to make of the destruction of death by Christ.[17] In biological terms nothing has changed. Saints die as well as sinners, and death remains the organic principle of the world's existence.

He begins his explanation by defining spiritual death as man's separation from life, from the giver of life, and ultimately from God. Death is the opposite term to the true life which is the light of man.[18] Man has rejected this life and so chose death – a choice which Schmemann defines as original sin. But there remains that 'mysterious inner certitude in man which no sin could ever destroy, which makes him always and everywhere seek salvation'.[19] 'Whole' death, he suggests, is not the biological phenomenon, but the spiritual reality whose 'sting is sin'[20] as man rejects the only true life given him by God. He chooses rather spiritual death which makes his life solitude, suffering, fear, illusion, enslavement to sin, emptiness, lust, and meaninglessness. Man's physical death then becomes the ultimate fruit of a death-filled life – total separation, total solitude, and total darkness. It was this spiritual death which Christ came to abolish, and from which he came to save man.

Man dies spiritually because he prefers something else to God, and desires his own life and his own will more than God's life. On the other hand Christ's life is made up entirely of his desire to do God's will, to save man, to free him from that death into which man has transformed his life, and to restore to man the life which he has lost in sin. So he suggests that Christ's death was truly deathless. There was no death in it because there was no desire in Christ's life to do anything other than serve God. He sums up: 'His death, being the ultimate manifestation of love as life and of life as love, removes from death its "sting" of sin and truly destroys death as the power of Satan over the world'.[21]

So Schmemann argues: Christ does not abolish physical death, because he does not abolish this world of which physical death is a principle of life and growth. But he does remove the sting of sin from death, as he fills it with himself, with his love and his life. Thus he transforms death into a joyful passage into a fuller life. Paul gave death a new meaning when he described it as being with Christ,[22] and death becomes the sign and the power of Christ's victory, by the way he transformed it.

Thus baptism into the likeness of Christ's death and resurrection means that in baptism the Christian begins his spiritual life. The likeness is there before it is fulfilled in the rite. It is the Christian's faith in Christ, his love for him, and above all his desire to do what he desired. In baptism the Christian is expressing a wish to be like Christ: 'We are saved not because we believe in his "supernatural" power – such faith he does not want from us – but because we accept with our whole being and make ours the *desire* that fills his life, which *is* his life and ultimately makes him descend into death to abolish it.'[23] Baptism expressed a desire for such a realization of faith that it truly can be described as death and resurrection. Thus it is the very firstfruit and work of faith itself. Christ was truly dead to this spiritually dead world – to its self-sufficiency, to the lust of the flesh and the lust of the eye, to the pride of life,[24] The baptizand seeks to share that reality of life in God which God experienced:

> Finally, it is impossible to know Christ without desiring to drink of the cup that he drinks of, and to be baptized with the baptism that he is baptized with (Matt. 20.22), without desiring, in other words, that ultimate encounter and fight with sin and death which made him 'lay down his life' for the salvation of the world.[25]

It is faith that desires baptism, it is faith that knows baptism to be truly dying and truly rising with Christ.

We must recognize that the views and emphases are primarily those of Schmemann himself and we must bear in mind the context in which he was writing, expecting his work to help ordinary Christians to rediscover the meaning of baptism in their lives, rather than to form an authoritative statement of the theology of baptism of the Orthodox Church. As a result, he may be forgiven some of the oversimplifications which he makes in sacrificing detail to the cause of communication. We shall continue to consider his work in the context of the baptismal Liturgy and its mystagogical explanation.

1. *The Liturgy of Baptism and its Mystagogical Explanation*

The Orthodox liturgy as we have seen above is one which remains in its ancient form, designed for adults and applied to infants with very little concession made to the different abilities of those infants. Although liturgically the form and structure have been preserved from the ancient traditions of the fourth century, the liturgy itself has been telescoped to enable rites which would have been celebrated on separate occasions over a two month period to be celebrated in a single service.

a) *The Reception of Catechumens*: The Liturgy begins with a brief office, 'The Prayers at the Reception of Catechumens'.[26] In the fourth century this would have taken place during the period of proximate preparation for baptism[27] which probably lasted about forty days. Hapgood's rubric and her explanation of it give us some clue to the difficulties encountered above by Schmemann:

> The priest looseth the girdle of the person who desireth illumina-

tion, and removeth it, and putteth it off from him; and placeth him with his face towards the east, clothed in one garment only, unshod and with head uncovered, and with his arms hanging by his sides; and he breatheth thrice in his face; and signeth his brow and his breast thrice with the sign of the cross; and layeth his hand upon his head.[28] The removal of the catechumen's garment signifies the putting off of the old man and his sinful life, inasmuch as this order is required only in the baptism of adults; that is of persons above seven years of age, who are received only after due examination and their own expressed desire to be baptized. With such also, the procedure differs, according as they may be Jews, Mahometans, or members of some other non-Christian body; in which case, each must specifically renounce the errors of his former belief. But the rite (*presumably from the point of insufflation*) is alike for all infants (that is, persons under seven years of age), whether they be of Orthodox or non-Orthodox parents; and of them, through their sponsor, only the third catechizing, to which the answer is the Symbol of Faith (the Nicene Creed) is required.[29]

Schmemann's solution to the problem he faces is advanced in his thesis, whereby he explains the liturgy in terms of the double rhythm of preparation and fulfilment. He uses this theme to explain that baptism always requires preparation even in the case of an infant only a few days old. He suggests that:

> The Orthodox Church, radically different in this from some 'rationalistic' sects, has never posited 'understanding' as the condition for baptism. She would rather say that true 'understanding' is made possible by baptism, is its result and fruit, rather than its condition. We are very far from the flat idea that baptism cannot be received unless it is 'understood' and 'accepted', and therefore is to be given only to 'adults'. Maybe the ultimate grace of baptism is needed that it makes us children, restores in us that 'childhood' without which, in the words of Christ himself it is impossible to receive the Kingdom of God. What preparation means therefore is a total act of the Church, the recapitulation by her of all that makes baptismal regeneration possible. For the whole Church is charged, enriched and fulfilled when another child of God is integrated into her life, and becomes a member of Christ's body.[30]

I am not sure that his understanding of the true teaching of some of the 'rationalistic sects' he criticized was not clouded by a difference in terminology'.[13] Certainly Cyril and Theodore expected at least an understanding of what was implied by faith in Jesus Christ from their catechumens. Otherwise one must ask what purpose was to be served at Jerusalem, for example, by the recitation of the creed, which the catechumen had learned by heart and had had explained in great detail *before* the act of baptism. Bishop Kallistos agrees that Schmemann is over-reacting to what he sees as 'rationalism' which is also probably demonstrated in his polemic against those who seek to have baptism understood.[32] He also points out that fallen man before baptism still possesses a certain natural power of understanding.

The first prayer of the office,[33] which as we have seen supersedes the enrolment of the candidate at the beginning of Lent, expresses the catechumen's flight from captivity in a world in which he has been deluded into serving the Devil and he comes seeking to be filled with 'true faith, hope and love which are in thee; that he may know that thou art the only true God with thine only begotten Son, our Lord Jesus Christ and thy Holy Spirit'.[34] The first act of the baptismal liturgy is an act of protection, as the bishop's hand was laid upon the catechumen, symbolizing the refuge of the salvation which Christ brought. Under this protection and rescued from his delusion the prayer asks that the catechumen's name might be inscribed in the Book of Life and united with 'the flock of thine inheritance'.[35] At the same time, the candidate's true life is described to him, as opposed to the life of the man lost in sin. The true life is described in these words: 'that he may render praise unto thee, may sing, worship and glorify thy great ᴀnd exalted Name always, all the days of his life'.[36]

The office continues with three exorcisms in which the Devil and all his works are laid under the Lord's ban. Once again, these have their history in the early Church rite, when the catechumens were instructed to attend regularly before the exorcist during their proximate preparation for the baptismal rite. Schmemann explains that although the tendency is to rationalize evil simply as the absence of good, the Church teaches that evil is a real presence, a force which must be rejected and hated. The view of the Devil which he puts forward is of one

among the very first, and the best creatures of God. He is, so to speak, perfect enough, wise enough, powerful enough, one can almost say *divine* enough, to know God and not to surrender to him – to know him and yet to opt against him, to desire freedom from him. But since this freedom is impossible in the love and light which always lead to God and to a free surrender to him, it must of necessity be fulfilled negation, hatred and rebellion.[37]

He goes on to point out that human beings know nothing about the initial catastrophe in the spiritual world, but only know about its effects in their own personal experience, as their pride prompts them to stand against God and to choose their own way. After this choice has been made, humans realize their fallen state, and must begin to seek a means of being reunited wth God. He concludes:

If there is only one thing we learn from spiritual experience, it is that evil is not to be 'explained' but faced and fought. This is the way God dealt with evil. He did not explain it. He sent his only begotten Son to be crucified by all the powers of evil so as to destroy them by his love, faith and obedience.[38]

It was Jesus' experience that immediately following his baptism in the Jordan by John, the descent of the dove, and his acknowledgement by God, he was driven away into the wilderness to face the temptation of the Devil. Similarly it is the Christian's experience that he meets the Devil at the very moment he makes the decision to choose to follow Christ, and also immediately after baptism, just as Christ did. In Schmemann's words:

In the baptismal rite, which is an act of liberation and victory the exorcism comes first because on our path to the baptismal font we unavoidably 'hit' the dark and powerful figure that obstructs this path. It must be removed, chased away, if we are to proceed. The moment that the celebrant's hand has touched the head of a child of God and marked it with the sign of Christ, the Devil is there defending that which he has stolen from God and claims as his possession.[39]

Schmemann describes exorcism as a *poem* in the deepest sense of the word in the original. It is a poem because 'it truly manifests and *does* that which it announces; it makes powerful that which it states; it again fills words with the divine energy from which they stem'.[40] And it is because it is given in the name of Christ that exorcism does this, for it is filled with the power of Christ as we see plainly from the Second Exorcism:

I abjure thee by the redeeming passion of our Lord Jesus Christ, and by his precious body and blood, and by his terrible coming-again; for he shall come and shall not tarry, to judge the whole earth; and he shall chastise thee and the confederate host with burning Gehenna, committing thee to outer darkness, where the worm ceaseth not and the fire is not quenched. For of Christ our God is the dominion, with the Father and the Holy Spirit, now, and ever, and unto ages of ages. Amen.[41]

It is through Christ's redeeming passion that he has broken into enemy territory and mortally wounded the enemy, and so he has earned the right to lay the enemy under his ban and abjuration.

Following the abjuration of the evil power, the priest performs the candidate's liberation from its power, and this liberation is the beginning of man's restoration. As the symbol of the act of purification during this prayer the rubric explains:

> *Then the Priest breatheth upon his mouth, his brow, and his breast, saying*: Expel from him (her) every evil and impure spirit which hideth and maketh its lair in his (her) heart. (And this he saith thrice.) The spirit of error, the spirit of guile, the spirit of idolatry, and of every concupiscence; the spirit of deceit and of uncleanness which operateth through the prompting of the Devil. And make him (her) a reason-endowed sheep in the holy flock of thy Christ, an honourable member of thy Church, a consecrated vessel, a child of the light, and an heir of thy kingdom; that having lived in accordance with thy commandments, and preserved inviolate the seal, and kept his (her) garment undefiled, he (she) may receive the blessedness of the saints in thy kingdom.[42]

Following the exorcism, the catechumen is thought to be restored to man's intended status as a free being, capable of a true freedom, the freedom to receive again the true life which comes from God and leads to God. Thus the way is prepared for the next step in the baptismal liturgy, the renunciation and profession, which, in Cyril's day, took place either on Good Friday or Holy Saturday, before the Baptism itself.[43]

b) *The Rite of Renunciation and Profession*. The rubric introduces this section of the service with the words: '*Then the priest turneth the person who is come to Baptism to face the west unclad, unshod, and having his hands uplifted*'.[44] Hapgood notes that from the west comes darkness; and Satan therefore has his dominion there. The uplifted hands of the Catechumen indicate the realm of the evil spirits of the air.[45] Schmemann also reminds us of Chrysostom's teaching regarding the catechumen's slave status, pointing out that:

> The catechumen is deprived of all that concealed from him his status as a slave, that made him appear to be a free man, not even knowing his enslavement, his misery, and his prison. Now, however, he knows that he was a captive – 'and the captives go naked and unshod'. He has put aside all that masked his captivity, his belonging to Satan. He 'knows from what evil he is being delivered, and to what good he is hurrying...' His uplifted hands indicate, that he surrenders to Christ, wants now to be his captive, seeks the captivity which according to St John Chrysostom 'changes slavery into freedom... drives one from foreign soil, and leads him to his homeland, the heavenly Jerusalem...'[46]

There seems to be a divergence of opinion in connection with the meaning of the catechumen's uplifted hands. Schmemann's suggestion seems to fit more closely the profession than the renunciation but by this point the catechumen has been turned to face the east, and has his hands lowered, and so I think I prefer Miss Hapgood's explanation as the more likely to fit in with the terms of the renunciation which follows, but by its nature symbolism is fluid and so symbols can have more than one meaning.

We discover that the renunciation is basically unchanged, even though it dates from a time when to be a Christian was to be radically opposed to the life of the people around, by adopting a non-conformist lifestyle. Today, for many Christians, Christianity has become so much a part of the world that the idea that there is anything to renounce is alien to them. As Schmemann comments:

> The very idea that a Christian has to *renounce* something and that this 'something' is not a few obviously sinful and immoral acts, but above all a certain vision of life, a 'set of priorities', a fundamental attitude towards the world, the idea that Christian life is always a 'narrow path' and a fight; all this has been virtually given up and is no longer at the heart of our Christian world view.[47]

This threefold renunciation remains, not discarded as irrelevant to the views of twentieth-century man, but there as a sobering reminder of the impossibility of serving two masters. For, to renounce Satan is to reject an entire world view built upon pride and self affirmation, pledging to have done with it and all that it implies. So the catechumen is instructed 'Breathe and spit upon him'.[48] Schmemann interprets this as a declaration of war upon Satan, a struggle whose real issue is either eternal life or eternal damnation. This struggle is the essence of Christianity.[49] Bishop Kallistos points out that spitting is also a gesture of contempt.

The profession is indicated by the rubric: '*And when he hath done this, the priest turneth him to the east with his hand lowered, and saith*: Dost thou unite thyself to Christ?'[50] Just as darkness proceeds from the west, so light comes from the east, the place of paradise.[51] It is from this position that the catechumen makes his profession of personal attachment to Christ. Schmemann reminds us that this implies an unconditional commitment to Christ.[52] The catechumen professes his faith in Christ as King and as God which reflects the earliest baptismal confession 'Jesus Christ is Lord', reminding the Christians of the unconditional obedience which they pledge to Christ.

The symbol of faith is then given back to the Church which first gave it to the candidate, as the catechumen recites the creed in the presence of the congregation. Schmemann comments: 'Now the knowledge *about* Christ is become the knowledge *of* Christ; the truth preserved by the Church in her tradition is to become the faith and life of the new member of the Church'.[53] This act and the profession itself is sealed by the candidate bowing down before the triune godhead as a symbol of reverence, love and obedience, just as the renunciation was sealed by the catechumen breathing and spitting upon Satan. The first office concludes with the prayer:

O Master, Lord our God, call thy servant, N, to thy holy illumination, and grant unto him (her) that great grace of thy holy baptism. Put off from him (her) the old man, and renew him (her) unto life everlasting; and fill him (her) with the power of thy Holy Spirit, in the unity of thy Christ; that he (she) may be no more a child of the body, but a child of thy Kingdom. Through the good will and grace of thine only begotten Son, with whom thou art blessed, together with thy most holy, and good and life-giving Spirit, now, and ever, and unto ages of ages. Amen.[54]

This prayer provides a clear summary of what has gone before.

  c) *Baptism*. The second office of the rite is the Office of Holy

Baptism which follows immediately. The rubric indicates that: '*The priest entereth the sanctuary and putteth on white vestments, and his gauntlets. And when he hath lighted all the tapers, he taketh the censer and goeth to the font and censeth round about it; and having given the censer to be held, he maketh a reverence*'. Hapgood explains the symbolism of his vestments and of the tapers by her statement that the white vestments and the light speak of the spiritual joy and illumination which come through baptism. Schmemann laments that this particular rubric is more honoured in the breach than in the observance, pointing out that this particular rubric is all that remains from the greatest of all solemnities of the early Church, the paschal celebration of baptism and the baptismal celebration of Pascha.[55] It is important for baptism to be performed with the participation of the people of God 'as an event in which the whole church acknowledges herself as *passage* – Pascha – from "this world" into the kingdom of God, as participation in the decisive events of Christ's death and resurrection'.[56] He deplores the reduction of baptism to a bare 'minimum' and reminds us 'that whenever and wherever baptism is celebrated, we find ourselves – spiritually at least! – on the eve of Pascha, at the very end of the great and holy "sabbath", at the very beginning of that unique night which every year truly makes us enter into the Kingdom of God'.[57]

The office begins with the solemn blessing of the water by the deacon, whilst the priest prays secretly for the catechumen and for himself. The deacon's prayer in litany form contains some very strong echoes of the fourth century teaching in Jerusalem and Antioch:

That this water may be sanctified with the power and effectual operation and descent of the Holy Spirit:
That there may be sent down into it the grace of redemption, the blessing of Jordan:
That there may come upon this water the purifying operation of the super-substantial Trinity:
That we may be illuminated by the light of understanding and piety, and by the descent of the Holy Spirit:
That this water may prove effectual unto the averting of every snare of enemies, both visible and invisible:
That he (she) who is baptized therein may be made worthy of the kingdom incorruptible:
For him (her) who is now come unto holy baptism, and for his

(her) salvation:

That he (she) may prove himself (herself) a child of the light and an heir of eternal good things:

That he (she) may be a member and partaker of the death and resurrection of Christ our God:

That he (she) may preserve his (her) baptismal garment and the earnest of the Spirit pure and undefiled unto the dread Day of Christ our God:

That this water may be to him (her) a laver of regeneration, unto the remission of sins, and a garment of incorruption:

That the Lord will hearken unto the voice of our petition:

That he will deliver him (her) and us from all tribulation, wrath and necessity:.[58]

It is the water which reveals to us the meaning of baptism, as we see from the prayer above, as it reveals the relation of Baptism to the world and to matter, to life and all its aspects. Schmemann suggests these essential dimensions of the symbolism of water from the Christian point of view:

> cosmical, because it is the sacrament of the new creation; ecclesiological, because it is the sacrament of the Church, eschatological, because it is the sacrament of the Kingdom. It is by entering into this *mystery of water* that we begin to understand why, in order to *save* a man, we must first of all immerse him in water.[59]

Then the priest formally blesses and consecrates the water in a prayer which is a solemn act of praise and thanksgiving. Schmemann points out that this eucharistic prayer has a preface, an anamnesis, and an epiclesis which begins with the bidding: '*the priest signeth the water thrice with the sign of the cross, dipping his fingers therein. And breathing upon it, he saith*: Let all adverse powers be crushed beneath the sign of the image of thy cross. (thrice)'.[60] As it continues the priest asks that the water be shown

> to be the water of redemption, the water of sanctification, the purification of flesh and spirit, the loosing of bonds, the remission of sins, the illumination of the soul, the laver of regeneration, the renewal of the Spirit, the gift of adoption to sonship, the garment of incorruption, the foundation of life.[61]

In this way the water is seen to be a means to an end, as indeed all matter is seen as a means to an end rather than an end in itself, and that end is man's knowledge of God, and communion with God. So the water is the vehicle of the re-creation of matter in Christ. 'It is the gift of that world to man. It is the gift of the world as communion with God, as life, salvation, and deification'.[62]

Following the blessing of the water, it is anointed with oil, the symbol of life, the life which Jesus came to bring, 'life in all its fullness'.[63] A similar pattern is followed for the blessing of the oil of gladness, First the oil is exorcized and restored to its true function, as revealed in its symbolism, of bringing healing, light, and thereby joy to man. Then follows an anamnesis, as the congregation and catechumens are reminded of the meaning of oil in the history of salvation, and a thanksgiving to God for the oil, and all that he has made it. Finally, there comes the anointing itself as the priest '*singing Alleluia with the people maketh three signs of the cross in the water with the oil*'.[64] After the water has been anointed with oil, then the catechumen is anointed as

> *The priest taketh of the oil with two fingers, and maketh the sign of the cross upon his brow, his breast, and between his shoulders saying*:
> The servant of God, N, is anointed with the oil of gladness; in the Name of the Father, and of the Son, and of the Holy Spirit, Amen.
> *And he anointeth his breast and shoulders. On the breast saying*:
> Unto the healing of soul and body.
> *On the ears*
> Unto the hearing of faith.
> *On the hands*
> Thy hands have made me and fashioned me.
> *On the feet*
> That he may walk in the way of thy commandments.[65]

So the catechumen is reshaped, restored and reconciled to God, and in God, to the world.

We now reach the climax of the service, the actual act of baptism itself. The rubric instructs:

> *And when his whole body is thus anointed, the priest baptizeth him, holding him upright and looking toward the east, as he saith*:
> The servant of God, N, is baptized, in the name of the Father, Amen. And of the Son, Amen. And of the Holy Spirit, Amen. At each invocation he immerseth him and raiseth him again.[66]

We note the threefold immersion, and the fact that the words of the rite point away from the human agency to the divine, using the passive rather than the active voice as with all the sacraments of the Orthodox Church. The sacrament is a personal application of the gifts which Christ makes available, as baptismal grace. It is the grace of the catechumen's participation in an event which is aimed at each one of us and

> was from the beginning and totally a gift which can and must be received, accepted, loved and appropriated by each one of us. In baptism, the death and resurrection of Christ are fulfilled as his death for me, his resurrection for me, and therefore my death in Christ, and my resurrection in him.[67]

The congregation as representatives of the whole Church affirms each of the three immersions with an 'Amen', testifying they have seen and experienced once more the death and resurrection of Christ, so that in him 'we may die to our mortal life and be partakers, here and now – of the "day without evening"'.[68] The final Amen continues into the singing of Psalm 32, which expands the affirmation of the Amens. The congregation has witnessed God's mercy and forgiveness, and has witnessed the recreation of the world and of man in that world. Once more they find themselves at a beginning, as they have witnessed a new man made again into the likeness of him who made him in a new world filled with God's glory. To all this the psalm bears fitting testimony and praise.

d) *Post-Baptismal Rites.* Immediately after this, the newly-baptized is dressed in his new robe. The white garment in which the candidate is vested is described by the priest as the robe of righteousness, and by the congregation as the robe of light:

> *Then, as he putteth his garment upon him, the priest saith:*
> The servant of God, N, is clothed with the robe of righteousness; in the Name of the Father, and of the Son, and of the Holy Spirit. Amen.
> *Then shall be sung the following Hymn (Tropar) in Tone VIII*
> Vouchsafe unto me the robe of light, O thou who clothest thyself with light as a garment, Christ our God, plenteous in mercy.[69]

John Chrysostom described the robe variously as a shining garment, a royal robe, a garment of immortality.[70] It symbolizes the state of spiritual purity and righteousness which God intends for his people, as it symbolizes the new life which begins at baptism.

The candidate is also given a lighted candle to hold, to

emphasize the relationship between baptism and enlightenment. Baptism is thus a sacrament of illumination, both of the candidate, and of the world through the candidate.

The next prayer begins the Office of Holy Chrismation[71] and following a prayer in which God's help is invoked for the newly-baptized to maintain his baptismal purity, the act of Chrismation takes place:

> *And after this prayer, he anointeth with the Holy Chrism, the person who hath been baptized, making the sign of the cross: On the brow, and on the eyes, and the nostrils, and the lips, and on both ears, and the breast, and the hands and the feet, saying each time:*
> The seal of the gift of the Holy Spirit. Amen.[72]

Hapgood points out that the purpose of the anointing of the newly-baptized with the holy Chrism is so that he may receive the gifts of the Holy Spirit to rear and strengthen him in the spiritual life and 'to render him strong, firm and invincible, in faith, in love, and hope; in boldness, that without fear he may confess before all men the name of Christ; that he may grow in all virtues, free himself from the Evil One, and all his guile, and preserve his soul in purity and righteousness'.[73]

Schmemann explains that chrismation is performed as the fulfilment of baptism, just as participation in the eucharist is the fulfilment of chrismation, and Hapgood points out that the child after chrismation can receive the eucharist without preliminary confession until he reaches his seventh birthday. The garment is bestowed upon the baptizand because he has been baptized and in order to be anointed.[74] The chrismation of the whole body imparts to the candidate the gift of the Holy Spirit[75] rather than gifts in the plural. Schmemann explains the significance of the personal Pentecost:

> Are we able to understand that the *impossible uniqueness* of this personal Pentecost is that we receive as *gift* him whom Christ and only Christ has by *nature*: the Holy Spirit, eternally bestowed by the Father upon his Son and who, at the Jordan, descends on Christ and on him alone, revealing Christ as the *Anointed*, as the beloved Son and the Saviour; that, in other words, we receive as gift the Spirit who belongs to Christ as *his* Spirit, who abides in Christ as *his* life?[76]

Thus chrismation sums up the union of the candidate with Christ, as adopted sons of the Father. It makes the candidate prophet, priest and king, and Schmemann begins to spell out

117

the implications of this fact in the life of the baptized.[77] Man, created as king in authority over the creatures of the world, has lost his kingship in the fall, and can only be restored to his role as a redeemed being. This redemption is revealed, manifested and fulfilled in the baptismal mystery, and his baptism into the likeness of Christ's death and resurrection.

In lamenting the neglect of the priestly dimension of the Christian he draws the attention of his readers to the early Church:

> As to the early Church, she firmly held and affirmed both the institutional priesthood *in* the Church and the 'royal priesthood' *of* the Church as the two essential and complementary dimensions of her very life: *essential* as stemming from her experience both of Christ and of his unique priesthood, *complementary* as revealing in their mutual correlation each other's place and significance in the life and work of the Church.[78]

The role of priest is to offer sacrifice, he says, and to be the mediator between God and creation, a role which man refused at the fall, and to which the baptized is recalled at baptism, but it remains the vocation of Christ.

> Their priesthood is not theirs but Christ's; their vocation is *to have no vocation* save the *personal* vocation of Christ, to assure the presence and the power of his priesthood in the Church, its continuity until the consummation of all things in God. As the Father sends his Son to save the world, the Son chooses and sends those whom he entrusts with the continuation of his saving ministry, the power of his unique priesthood.[79]

He explains the prophetic role of man originally in terms of God speaking to Adam,[80] and of man's rejection of this role at the fall by his pride. Man at baptism is restored by Christ through the sacrament of the Holy Spirit to his role of prophet which Schmemann describes as the gift of sobriety:

> Sobriety is that inner *wholeness* and *integrity,* that harmony between soul and body, reason and heart, which alone can *discern* and therefore *understand* and therefore *possess* reality in its totality, *as it is*, to lead man to the only true 'objectivity'. Sobriety is understanding because it *discerns* first of all and in everything – in almost unconscious movements of the soul as well as in 'great events' – the good and the evil, because it 'sees through' evil, even when evil vests itself, as it usually does, in garments of light. Sobriety is possession because, being the openness of the whole

man to God, to his will and to his presence, the constant awareness of God, it makes man capable of receiving everything as coming from God and leading to him, or, in other words, of giving everything meaning and value.[81]

This particular role also highlights the task of the baptized to witness to the world.

But, primarily, the candidate at chrismation receives the Holy Spirit himself. Schmemann then poses the question of what this means for the baptized. He explains that the knowledge of the Holy Spirit is only possible by his presence in the Christian, a presence which is manifested above all by ineffable joy, peace, and fullness. He describes the gift of the Holy Spirit in these terms:

> Such is the gift of the Holy Spirit, the meaning of our personal Pentecost in the sacrament of the holy anointment. It *seals*, i.e. makes, reveals, confirms, us as members of the Church, the Body of Christ, as citizens of the Kingdom of God, as partakers of the Holy Spirit. And by this *seal*, it truly makes us into ourselves, 'ordains' each one of us to be and to become that which God from all eternity want us to be, revealing our *true personality* and thus our only self-fulfilment.[82]

Following the chrismation, the priest and the sponsors together with the newly-baptized, make a processional circuit of the baptismal font, singing three times the words: 'As many as have been baptized into Christ have put on Christ. Alleluia'.[83] The circle is the liturgical type of eternity. The triple circling of the font with the lighted tapers signifies that the newly baptized and illumined person has entered into an eternal union with Christ the Light of the World. Then the service proceeds with the epistle and gospel[84] followed by prayers, first for the sponsor, his mercy, life, peace, health, salvation and remission of sins and then for the neophyte.[85]

Schmemann then explains to his readers the interdependence of the sacraments of baptism, chrismation, and the eucharist, seeing the eucharist as *the* sacrament of the Church, rather than *one of the* sacraments of the Church, but to examine this at length will take us outside the scope of this study. So we note the relationship and pass on.

This is usually followed by a part of the service which comes from the Rites of the Eighth Day, when the neophyte was brought again to the Church for the concluding act of the rite of baptism. Now this time lapse is disregarded, and the Ablution and Tonsure are now performed as part of the same service as the preceding Offices. Originally, the Rite of the Eighth Day followed the week of mystagogical instruction following baptism itself,[86] but such teaching and close fellowship enjoyed by the newly-baptized had to have an end, and the newly-baptized had to return into the world. So the baptismal liturgy concludes with rites which express the return of the Christian into the world, and which signify the beginning of Christian life as mission and witnessing, and the commissioning of the newly-baptized to witness to the light of Christ in the world.

The first rite of the Eighth Day is the Washing Off of Holy Chrism which prepares the newly-baptized for that fight which is the content of the Christian life. The first prayer is phrased in a context which befits a fight or struggle:

> Maintain the shield of his (her) faith unassailed by the enemy. Preserve pure and unpolluted the garment of incorruption wherewith thou hast endued him (her), upholding inviolate in him (her) by thy grace, the seal of the Spirit, and showing mercy upon him (her) and unto us, through the multitude of thy mercies.[87]

The second prayer is similar: 'Keep him (her) ever a warrior invincible in every attack of those who assail him (her) and us; and make us all victors even unto the end, through thy crown incorruptible'.[88] Then the external symbols of the liturgical rite can be removed as superfluous, for from now on nothing that is merely external can be of any help. As Schmemann points out: 'only the inner appropriation by man of the gift of grace, faith, and faithfulness will sustain him. When the real fight begins, the bright and colourful uniform is of no use and is replaced by battle fatigues'.[89] So the white garment is removed. Chrism is removed as it was given to be transformed into the life of the neophyte. So the neophyte is addressed by the priest with these words, as the holy chrism is washed off:

> Thou art justified. Thou art illumined. Thou art sanctified. Thou art washed: in the Name of our Lord Jesus Christ, and by the Spirit of our God. Thou art baptized. Thou art illumined. Thou hast received anointment with holy chrism. Thou art sanctified. Thou art washed; in the Name of the Father, and of the Son, and of the Holy Spirit.[90]

The last rite is that of the Tonsure, or the cutting of the hair, and Hapgood points out: 'The shearing of the hair signifies that the newly baptized person had dedicated himself to the service of God, and to obedience; because the cutting of the hair has always been the symbol of submission and servitude'.[91] Schmemann has some very interesting comments on the way in which a man's hair becomes the symbol of his national identity, or of pathological deviations in man.[92] It is also the symbol of the offering of the first fruits to the Lord: 'Bless, now, thy servant, N, who is come to make a first offering shorn from the hair of his head'.[93] So the new life begins by sacrificing to God and making him an offering – 'man's first free and joyful sacrifice of himself to God'.[94] Now the neophyte is ready to live his life for God, in God's world, in the strength he has received through his baptismal experience. Schmemann sums up:

> Just as the whole life of the Church stems from Pascha and takes us through Pentecost and the time 'after Pentecost' to another Pascha, our whole life stemming from Baptism has been made into a 'passage' – the pilgrimage and the ascension towards the 'day without evening' of God's eternal Kingdom. And as we proceed and fight and work, the mysterious light of that Day already illumines our way, shines everywhere, transforms everything, makes everything life in God, and the way to God. It is when the baptismal liturgy is accomplished that baptism begins to work in us.[95]

6

The Roman Catholic Church in the United Kingdom

1. *The Theology of Baptism and its Catechetical Explanation*

In 1960, the official norm of Roman Catholic teaching about the theology of baptism was summarized in *A Catechism of Christian Doctrine*.[1] This defines the sacramental effect of baptism in terms of cleansing, forgiveness, and of making a person Christian. The definition included the renunciation of Satan, and although it affirms baptism is necessary for salvation, it does not include allegiance to Christ as the counterpart to the renunciation of Satan. It is plain too that the norm is infant baptism in that 'the child' is specifically mentioned in answer to the question 'How is baptism given?'[2]

However, since Vatican II this definition has been qualified and expanded. The current *General Catechetical Directory*,[3] in its early section, notes the problem of indiscriminate infant baptism which has resulted in a situation in which there are 'many baptized persons who have withdrawn so far from their religion that they profess a form of indifferentism or something close to atheism'.[4] Vatican II constantly urged the renewal of the ministry of the word in the Church. The *General Catechetical Directory* comments that this renewal is entering a period of crisis because the thinking upon which it was based has not been fully understood. A thorough renewal of the catechetical plan is involved to provide a continuing education in the faith for both children and adults.[5] It stresses that renewed catechesis belongs in the context of pastoral renewal, and is always related to the task of evangelization, whether or not the subjects of that evangelism are baptized.[6]

Bishops have the clear responsibility of providing adequate pastoral support and teaching, and they are reminded by *GCD* of the emphasis of Vatican II upon the catechesis for adults, considering it 'the chief form of catechesis'.[7] All the other forms of catechesis are to be seen within the orientation of the adult programme. The maturity of faith of all those within their care is to be a priority upon their episcopal activity.

As a result, *GCD* in its definition of baptism applies the principles of catechesis enunciated in the Directory:

> Baptism cleanses man from original sin and from all personal sins, gives him rebirth as a child of God, incorporates him into the Church, sanctifies him with the gifts of the Holy Spirit, and impressing on his soul an indelible character, initiates him in Christ's priestly, prophetic and kingly roles (cf. 1 Peter 2.9).[8]

A number of factors indicate far more clearly the role of the personal faith of the candidate, and the move towards adult baptism as the norm. The role of faith is emphasized in the preceding section. There is a much closer link between personal sins and original sin, the element of sanctification has been added, and sharing the priestly, prophetic and kingly roles of Christ result from the initiation of the candidate. The definition of confirmation is even more radical as it takes up the emphasis on the witnessing role of the Christian in the world[9] from the *Dogmatic Constitution on the Church* and the *Decree on the Church's Missionary Activity*.[10]

The teaching of *GCD* found flesh in the booklet *Basic Teaching for Catholic Religious Education*.[11] This defined the recommended syllabus thus:

1. Mystery of one God, Father, Son and Holy Spirit.
2. True Worship of God in a world that ignores Him.
3. Knowledge of God and the witness of Christian love.
4. Jesus Christ, Son of God, the First born of all Creation and Saviour.
5. Creation, the beginning of the History of Man's Salvation.
6. Jesus Christ the Centre of all God's Saving Works.
7. Jesus Christ, true man and true God in the Unity of the Divine Person.
8. Jesus Christ, Saviour and Redeemer of the World.
9. The Holy Spirit in the Church and in the Life of the Christian.
10. The Sacraments, actions of Christ in the Church (the Universal Sacrament)
11. Religious Instruction of the Sacraments.
12. The Eucharist, the Centre of all Sacramental Life.

13. The sacrament of Matrimony.
14. The New man in the Spirit.
15. Human and Christian Freedom.
16. The Sins of Man.
17. The Moral Life of Christians.
18. The Perfection of Christian Love.
19. Specific in the Teaching of Morality.
20. The Church, People of God and Institution for Salvation.
21. The Church as a Community.
22. The Quest for Unity.
23. The Church as the Institution for Salvation.
24. Mary, Mother of God, Mother and Model of the Church.
25. Final Reunion with God.[12]

Contemporary with the thinking crystallized by Vatican II came the publication of *A New Catechism* which emanated from the Netherlands.[13] Subtitled *The Catholic Faith for Adults* this book took seriously the spirit of the statement in the *Constitution on the Sacred Liturgy* which it anticipated that: 'The catechumenate for adults... is to be restored and to be put into use'.[14]

The syllabus they developed may be summarized from the table of contents:

Part One   The Mystery of Existence
Part Two   The Way to Christ
            A. The Way of the Nations
            B. The Way of Israel
Part Three The Son of Man (a chronological account of the gospels)
Part Four   The Way of Christ (covering the growth and history of the Church, the Sacraments, Sin and Redemption, Faith, Hope, Love, Christian Prayer, Sunday, Words of Eternal Life, the Eucharist, Priestly People, Pastoral Priesthood, Marriage and the family, the Evangelical Councils, Church and State, Reverence for Life, Possessions on Earth, Helping the Needy, the Business of Living. The Quest for Truth, Failures of Christians, Forgiveness).
Part Five   The Way to the End.[15]

Beginning with John the Baptist, the authors examine the

place and nature of the baptism which he offered those who responded to his call to repentance, seeing it as a preparation for the baptism with the Holy Spirit of 'He who comes', and as an opportunity to demonstrate their readiness for conversion and their openness to Christ. John's baptism is thus seen as pointing the way to the coming of Christ,[16] and so it is not surprising 'that the whole kernel of his mission will become apparent'.[17] However, the authors explain that in the account of Jesus' baptism by John outward imagery is used as the expression of a reality which cannot be fully articulated, the contact of the Father, with Jesus, and the power of the Holy Spirit.

> Hence the baptism is a sign of Jesus' role as servant, of his submission and suffering, indeed of his death. Twice Jesus was later to describe his death by the word 'baptism' (Mt. 20.33; Lk. 12.50). The beloved Son dedicates himself as servant, sets out on his path of lowliness to be the lamb who bears all sin. This is his vocation.[18]

The gospel narrative makes it very plain that Jesus' choice of the servant role led him along the path of temptation and ultimately to death, as it brought him into conflict with Satan, and the temptations, the opposite of his baptism.[19] The authors sum up the significance of Jesus' baptism: 'His baptism signified readiness to submit and suffer, to share the common lot, to be a servant unto death. In a word he chose not success but service. To be faithful to his task was his joy, and it brought a new joy into the world'.[20] We are reminded that because Jesus was strengthened at his baptism by the descent of the Spirit, the ablutionary baptism of John is given a new spiritual significance and becomes a symbol of the baptism with the Spirit which will be conferred on all future believers.

When the authors apply their teaching to the Church today they define baptism as 'the visible sign under which we enter the people of God',[21] and follow 'step by step the ceremonies of the solemn celebration of the baptism of adults'.[22] These ceremonies begin with the admission to the catechumenate, which in fact takes place outside the door of the Church, and which is a rite rich in the symbolism of preparation. It is intended that these ceremonies should emphasize to the candidate his distance from his ultimate goal of union with

Christ, and eternal life. The candidate comes to realize his inadequacy to attain his goal apart from the gift of faith. His identity and motivation are publicly established, as is his preparedness for baptism, and the rite concludes with the priest performing Jesus' paschal gesture of breathing upon the candidate, expelling evil spirits, and preparing for the Holy Spirit.

The authors then explain the significance of exorcism and its place in the baptismal ceremonies. In the rite of exorcism, the battle of good against evil is starkly demonstrated with no room for any compromise with evil, because 'the ceremony is a brief and vital statement of a vital hour'.[23] The conversion struggle against evil by the candidate is summed up without nuances with a biblical succinctness and profundity. The candidate's awareness of the temptation dilemma with its darkness, and despair, is tempered by the reminder of God's peace, goodness, and joy shown in his signation with the cross and its assurance of the candidate's ability to triumph over all evil in the victory of the cross. The rite of admission to the catechumenate concludes with the giving of salt in place of the eucharist, symbolizing preservation against corruption, creating a thirst for water, and heralding a new life savouring the things of God.

Describing the second ceremony the authors show that this also depicts the struggle between God and Satan. This involves the candidate's recitation of the Lord's Prayer and the Apostle's Creed. In public and before God, he calls God his Father and affirms the faith of God's people, for his faith is part of 'a dialogue where the man answers audibly in the frame-work of the ecclesiastical community'.[24] Evil is bidden to depart, and the candidate is exorcized. This is followed by the 'Eph-phatha'[25] symbolizing the opening of the senses to the power of Christ. Finally the candidate is anointed between the shoulders with the oil of catechumens, signifying suppleness and strength for the combat, just as we have seen above in Chrysostom.[26] This too is 'an answer from Christ, given through the sign performed by his Church – the strength to be steadfast.'[27]

The writers anticipate the spirit of Vatican II closely in commenting upon the particular suitability of the Easter Vigil as a time for baptism. The liturgy of the Easter Vigil concentrates on the tremendous significance attached to water in Scripture, and the authors suggest various examples from contemporary scientific thought to enhance the significance of the element. They particularly emphasize the connection between water and birth, to show that the candidate enters the Church by a new birth, receiving in baptism the new life of water and the Holy Spirit.

Baptism takes place by affusion in the triune name, and is followed by the anointing of the neophyte with chrism. Thus at baptism the neophyte becomes a new creation in Christ, living his life, which is only made possible by the Holy Spirit. The sign of the old life is washed away in the flowing water of baptism which signifies cleansing. Actual sin is washed away, the roots of sin are conquered by this contact with Jesus, and the neophyte is strengthened in his whole life-struggle to overcome sin. It is plain that light has conquered the darkness in his life.[28]

Following their chrismation the neophytes are blessed, and given a white garment and a lighted candle as symbols of purity and light. The baptismal cleansing is a once for all event, and this is expressed by the statement 'that baptism of water confers a character which can never be effaced.'[29] The *Supplement*[30] explains further that through baptism the neophyte is participating in the priesthood of Christ, and so the character of baptism is as indelible as the sacraments of confirmation and ordination.[31]

The Catechism then develops the concept of sharing Christ's burial in baptism, and they indicate the double significance of water – salvation and destruction. Beginning from Romans 6.3–4, they point out that the symbolism of these verses is best served by the practice of immersion. As the old man is destroyed and vanishes, then the life of the baptized is transformed, and conformed to Christ's way of service, of suffering, and finally of death. In terms reminiscent of Schmemann, they teach:

> Our death is our truest baptism. We accept it like Jesus, with Jesus, and in Jesus. The fact that our Lord has redeemed us does not mean that he has set us beyond sin and suffering. It means that we must join him in redeeming ourselves and others in *his* way.[32]

Thus death in this life is the final act of Christian service, which sets the Christian wholly free to serve his Lord. They further explain: 'When we enter the water, it is a symbol of death; when we leave it, it is the symbol of resurrection and rebirth. That is why baptism is conferred on the happy night of Easter'.[33]

Baptism is a rite which 'builds new stones into the Church',[34] and thus the corporate aspect of baptism is stressed. It causes the adoption of the baptized into the fellowship which seeks to be a servant along with Jesus:

> Together we pass through the Red Sea, to be obedient to our call and to place our little lives and our death under the sign of service. We become little ones by joining in with God's little ones, just as Christ joined in and became a common man along with us. And likewise we break with the opposite attitude to life.[35]

So baptism divides humanity between those who make Christ's baptism unto death come true in their own lives, through the baptism of service, and those who make Satan's temptation of power the pattern for their way of life. The decisive factor is whether baptism is allowed to 'come true' in the life of the baptized. But this division runs right through the self, as part responds to the call of Christ 'I am ready', whilst the other part responds 'I will not serve'.[36]

This wider view of baptism to service leads the authors to acknowledge the reality of the baptism of those baptized outside the Roman Catholic Church, and to teach that 'everyone who is prepared to be "obedient unto death" is touched by Christian baptism'.[37] This is because every human makes contact with Jesus through their birth because 'they have Jesus as their fellow man'.[38] However this does not mean that baptism should be omitted and they reaffirm its function: 'It shows that we need the forgiveness which it brings. It proclaims that the Lord is in contact with us. It gathers us, visibly and tangibly, as one people to which the Spirit is given and where forgiveness is at work'.[39] The authors of the *Supplement* add the idea of rebirth through the Spirit to the third element of the definition.[40] The gift of the Spirit, which is bestowed in baptism is strengthened in confirmation, which they describe as the 'Pentecostal finale' of baptism. They also remind their readers of the original timing of baptism and confirmation together, as part of the same rite.[41]

In concluding the baptismal section, the authors plead for baptism to be seen as part of a totality, rather than in isolation:

It is important not to isolate baptism and envisage it only as something individual and momentary, which takes place between God and the soul. As soon as the baptism of water is taken out of the whole great context, strange problems arise, as the history of the Church has shown. Just as the hand is only really a hand in the totality of the body, so too baptism is only a genuine sign of Christ in the totality in which he gives it to us, the totality of our life and death, the totality of Christian upbringing, of the fellowship of the Church and of mankind'.[42]

Although this document predates *RCIA* and bases its catechesis on the previous service of baptism of adults, it does incorporate the thinking of Vatican II into its explanation of the service and in so doing represents a contemporary attempt to demonstrate catechetically the spirit of that Council.

In 1976 *The Teaching of Christ*,[43] a more orthodox Catechism, was published. It very closely models its teaching on the syllabus outlined in the *GCD*[44] and its claim to respectability is greatly enhanced by the preface subscribed by the Prefect of the Sacred Congregation of the Clergy.

Its authors state that baptism is conferred by water and the Holy Spirit and, at confirmation, the Christian receives a strengthening in the power of the Holy Spirit. The work of the Holy Spirit is to make Christians holy, and by baptism the Christian is born to newness of life. Christ himself is always the minister of baptism:

> Though men serve as agents for Christ, Christ himself is the principal minister of baptism and of every sacrament. For this reason the Church declares that the sacred signs we call sacraments are deeds of Christ in his Church. Sacraments are outward signs instituted by Christ to give grace.
>
> Sacramental participation underscores both aspects of the mystery of grace. The initiative is entirely the Lord's. The sacraments are his actions, his saving deeds, performed by him, through his ministers. But they are fruitful in an adult, only when there is in the recipient a free inner disposition, a willing response to grace.[45]

However, it is perhaps indicative of the attitudes to *RCIA*, which we shall see below, that this catechism, subtitled 'A Catholic Catechism for Adults', begins its major section on baptism and the sacraments of initiation with a definition from the Introduction of the revised Rite of Baptism for Children.[46]

The three sacraments of Christian initiation closely combine to bring the faithful to the full stature of Christ and to enable them to carry out the mission of the entire people of God in the Church and in the world.[47]

They start with the meaning of baptism which is richly expressed in the liturgy of the Holy Saturday vigil. The first reading (Gen. 1.1–22) is seen as a symbol of the new creation which actually takes place in baptism, the sacramental climax of the vigil. The second (Gen. 22.1–18) is seen as a fore-shadowing of Christ's sacrifice in obedience to the command of God, a sacrifice from which baptism receives its power. The third (Exodus 14.15–15.1) emphasizes the idea of deliverance through water. The symbolism of water is twofold, demonstrating death and destruction as well as life and salvation, and this becomes even clearer in the allusion to Noah in the fourth reading (Isaiah 65.5–14) as God destroys his enemies by the deluge, but saves those who are faithful to him. The remaining readings (Isaiah 55.1–11; Baruch 3.9–15, 32–44; Ezekiel 26.16–17a, 18–28) celebrate God's wonderful use of water and point forward to the new creation by promising a new heart and a new Spirit to men. So the vigil sets the scene for the celebration of the events of the fullness of time, when John the Baptist proclaimed the need for baptism for repentance and for the forgiveness of sins. Through the obedience of Jesus and his identification with man by his participation in John's baptism, Jesus brings this long sequence of water events to completion. 'Sinless himself, he leads his people from sin through the waters of baptism to a new covenant with the Father'.[48] Thus by the waters of baptism, sin and evil are destroyed and the neophyte rises to a new life sharing in the resurrection of Jesus.[49] The whole paschal mystery of the dying and rising of Christ as it envelops the baptized is summarized by Paul in a passage read on Easter morning: 'If then you have been raised with Christ, seek the things that are above, where Christ is, seated at the right hand of God. Set your minds on things that are above, not on things that are on earth. For you have died and your life is hid with Christ in God.'[50]

So the authors set their baptismal catechesis against the biblical and liturgical background of salvation history culminating in Christ. Beginning from the events preceding the baptismal rite, they mention the lengthy catechumenate for adults which is completed by the Easter Vigil and continue to relate their catechesis to this service. They describe the procession of the paschal candle, the diffusion of its light throughout the congregation and the other preparations for the passage of the neophytes through the waters of baptism to the resurrection Christ offers them. The prayer of blessing over the water sums up the salvation history recounted in the readings above, and the paschal candle symbolizing the life of the risen Christ is lowered into the waters. The font now becomes life-giving because, as 'the womb of the church, (it) will bring forth children of God, as once more the Spirit of God is "moving over the face of the waters"'.[51] Following the baptismal promises and the profession of faith there is the baptism itself, and then the anointing with chrism, recalling Christ's anointing by the Spirit which is now showed by the new Christians. Thus the baptized become members of the community and will be able to share in the 'holy priesthood'. The ceremonies are completed by their investment with a white garment, symbolizing baptismal innocence. Then they are ready to share in the eucharist with which the vigil concludes.

The authors comment that there is strong emphasis on the community aspect of baptism, and baptism is both a rite which incorporates the candidate into the Christian community, and a rite which ministers to the whole community through the preparation for baptism.[52] They proceed to discuss the effects of baptism and point out that the spirit of the paschal mystery should always penetrate its celebration.[53] Baptism itself is administered by triple immersion or affusion in the name of the Trinity, and symbolizes the new life to which the candidate is called. It may be administered ordinarily by bishops, priests, and deacons, and each candidate should have at least one godparent who should be a mature practising Roman Catholic.

The manner of man's justification through grace concerns the authors next. Through the graciousness of God the candidate at baptism receives a true inward renewal.[54] 'By baptism men are plunged into the paschal mystery of Christ; they die with him, are buried with him, and rise with him. Baptism produces all its effects by the power of the mystery of the Lord's passion and resurrection'.[55] When the baptizand passes through the cleansing waters of baptism, the old self dies and the baptized is set on a new way of life. Both original and personal sins are remitted at baptism when the candidate sincerely repents, but he is not freed from the inclination to sin by his rebirth in baptism.[56] This is left for the candidate to wrestle with, and involves the baptized in a lifelong sharing in the dying of Christ. They suggest that God permits this struggle so that the faithful may share more fully in the great work of their own redemption.

The baptized die with Christ only to rise with him to share his life. It is this sharing of the life of Christ which produces the interior renewal which he experiences. This in turn means to become a member of the community where his risen life is celebrated. Baptism also effects a new birth so that the baptized become the children of God, albeit by adoption,[57] and this means that the candidate in some way shares in the nature and life of God if he is truly a child of God. The Church has a priestly function, and the authors point out that one effect of baptism is the incorporation of the candidate into the royal priesthood of which Peter speaks.[58] The baptized have a role to fulfil 'in worshipping God fully, consciously, and actively'.[59] They are speaking of worship in the wider sense of embracing and sanctifying all the duties of life, and they sum up these ideas by quoting the Rite of Baptism for Children which states: 'Baptism is the sacrament by which men and women are incorporated into the Church, built into a house where God lives, in the Spirit, into a holy nation and a royal priesthood.'[60]

They remind their readers that the Church taught the necessity for baptism for entry to the kingdom of heaven, and then explain the difference between sacramental baptism, baptism in blood, and baptism of desire, in similar terms to that of the new catechism.[61]

Finally they consider the baptismal character, as baptism imprints a permanent character or sign on the life of the baptized. This marked the baptized as belonging to Christ, just as the 'seal' had done in biblical times. The authors define the baptismal character in these terms:

All participate in a basic way in the royal priesthood of Christ, are designated for divine worship, and are rendered capable of offering their whole lives in union with his sacrifice. Even if they fall they can be reconciled to the Church by the sacrament of penance without a repetition of baptism.[62]

It is the sign at once of the Christian's permanent vocation, of his call by Jesus Christ, and of God's initial and undiscouragable love.

The emphasis of the *Teaching of Christ* is placed on what the sacraments do for the baptized rather than on the faith expressed by the baptized in obedience to Christ, and in response to the love of God. This seems to be a retrenchment of the position from some part of *RCIA*. Similarly the insistence of separating confirmation from baptism and the suggestion of a special propriety in its conferment by the bishop[63] is also moving back from the position expressed in *RCIA*'s interpretation of Vatican II. This gives weight to the fears expressed by Ralph Keifer in connection with his comments about the new initiatory rites which he welcomes but comments:

> They are in many ways out of step with the presuppositions of those who must use them. They also provide a possible critique of church life as it is presently lived. For those reasons they are not apt to be received with open arms and they will not be easily understood.[64]

2. *The Liturgy of Baptism and its Mystagogical Explanation*

Turning our attention to the contents of the rite itself, we note once again even greater intertwining of catechesis and mystagogy in the twentieth century than in the fourth century. The primary source of the mystagogy is the rubric and study edition of the rite, supplemented by some American material produced by those using the new rite, which was recommended by various correspondents.

The new typical edition of the *Rite for the Christian Initiation of Adults*, which replaced the rite in use at that time, was authorized for use by the decree of the Sacred Congregation for Divine Worship on January 6th 1972.[65] This rite makes an important advance in the thinking of the Roman Catholic Church, prompted by the decrees of Vatican II, and thus it provides a further variation on the baptismal theme. This Church looks back to the ancient practice of the Church, and seeks to model its present-day practice upon that insofar as it is relevant.

The rites of the catechumenate are restored in the new rite following the decrees of Vatican II.[66] The purpose of the catechumenate, particularly in missionary work, is defined in the *Decree of the Church's Missionary Activity.*

Those who, through the Church, have accepted from God a belief in Christ should be admitted to the catechumenate by liturgical rites. The catechumenate is not a mere expounding of doctrines and precepts, but a training period for the whole Christian life. It is an apprenticeship of appropriate length during which disciples are joined to Christ their Teacher. Therefore, catechumens should be properly instructed in the mystery of salvation and in the practice of gospel morality. By sacred rites which are to be held in successive intervals, they should be introduced into the life of faith, liturgy, and love, which God's People live.

Then, when the sacraments of Christian initiation have freed them from the power of darkness (cf. Col. 1.13) having died with Christ, been buried with him, and risen with him (cf. Rom. 6.4–11; Col. 2.12–13; 1 Pet. 3.21–22; Mk. 16.16), they receive the Spirit, (cf. 1 Th. 3.5–7; Acts 8.14–17) who makes them adopted sons, and celebrate the remembrance of the Lord's death and resurrection together with the whole People of God.

It is the desire of this Council that the liturgy of the Lenten and Easter seasons be restored in such a way as to dispose the hearts of the catechumens to celebrate the paschal mystery at whose solemn ceremonies they are reborn to Christ through baptism.

But this Christian initiation through the catechumenate should be taken care of not only by catechists or priests, but by the entire community of the faithful, especially by the sponsors. Thus, right from the outset the catechumens will feel that they belong to the People of God. Since the life of the Church is an apostolic one, the catechumens should also learn to co-operate actively, by the witness of their lives and by the profession of their faith, in the spread of the gospel and in the upbuilding of the Church.

Finally, the juridical status of catechumens should be clearly defined in the new code of canon law. For since they are joined to the Church they are already of the household of Christ. In many cases they are already leading a life of faith, hope and charity.[67]

This is a key passage indicating the changes which are made through the new rite. We shall see that the reference to the important role of sponsors is reflected in the liturgy. We also see the problems for the Church of those who are baptized as infants, but who have 'withdrawn so far from their religion that they profess a form of indifferentism, or something close to atheism'.[68] The purpose of catechetical training is defined as that which will make men's faith become living, conscious and active, through the light of instruction. This purpose is achieved by instruction based on 'sacred Scripture, tradition, the liturgy, the teaching and life of the Church'.[69] It is the clear responsibility of bishops to 're-establish or better adapt the instruction of adult catechumens'.[70]

The introduction to the rite sets the initiation of catechumens within the overall life of the Church.[71] The process from precatechumenate throughout life is described as a journey towards the new man perfected in Christ:

> This conversion, to be sure, must be regarded as a beginning. Yet it is sufficient that a man realize that he has been snatched away from sin and led into the mystery of the love of God, who has called him to enter into a personal relationship with him in Christ. For, by the workings of divine grace, the new convert sets out on a spiritual journey. Already sharing through faith in the mystery of Christ's death and resurrection, he journeys from the old man to the new one, perfected in Christ (cf, Col. 3.5–10; Eph. 4.20–4).[72]

The rite's introduction defines the journey towards baptism in terms of precatechumenate, catechumenate, purification and enlightenment and post-baptismal mystagogies, and the transition between each stage is marked by the liturgical rites of becoming a catechumen, of the election, of the celebration of the sacraments respectively. The final period of post-baptismal mystagogia goes on throughout the Easter season; 'it is a time for deepening the Christian experience, for gaining spiritual fruit, and for entering more closely into the life and unity of the community of the faithful'.[73]

The rite intends to restore baptism for adults to its paschal setting. *The Constitution on the Sacred Liturgy* demonstrates the twofold character of the Lenten season, as it recalls baptism and prepares for it, and it stresses a penitential spirit. It decrees that both baptismal and penitential themes should be more pronounced in the liturgy, and urges that wider use be made of the baptismal features proper to the Lenten liturgy.[74] The Easter Vigil is considered to be the proper occasion for the sacraments of initiation because these are described as 'the first sacramental sharing in the death and rising of Christ'.[75]

The proximate preparation for sacramental initiation

begins with the celebration of the election or enrolment of names. This rite marks the completion of the lengthy formation of the mind and heart which has preceded during the catechumenate. At this rite the catechumen is expected to demonstrate a conversion of mind and morals, a sense of faith and charity, and a sufficient knowledge of Christian teaching. He must have an enlightened faith, and a deliberate intention of receiving the sacraments of the Church.

The rite of election or enrolment[76] enables the Church to hear the testimony of the godparents and catechists.[77] The candidates also reaffirm their intention and their faith. Then the Church passes judgement on their state of preparation and decides whether they may go on to the Easter Sacrament. Those elected then have their names enrolled in the book of the elect, and from this point onwards are called 'the elect'. The rite normally takes place on the first Sunday in Lent because of the liturgical benefits which the Lenten season brings with it. The rite lays a heavy stress upon the support from the community which has been and must continue to be given to these mature catechumens.[78] Thus it is the entire congregation of the faithful who are asked to assent to the enrolment of the candidates.

The spiritual preparation of the elect is completed through the scrutinies and presentations during the Lenten period. The scrutinies are intended to purify and strengthen the elect so that they may progress in their efforts to love God more deeply.[79] Their purpose is to identify both strengths and weaknesses in the spiritual lives of the elect,[80] and to help them to know themselves better. They are helped in this by the rite of exorcism which frees the elect from the effects of sin and the influence of the Devil, and, strengthening them in their spiritual journey, opens their hearts to receive the gifts of the Saviour.[81] During these scrutinies they are accompanied by their sponsors who encourage and strengthen them by placing their right hand upon the shoulder of the one they are sponsoring. This not only strengthens them by assuring them of the support of their particular sponsor, but also heightens their awareness of being surrounded by the prayers of the faithful.

The presentations are intended to be given at a weekday mass when the Church entrusts to the elect documents which are considered a summary of its faith and prayer from ancient time. The intention of the presentation is to deepen the faith and joy of the elect as their salvation is recalled in the Profession of Faith, and to remind them of their sonship of the God they call Father in the Lord's Prayer.[81]

It is intended that Holy Saturday should be used as a real time of spiritual preparation for baptism, and it is suggested that the elect should use it as a time for prayer and fasting.[83] Some of the rites immediately prior to baptism may also be celebrated on this day, such as the recitation of the the the profession of faith, the *ephphatha*, the choosing of a Christian name, and the anointing with the oil of catechumens.[84] The recitation of the Profession of Faith is to prepare the elect to profess their baptismal faith, and to teach them the duty of proclaiming the gospel message throughout their Christian lives. This is emphasized in the prayer.[85] The rite of *ephphatha*, the opening of the ears and mouth, demonstrated the need of grace if anyone is to hear the word of God and to work for salvation. The new Christian name helps to emphasize the newness of life to which the candidate is raised following baptism.[86]

The three sacraments of baptism, confirmation and the eucharist complete the initiation of the elect into the people of God. They receive adoption as the sons of God, and are led by the Holy Spirit, in the eucharistic sacrifice and meal, to the banquet of the kingdom of God.

The introduction of the rite explains that preparation for the celebration of baptism is by means of the blessing of the baptismal water and the profession of faith. The blessing of the water recalls the dispensation of the paschal mystery, and the choice of water for the sacramental operation of the mystery, and so the paschal mystery is plainly set forth in the blessing of the water.[87] This is linked with the rites of the renunciation of sin and the profession of faith which

also recall, in the active faith of those to be baptized, the same paschal mystery which has been recalled in the blessing of water and briefly professed by the celebrant in the words of baptism. Adults are not saved unless they come forward of their own accord and are willing to accept the gift of God by faith. Baptism is the sacrament of faith, not only the faith of the Church, but also the candidates' own faith, and it is expected that it will be an active faith in them. When they are baptized, they should not receive such a sacrament passively, for of their own will they enter into a covenant with Christ, rejecting their errors and adhering to the true god.[88]

The emphasis is laid upon the adults' free choice to be baptized and thus to be saved, and upon their need to accept willingly the gift of God. Although there is a grey area with regard to the actual point of a person's commitment, this is the baptism of believers.[89]

Much of the imagery of Satan as a dreadful tyrant is gone from the rite of renunciation and he is depicted as a confidence trickster, because all his empty promises are renounced by the candidate.[90] The congregation are bidden to pray for courageous hearts for the elect as they renounce Satan and profess their faith in Christ.[91] The rite of profession is now formalized into an affirmation to the Apostles' Creed, divided into the three questions thus:

> N, do you believe in God, the Father Almighty, Creator of heaven and earth?
> Answer: I do.
> Do you believe in Jesus Christ, his only Son, our Lord, who was born of the Virgin Mary, was crucified, died, and was buried, rose from the dead, and is now seated at the right hand of the Father?
> Answer: I do.
> Do you believe in the Holy Spirit, the holy catholic Church, the communion of saints, the forgiveness of sins, the resurrection of the body, and life everlasting?
> Answer: I do.[92]

Following this comes the rite of immersion which is seen not merely as a rite of purification, but as the sacrament of union with Christ,[93] and signifies the neophyte's participation in the paschal mystery of Christ. However, Father Dujarier comments that: 'We do find it somewhat surprising that after stressing so much that Baptism is primarily participation in the death and rising of Christ, the new rite continues to speak of baptism as a "washing"' (*RCIA* 28 and 31).[94] The rubric specifies that decency and decorum should prevail, and that the immersion or affusion should be threefold. Immediately upon his baptism, the welcome of the church community is expressed by the sponsors with a physical greeting.[95]

Then may follow three complementary rites which help to reinforce the significance of what has just been effected in the rite of baptism. These are the anointing with chrism, the giving of the white robe, and the giving of the baptismal candle. The anointing with chrism is a sign of the enrolment of the neophyte in the fellowship of the people of God, and as such of his task to share in the ministry of Christ as prophet, priest and king. Similarly the neophyte is reminded of his new status as a new creation, clothed in Christ by the giving of the white garment which he is told to keep clean as a symbol of his new life in Christ. The candle reminds the candidate of his enlightenment by the light of Christ, and of the flame of faith burning within his heart.[96]

The Celebration of the Confirmation of Adults raises some interesting questions and problems in its introduction and its rubric. The introduction begins:

> According to the ancient practice maintained in the Roman liturgy, an adult is not be be baptized unless he receives confirmation immediately afterwards (See No. 44), provided no serious obstacles exist. This connection signifies the unity of the paschal mystery, the close relationship between the mission of the Son and the pouring out of the Holy Spirit, and the joint celebration of the sacraments by which the Son and the Spirit come with the Father upon those who are baptized.[97]

Paragraph 44 picks up the intention of the *Constitution on the Sacred Liturgy* concerning the restoration of the catechumenate for adults, and makes it plain that the bishop should make his priority the active role in the catechumenate. Kavanagh draws attention to the point that although bishops are urged to preside at the rite of election and at the Lenten catechumenal liturgies, and to preside at the sacraments of initiation during the Easter Vigil, their necessary absence from the latter should not continue to force confirmation to be celebrated apart from baptism and the eucharist.[98] Indeed the document defines quite broadly the presbyters who may act as the delegates of the bishop in the celebration of confirmation immediately following baptism, the main criterion of those added being their connection with the candidates during their catechumenate.[99] This change affects the traditional episcopal hegemony regarding confirmation, but it does make a closer connection between all three sacraments making up the rite of initiation practicable. Kavanagh believes that this will remove the restriction which limited the bishop's role to confirmation and will 'enhance this ministry by emphasizing the real sacramental importance of the bishop as the one who normally should preside throughout the whole process of Christian initiation'.[100] It also stresses the importance and responsibility of the local church which is a vital element throughout the whole of the liturgy of *RCIA*.

The question of baptism and confirmation being celebrated in the same liturgical event only for adults and children of catechetical age is implicit in *RCIA* 34. Kavanagh interprets this to imply that 'all those deemed fit for baptism, no matter what their physical age, should also be confirmed within the same liturgical event'.[101] He questions whether age should be a serious obstacle to the reception of the sacraments, and concludes: 'But if this is proved, then it is inevitable that the same question be posed about baptism of infants: if age is a serious obstacle to receiving confirmation, why then is age not a serious obstacle to receiving baptism?'.[102] Kiesling avers that any suggestion to abandon the practice of infant baptism stresses too greatly the meaningfulness of the ceremony and the conscious participation of the subject. This stress is made at the expense of an emphasis upon 'the more important gift of God's grace which is already at work in the gift of upbringing by Christian parents and the Christian community, and which the ceremony of baptism celebrates'.[103] However, Kiesling does allow that some changes in indiscriminate infant baptism are inevitable if the Church is to be consistent with the implication of adult initiation. He suggests that such changes would include a restored and intelligible initiation sequence:

> Such a restored sequence may well involve as normal:
> a) enrolling infants as catechumens at an early age; b) guiding them through the catechumenate in a careful progression until an age of free acceptance of Christ and his Church is determined by catechist, family, pastor and congregation; c) full initiation through Lenten observance, baptism – confirmation – eucharist on Holy Saturday – Easter and post-baptismal catechesis through that Eastertide. This is largely what we do now, except that we baptize infants at a) reconcile them through penance and education and communicate them at b) and confirm them at c) with some more education.[104]

Braxton points out that the present practice of making confirmation a kind of adult initiation implicitly states that infant baptism is in fact functioning as an enrolment in a catechetical process. He reports a statement issued in December 1973 on the tenth anniversary of the *Constitution on the Sacred Liturgy*, and suggests that this is a representative cross-section of American opinion:

1. The rite of Christian initiation should normally consist of the unified sacramental event in which the three now separated moments (Baptism, Confirmation, Eucharist) are integrated. The full rite is to be used at *any* age when a person is initiated [emphasis added]. As an act of the Church, the rite of initiation is most properly celebrated in the midst of the congregation.
2. Within the economy of the sacraments, adult initiation should be the practical norm. The Church's understanding of baptism is most fully demonstrated when an adult is baptized.
3. Infant baptism derives from the adult form. It places specific responsibilities on the adult community. When parents and the congregation accept these responsibilities, the celebration of infant baptism proclaims the initiative of God's love.
4. The entire Easter season from Lent to Pentecost is derived from the public practice of adult Baptism. The meaning of Baptism is best demonstrated when it is celebrated within the context of the Church's dramatic shaping of time, whose climax is the Easter Season.
5. For children of responsible Christian parents, two different patterns of initiation might well co-exist; the celebration of the full rite of initiation (Baptism, Confirmation, Eucharist) shortly after birth, to be followed by catechesis appropriate to succeeding stages of development; or enrolment of the infant as a catechumen, with initiation to be celebrated at a later stage after catechesis.
6. Catechumenate. The development of viable and visible catechumenate structures on a parish, inter-parish, or diocesan basis is essential to the renewal of the sacrament of initiation. We urge that everywhere this thoroughly restored and fully celebrated rite be implemented and adapted and that the simpler forms of the new ritual be reserved for extreme exceptions'.[105]

Keifer suggests that a repeatable rite for the reaffirmation of baptismal commitment could hold the solution to the problems being experienced by those taking *RCIA* seriously.

Following confirmation, the full rite moves onward to the celebration of the eucharist at which the neophytes for the first time have the full right to participate. Their presence is marked in the prayers and they may carry the gifts when they are brought to the altar. Significantly this is also the first occasion on which they say the Lord's Prayer, identifying their family links with their fellow Christians.[106] *RCIA* also points out that 'It is most desirable that the neophytes receive communion under both species, together with their godparents, parents, sponsors and catechists'.[107] Emphasis is once again placed upon the place of the community in *RCIA*, and it needs the community to participate at every stage. This is a marked contrast to the earlier practice described by Hovda:

> As a former adult candidate for admission into communion with the Roman See, I cannot help thinking, however, that it would have been kind of nice to have had some slight indication, back in 1943, that the faith community I was joining was just a bit interested in me, even if it were manifest in prying. There was no prying, no snooping, and no apparent interest. Working with the warm bodies of one priest and one sponsor, I had to conjure up a Church.[108]

He welcomes the fact that in *RCIA* 'initiation becomes a project of the local church'.[109]

RCIA then lays down guidelines for the periods of post-baptismal catechesis which is recognized as the final stage of the neophyte's initiation. The aim is that, through this period, the neophyte should 'obtain full and joyful insertion into the life of the community'.[110] This should be assisted by the experience of 'frequenting the sacraments'. The process is mutually beneficial and the ministry to the neophytes through the Scriptures is balanced by their ministry to the community as they bring to the faithful renewed vision, and a new impetus.[111] *RCIA* recognizes that although post-baptismal catechesis never really finishes, just as 'there is no such thing as a fully "mature" Christian this side of the eschaton',[112] the immediate period of post-baptismal catechesis should close around Pentecost with some form of celebration.[113]

Kemp, writing of his experience of using the rite in his Washington parish, describes this as a period for 'experiencing the family history as our own, a time for celebrating the power that the Lord has shared in allowing us to be called his daughters and sons. This is a seven week period of coming home for the first time'.[114] He suggests that this feeling of being at home is essential if the neophytes are to feel comfortable in bringing the family a renewed vision of what being 'in Christ' means to them. He encourages both neophytes and sponsors to share freely with the whole community about the personal impact of initiation.[115] Using both midweek and Sunday occasions, he suggests that 'By Pentecost the Eucharist assembly should have heard from every neophyte and sponsor at least once.... The neophytes are the ministers of the Easter season to the whole parish'.[116] His prayer, as parish priest, is that the enthusiasm of the neophytes might become contagious. Dunning points out that each neophyte should also be encouraged to discern what service or ministry they might offer to the Church, and to celebrate that decision at a Commitment Sunday.[117]

RCIA suggests that some note should be taken of the anniversary of baptism.[118] Although this could be seen as a divisive factor, Dujarier mentions the practice of some parishes who encourage members who will celebrate the first, tenth, and twentieth anniversaries of baptism that year to participate in a communal retreat for recollection. Such retreats can coincide with a public recognition of the ministries and vocations which the former neophytes have been called to and have accepted.[119]

All in all this constitutes a very exciting revision and reappraisal of the Roman Catholic Church's thinking about the meaning of baptism, and its effect will continue to be felt for some years to come. Some of its enthusiasts describe it thus:

> The New Rite of Christian Initiation of Adults (*RCIA*) of 1972 is one of the best kept secrets since Vatican Council II.
> For some it denotes an ominous department of the American intelligence community. For others it is just one more document, written in the dry language of 'Vaticanese', imposed on us by the rite-makers immediately after the Council. Still others claim either it is one more archaism based on the principle that 'old means better', or it is obviously written for missionary countries and not for lands supposedly firm in faith (as if the Church could ever be not-on-mission).
> Perhaps others intuitively sense that this rite confronts our most fundamental assumptions about Church and with good reason keep their distance. Perhaps they sense that the *RCIA* is indeed new wine.[120]

Dujarier describes it as the most far reaching and ambitious of all the post-Vatican liturgical reforms.[121] Keifer comments about the irony that, having often cried out to Rome for reform, many have been unable to perceive radical revision and drastic change when Rome provided it. He suggests that the *RCIA* represents a reversing of a thousand years of practices and attitudes, and yet this change has gone unnoticed, virtually without comment, and with scarcely a word of dissent:

> Under the aegis of an Ecumenical Council, with the approval of the Roman See, and over the signature of the Roman pontiff, the primary rites of initiation (those for the baptism and confirmation of adults and the baptism of children) have been turned upside down and inside out, heralding a cry to bring a reform and renewal of the most radical sort.[122]

Sadly the implications of this change have not yet shown much sign of being grasped by Roman Catholics in England and Wales.[123] The solemn rite seems to have been rarely used, and probably its first significant use was its use by Pope John Paul II at Westminster Cathedral as part of the Papal visit in May 1982. The thinking behind the rite has been used as a catechetical basis, and as an encouragement to renewal, stress being laid upon it at the National Pastoral Congress in Liverpool in May 1980. It has been adopted 'as normative for all catechesis, not only for sacramental preparation'.[124] The prevailing attitude, however, seems to be that *RCIA* is more relevant to the missionary church than to the 'established' Roman Catholic Churches, and that, in established situations, there are few completely unchurched adults available for initiation. However from America we see a commitment to look for the unchurched, and from this and other situations, the 'established' Roman Catholic churches must be willing to learn.

The eloquent testimony from America is that the Church which dares, wins. Neophytes, as they challenge the community with their new life and their new faith, will encourage that community to attract new members to a commitment to Christ, and only then will the precatechumenate get under way. Kemp stresses this: 'Not to be missed are the possibilities inherent in the neophytes sitting with interested inquirers and assisting and strengthening their desire at least to try the precatechumenate stage which will begin immediately after Pentecost'.[125] Thus we see a contrast between the catechesis of some of the American Roman Catholics, who are thoroughly committed to taking seriously both the theory of Vatican II, and the liturgical revision which it instituted and the non-action of the British Roman Catholics who are only slowly grasping the implications of the reversion to the fourth century, and to a perception of the Church with a real missionary task. The fundamental documents are the same for both sides of the Atlantic, but the activity based upon the documents varies radically.

The rite re-establishes the community of faith in a vital place, and the personal faith of the candidate is placed once again in a high priority. Whether ultimately the 'established' national Roman Catholic Church will accept this emphasis from the 'missionary' churches or whether it will be pigeon-holed is still in a state of flux. So it will take the passage of more time to assess the full response of the English Roman Catholic Church to the insights and suggestions of *RCIA*.

7
Baptist Churches in Britain

Historically, the Baptists belong to the Protestant Free Church branch of the Christian Church, drawn together on the basis of their belief in the authority of Scripture, the independence of the local church, and a belief that baptism should be administered only to those with a personal faith in Christ. This is plain from the first point of the Declaration of Principle enshrined in the constitution of the Baptist Union of Great Britain and Ireland, representing 2070 churches:

> '1. That our Lord and Saviour Jesus Christ, God manifest in the flesh, is the sole and absolute authority in all matters pertaining to faith and practice, as revealed in the Holy Scriptures, and that each church has liberty, under the guidance of the Holy Spirit, to interpret and administer His Laws'.[1]

This results in a spirit of independence, rather than interdependence, and any grouping of churches beyond the local church is a matter of voluntary association. Thus it has been necessary to seek to establish the degree to which the views expressed in the various catechetical leaflets are held. It has also been necessary to delve deeper than the leaflets to discover expressions of the underlying theology of baptism upon which at least some of the catechetical material will have been based. However, as Payne reminds us, 'Baptists have no standard, authorized procedure'.[2]

1. *The theology of Baptism and its Catechetical Explanation*

A survey of 330 Baptist Ministers taken by the author in 1981[3] revealed a syllabus taught either before or after baptism:

The work of Christ and man's response.
Baptism
The Bible
Prayer

The Holy Spirit
Church Membership and Worship
Stewardship
Christian Service and Commitment
The Person of Christ
Witnessing
Belief in God
The Christian Heritage and the Baptist Family.
Additionally, teaching may be included on: Knowing God's will, Maturity and Growth, Temptation and evil, Suffering, Eschatology and Eternal Life, the Trinity and Assurance of Salvation.[4]

The survey revealed that the seven most frequently used syllabuses[5] explain the ordinance of believer's baptism at some length, adapted to various levels of understanding.[6] The theology of baptism passed on to the candidates depends upon the quality of source material which is chosen for them, and the depth of preparation which they receive. So we begin our study by considering the background theology of baptism from the 1960's, a period when many of the ministers were receiving their training in pastoral theology.

The Declaration of Principle referred to above contains a definition of baptism:

2. That Christian Baptism is the immersion in water into the Name of the Father, the Son and the Holy Ghost, of those who have professed repentance toward God and faith in our Lord Jesus Christ who 'died for our sins according to the Scriptures: was buried, and rose again the third day'.[7]

Underwood[8] provides a summary which illustrates some of the diversity of thought amongst Baptists. Some Baptists are content to view baptism in symbolic terms, as a symbol of the inward experience of conversion, and of the experience of dying to the old sinful life and rising again to newness of life in Christ. It is also an act of obedience to the command of Christ. Other Baptists have however abandoned this view in favour of a more sacramental interpretation of believer's baptism although they would refuse to make the form of baptism necessary for salvation. In their view, all that can make a man Christian is a personal response to the grace of God in Christ. However, they point out the relation in the New Testament between baptism and the gift of the Spirit which is also part of the conversion experience, and that those baptized as believers find themselves carried beyond symbolism by the actual experience of baptism to:

> an unforgettable religious experience of the first rank, in which God does something for them in response to their repentance and faith. They receive from him a further endowment of the Spirit and further power to walk in newness of life. It makes their surrender to Christ more absolute and enhances their union with him. It quickens their sense of responsibility to him as Lord, deepens their service of pardon and sin forgiven, and brings them a profounder experience of that Divine grace they had already embraced by faith at their conversion.[9]

Thus they would want to say that baptism was something more than a sign and a statement. It is in fact a genuine sacrament, a means of grace in which God, in response to the candidate's faith, uses material media as the vehicle of his grace. Baptism by immersion contributes to this sacramental experience as it demonstrates the candidate's complete surrender to Christ, death to sin, burial with Christ, and resurrection to a new life in him. This fuller doctrine advances the early Baptists' claim that their loyalty to the New Testament prevents them from modifying a scriptural ordinance, to a further claim that they alone preserve the full sacramental value of believer's baptism as a means of grace. Baptism is impoverished of its divine intention of enriching the soul of the recipient when it is administered to any who have not already made a personal surrender and commitment to Christ. Underwood suggests that if most Christians safeguard the sacramental value of the Lord's Supper by limiting it to professing Christians, then Baptists claim that similar limits apply to Baptism.[10].

Writing in *Concilium*, McClendon, a Southern Baptist from the United States, sees Baptist practice in these terms:

> Baptists first seek to proclaim the Gospel. When (and only when) hearers, whether our own children or outsiders, respond by confessing faith in Christ as Lord and Saviour, are they accepted as candidates immersed in the triune name in the presence of the congregation by the Minister, and (in most churches) thereby admitted to membership in the congregation as brothers of Christ.[11]

In his view, the New Testament evidence points without exception to the baptism of those who came to baptism expressing their own faith-commitment. Early Christian baptism retained some elements of John's baptism in that it was conversion-baptism, forgiveness-baptism, and it was baptism that admitted to the eschatological community, but it contained some new elements as well in that it was baptism in Jesus' name, it was confession-baptism, and it was baptism in the Holy Spirit.

Clark, an English Baptist, takes a very sacramental approach to baptism. He points out that the apostles defined the limits of Jesus' earthly ministry by reference to his baptism by John and his death, resurrection and ascension. Jesus' participation in the baptism of John had profoundly altered that baptism: 'It was, at one and the same time, broken and remade, negated and fulfilled ... If the old was taken and used, it was also transformed'.[12] However Jesus' baptism is, in the end, his cross, and Clark reminds us of this: 'It is from his side that the water flows (cf. John 19.34); it is his crucified and risen body that links Johannine and Christian baptism together and bridges the gulf between them.'[13] He states that the initiation of the baptizing mission of the church belongs inevitably to the risen and ascending Lord. Thus Christian baptism becomes possible at the ascension of our Lord. He develops his argument thus

So it is that the passing of the baptism at Jordan through the cross/resurrection by those who live in the light of the ascension produces the constant threefold emphasis of New Testament baptismal theology. Baptism in this normative period, implies, embodies, and effects forgiveness of sin, initiation into the Church, and the gift of the Holy Spirit. Each and all stem from John's baptism and the participation of Jesus in it, each and all are transfigured by the fulfilment that the cross and the resurrection provide; each and all are marked by the tension between the 'now' and the 'not yet' which characterizes the Christian era. The baptism of Jesus was a 'baptism of repentance for the forgiveness of sins' (Luke 3.3) and this emphasis is taken up in the Acts and unwarrantably heightened in the early Fathers; but the Epistles of Paul subject this note to the richer and more positive concept of new life in Christ, as the christological criterion begins to overwhelm the inheritance of the past and the original symbolism of the baptismal act (Romans 6.3,4).

Baptism effects initiation into the life of the blessed Trinity and all the blessings of the new 'age', and so, embodies the wholeness of redemption. It is 'into Christ', into the crucified, risen and ascended Lord, into the drama of his redemption achievement. We are incorporated into Christ that we may be crucified with Christ. We are crucified with Christ that we may share his resurrection. But 'in Christ' ... is primarily an ecclesiological formula. That is to say our incorporation is into the crucified and risen body of the Lord, the organic unity animated by the Holy Spirit, Christ in his Church, *totus Christus*, the whole Christ, head and members.[14]

Hurley, in a second article in *Concilium*, describes Clark's theology of baptism which followed as 'highly controversial writing for a Baptist'.[15] He also refers to the views of Beasley-Murray, who sought to face the problem as to why Baptists resist sacramental theology, retreating to the defence of an apparently ineffective symbolic ordinance. He explains the problem in these terms:

On the one hand they have reacted strongly to a type of sacramentalism that has savoured to them more of superstition than of Christ's true religion, and on the other hand they have been intensely concerned to observe the spiritual reality of baptism, namely participation in the redemption of Christ through faith – union with him and the reception of his Holy Spirit.[16]

Personal religion and freedom of the individual under the lordship of Christ are watchwords that dominate Baptist life. However a stress on the symbolism of baptism places the emphasis upon the baptizand, and his obedience and witness, rather than on Christ and his gracious work.

He suggests that the apostolic writers do not define baptism in purely human terms, nor do they separate it from conversion.[17] For them the essence of believer's baptism has been that it was conversion-baptism. Conversion is fulfilled and expressed in baptism, and baptism is conversion, itself a work of the Spirit, and filled with the Spirit's gift to the penitent convert.

Child[18] makes a further contribution to the symbol or sacrament debate. He defines baptism as:

a form of symbolic action, and ... one which is particularly rich in meaning and power because it is used in a religious setting. The Church, through its ministers acting in God's name, uses certain words and performs certain actions as the divinely appointed means whereby men are made more deeply aware of the reality of God's presence, and more susceptible of his truth and grace.[19]

The clue to the relationship between sacrament and symbol is that every symbol takes its character from what it symbolizes or represents.[20]. Baptism reminds everyone of the sovereign work of Christ on the cross for all mankind, and it proclaims the ongoing work of repentance and renewal in which Jesus Christ is acknowledged as Lord.[21] In the New Testament baptism 'transformed the individual experience of the candidate into a corporate fact ... they were in very truth "members one of another"'.[22]. The most important participant in baptism is God, under whose authority the rite is administered. Whilst baptism gives the candidate the opportunity to testify openly to his repentance and allegiance to Christ, it is God alone who is able to make baptism effective.[23]

In 1965, we find some Baptists engaged in ecumenical dialogue.[24] Significantly they are the contributors[25] to Gilmore's book,[26] but their comments give us a clue to the Baptist view of baptism current in 1965. Gilmore himself comments on the primeval connection between creation and water, and concludes that water should also be used for re-creation.[27] However, in the baptism of Jesus, God is concerned with the re-creation of fallen nature, citing Gregory of Nyssa's description of Jesus elevating the whole world as he emerged from baptism.[28] The baptized experiences the transformation of his whole world view as he shares in Christ's work of creating and sanctifying the world. Although this is not confined to immersion, baptism does point to death, the gateway to life, as the old is surrendered to make way for the new. His share in Christ's work is most faithfully and consistently fulfilled where there are people who offer themslves and their world to God, particularly through the focal point of the rite of Holy Communion. So he argues that because it is the continual re-creation of God's people which is focused in Baptism and the Communion, and because it is the believer who is committed to this task of offering himself to God, 'the act of baptism which initiates the process of sharing in creation, should be reserved for those who are able, in knowledge and understanding, to commit themselves to it'.[29]

Clark contributed a paper on 'Baptism and Redemption' based on the precept that a basic understanding of baptism can only derive from the Christ-event, and insists that 'the historical basis of the baptismal rite and the historic actuality of the incarnate Jesus (must) be allowed to remain properly normative'.[30] The theology of baptism comes from the twin realities of the baptism of Jesus at Jordan, and its fulfilment at the cross and resurrection which modifies John's baptism of repentance, and which binds Christian baptism after Pentecost with Jesus' baptism. It is the risen and ascending Lord who initiates the Church's mission to baptize. Whilst this baptism continues the significances inherent in Jordan baptism – forgiveness of sin, initiation into the Israel of God, the gift of the Holy Spirit – all have been transformed and are now controlled by the redemptive act of Calvary. So Christian baptism is a reality which belongs to the period between Pentecost and parousia, and in terms reminiscent of Theodore, Clark points out both a unity and a distinction in the understanding of redemption expressed in baptism:

> There is unity. The Christ who has come is the Christ who will come. There is distinction. At the cross and resurrection we were redeemed. At the parousia we shall be redeemed. This is the tension of eschatology. Between the redemptive realities of past and future and under the eschatological tension is the Church, the saving community, charged by word and baptism to extend the redemptive purpose of God. Baptism is incorporation into this body'[31]

He describes baptism as a sacrament of inaugurated eschatology, and it is neither the declaration of a redemption already accomplished nor the guarantee of a redemption which at last will be. It is rather the incorporation into Christ of the baptized, and the initiation of the baptized into the servant people of God.

Winward's contribution was a comment on Davis' paper 'Baptism, Confirmation, and the Eucharist' and his comment considers the relation between confirmation and baptism.[32] Davis states quite plainly that the Holy Spirit and his gifts are present in the baptized, from the moment of baptismal regeneration, and that baptism is the door into the life of the community, and achieves the oneness with Christ which carries the entire gift of salvation with it. Winward understands Davis' argument to be: 'Confirmation is an act of commissioning for the work of witness at which an additional gift of the Spirit is imparted for that vocation'.[33] However Winward cites the New Testament evidence which, without exception, ascribes this gift to baptism. It is through baptism that we are united with Christ, share his risen life, possess the Holy Spirit, are consecrated to God, and made members of his Church.[34] The laying on of hands with prayer underscores the acceptance of the catechumen into the community, and marks his commissioning because he is accepted into a community whose nature is mission. Both baptism and the laying on of hands should be seen as two aspects of one individual whole. Winward also stresses the importance of preaching and of a response to the proclaimed word in repentance and faith before the administration of any of the sacraments of initiation.[35].

In their more recent study, Donald Bridge and David Phypers, both theologically conservative, cover very similar ground.[36] They affirm that although they are administered independently, baptism in water and baptism in the Spirit belong to each other. 'They are different aspects of one great initiation complex which includes the *inward attitudes* of repentance and faith, the *outward marks* of water baptism and the laying on of hands, and the declaration by God of sin's forgiveness and heart renewal.'[37] They also point out the appropriateness of the symbol of baptism to the elements of salvation in the New Testament, especially the portrayal in baptism of the death, burial and resurrection which the Christian shares with Christ. This association in itself makes it plain that baptism is also a sacrament – a means of God's grace, and they conclude 'To the New Testament writers there is no problem. Baptism is integral to the salvation process, of value in itself, bringing with it the full blessing of God upon the Christian'.[38] They affirm the vital part which the individual's response in faith to the grace of God in Christ must play in any act of initiation, and this element must be the key to any Baptist theology of baptism.

This background theology is interpreted in the printed word of the catechetical leaflets, and we shall begin with *The Way of Christ*.[39] Beginning from the New Testament, Neil suggests that for the first Christians, baptism was the inevitable development of faith in Christ, an experience which could be analysed into four stages, viz., repentance, faith, baptism and belonging to the fellowship, and the omission of any of these stages would result in an incomplete view of what was involved in becoming a Christian. Baptism is an act of obedience to the command of Christ[40] and follows commitment to Christ as his disciple, and is the outward declaration of an inward act of repentance and faith. For the candidate it also marks the beginning of a life of obedience in acknowledgement of the lordship of Christ. Baptism is a declaration of the union of the baptized with Christ, and this is reinforced by the act of immersion in water in the name of Jesus which is an acted parable of the death and resurrection of Jesus Christ.[41] The ordinance demonstrates the outward act which declares the response of God to the faith of the baptizand as he receives new life in Christ. Neil emphasizes the link between faith and baptism, describing them in Denney's quotation: 'Baptism and faith are but the outside and the inside of the same thing', and he suggests that when baptism is the expression of personal faith, 'we can better understand the New Testament teaching that baptism results in the forgiveness of sins (Acts 2.38), union with Christ (Galatians 3.27) and the gift of the Holy Spirit (Acts 2.38).'[42]

Returning to Galatians 3.27–28,[43] he points out that baptism is the mark of entry into the Church, and suggests that one way for the phrase 'baptized into Christ' to be understood is that the baptizand is being baptized into the Christian community. Thus baptism involves a firm commitment to the life and work of the people of Christ. His final point again reverts to the New Testament practice when he emphasizes that baptism is an act of public declaration of allegiance to Jesus Christ as Lord.

Produced by the same publishers is *Invitation to Baptism*.[44] Its subject is baptism, whereas Neil's subject is a life of committed discipleship. The greater depth of White's treatment, possible because of his narrower subject, results in a closer comparison with some of the Roman Catholic material which we have considered above. He makes a similar beginning, considering the baptism of Jesus by John, and linking this to Jesus' call to the first disciples to follow him. Such discipleship, White suggests, involves the deliberate surrender of all life's decisions to his direction and control, just as Jesus' baptism by John was 'a supreme instance of his unhesitating obedience to every call of God, however it came'.[45] His obedience provided an opportunity for a public identification with the word and work of God in his generation, and the candidate's baptism not only provides him with a similar opportunity, but Jesus' baptism also earths the faith of the candidate through baptism to the historic events of Jesus' ministry, death and resurrection. Thus, following Christ's example, and his command to his disciples, the Church possesses Christ's own authority to baptize in his name. Referring to Jesus baptizing at the hands of his disciples,[46] a rarely used passage, he stresses the identity of baptism with Christ. He sums up thus:

> In passages like these the apostolic Church expressed its deep conviction that Christian baptism derived from the express command of Jesus. Behind that conviction lay also their knowledge that he himself had been baptized. And that knowledge was given added weight and importance by the fact which is virtually certain, that only Jesus himself could have described for them exactly what happened.[47]

From the standpoint that nothing Jesus shared could possibly be meaningless, he suggests that the baptized also must expect some positive, spiritual and permanent effect from baptism. He summarizes the four things which happened to Jesus in his baptism as acknowledgement, empowering, commissioning and temptation, and suggests that the New Testament provides evidence for believing that 'we would hesitate to conclude that anything like this should happen to us in baptism, if the New Testament did not give us (as we shall see) considerable ground for believing that'.[48]

In the next chapter White examines the meaning of John's baptism emphasizing the concept of cleansing from the defilement of sin. In a passage reminiscent of Tertullian, he examines the biblical evidence and shows that the root idea of baptism as purification is an important part of Christian thought.[49] Thus baptism expresses confession, repentance and pardon, but of necessity, must be sincere.[50] His description of baptism as 'one deliberate, public and irrevocable act' which can never be undone is reminiscent of the Roman Catholic teaching on the character of baptism. It is an act which expresses once and for all the candidate's break with sin, and his faith in the forgiveness of God.

White next turns his attention to the relationship between faith and baptism, remarking on the revolutionary nature of the confession 'Jesus Christ is Lord' in the days immediately after the crucifixion. Once the crucial confession was made, the next step for the early Christians was to share symbolically in the death, burial, and resurrection of Jesus, and to be baptized into his name, thus passing their lives into the ownership of Christ. White insists that there is a real place in a baptismal service today for just such a confession of the lordship of Christ. Baptism unites the candidate to the Church, and this supports the stand which he is making, and witnesses to the power of Christ at work in his life.

Sharing in the fellowship is a real part of what it meant to be baptized in Christ but the major part of being in Christ was dependent upon the candidate's real and living relationship to Christ himself. So he states that in baptism

> Christ is present when in the fellowship of the gathered Church, a new convert makes his act of repentance, confession, obedience, faith, imitation, resolve, commitment and witness. An act so richly significant, to which the heart has been led by the Holy Spirit himself, must receive blessing. And the blessing is, that Christ receives the baptized into fullest fellowship and union with himself.[51]

Developing more fully the concept of baptism into the death of Christ, he indicates that 'something in us must die if the Christ-life is to survive and flourish.[52]. Essentially this is just a restatement of the truth of repentance, but the concept is strengthened by the addition of the element of identification with Christ, and of the transformation in Paul's thinking of the baptistry from a pool of cleansing to a tomb.[53]. Thus following baptism, the neophyte is pledged with Christ to oppose all evil, and to be dead to everything to which he died.[54].

White demonstrates the difference between the Baptist and Roman Catholic ecclesiology in his chapter 'Baptized into one Body' when he stresses the authority of the local church to baptize. The minister acts alone on the authority of that local church and this authority should be exercised responsibly in Christ's name.[55] He also emphasizes the expectation by the church of the candidates that they should love, defend, serve and support the church into which they come.

Proceeding to note the connection of the Holy Spirit with baptism, White suggests that following the sincere commitment and obedience of the candidate, 'the Spirit who has led him to baptism will come upon him in altogether the new fullness and power, and abiding with him, lead, empower, and sanctify him, and see him safe to glory'.[56] However he questions the association of laying-on of hands with the coming of the Spirit within the baptismal rite, suggesting that its use in Acts was to regularize the baptism of the Samaritan Christians,[57] and to complete the baptism of John received by the disciples at Ephesus.[58] He feels that it should be used as an exceptional supplement to an inadequate baptism. Its normal use 'is simply a gesture of solidarity among believers'.[59]

In conclusion he looks at the doubts which may prevent or delay a request for baptism, and emphasizes the christocentric nature of baptism:

> In the last resort Christ himself is the baptizer, as he is the head of the Church we join, giver of the Spirit we receive, host at the table where we shall be renewed. Minister, congregation, Church Meeting are agents of his action. The promise is 'He shall baptize you....'[60]

White's approach illustrates well the lack of any form of 'official' view among Baptists, and, for example, his view of the laying-on of hands would not be universally accepted or expressed.

Another booklet produced by the Baptist Union is Winward's *Your Baptism* subtitled 'A booklet for the instruction of candidates for baptism and Church Membership'.[61] A sacramentalist among Baptists, he too stresses the unity of faith and baptism.[62] He thinks first of what the candidate receives in baptism, and emphasizes the fact that the neophyte is in union with Christ, a phrase which describes the relationship of the Christian with the risen and glorified Lord. This unity makes the baptizand a Son of God,[63] and makes possible the baptizand's sharing of the death, burial and resurrection of Christ.[64] He develops this point in a very similar fashion to White.[65] Through this union with Christ the baptizand receives the promised forgiveness of sin, which God alone could effect through the perfect sacrifice of Jesus Christ.[66]

Winward is sure that 'the baptism of the disciple, like that of the Master, is with water and Spirit',[67] and although he freely admits that the Spirit is at work in the candidates' lives long before the administration of baptism, he suggests that the gift of the Spirit in baptism is related to Christ, to the Church, to the neophyte's vocation, and to his response.[68] By the Holy Spirit, God anoints and seals the baptizand as his own in baptism. The Holy Spirit also joins the baptizand to his brethren in Christ, and this brings Winward to his next point: membership in the Church. This he defines as 'that in which all former divisions between men are destroyed and all are one in Christ'.

Winward sees all this in terms of what Christ does for the candidate in his baptism. He proceeds to suggest that the baptizand makes a threefold response. The response begins with the candidate's obedience to the Lord's command, an element which was strongly shown in Jesus' own baptism, and which he expected from his disciples in response to his command.[69] This leads to the candidate's public confession of a personal faith in Christ, which gives joy to the Lord to whom the confession is made, and it confirms and strengthens the faith of the candidate. This good confession is used by the Holy Spirit to create or strengthen faith in those present among the witnesses who have not yet come to faith and baptism. For Winward, the simple confession 'Jesus Christ is Lord' has far-reaching implications:

> We confess our faith in the one eternal God, the Sustainer of the Universe, our Maker, known through Christ as our Father, active in Christ as our redeemer. We confess our faith in Jesus Christ as Lord and Saviour, as God manifest in the flesh, who has saved us from sin and death. We confess our faith in the Holy Spirit, who sanctifies the people of God, the Paraclete who guides, helps and strengthens us.[70]

He also reminds his readers that in their baptism they are pledging their allegiance to Christ, and uses the analogy of the Roman soldier's *sacramentum*, the oath of allegiance to the emperor, adding to this the allusion of 1 Peter 3.20–22 of the pledge arising from the interrogation and consent by two parties to a contract. Such allegiance, he suggests, must be affirmed publicly to strengthen their resolve, and in recognition of the frailty of human nature.[71]

Winward sums up this section of his leaflet: 'And so, in obeying, in confessing and in promising we make full response to him who unites us with Christ, cleanses us from sin, seals us with the Holy Spirit, and makes us members of his Church.[72]

He also produced a booklet of daily Bible readings for baptismal candidates.[73] In it he has collected the references to baptism from the New Testament, and comments upon each passage in about 200 words. They act as reinforcement to the previous leaflet, but he makes a few additional points. He notes the reference in John[74] to Jesus baptizing disciples and suggests that this was why the first Christians practised baptism immediately after Pentecost.[75]. In the readings in Acts he traces a pattern of conversion, baptism, the gift of the Holy Spirit, and incorporation into the fellowship of the Church through the laying-on of hands, although he notes that there were variations in the order of these events.[76] He interprets the laying-on of hands as confirmation, and urges that conversion, baptism, confirmation and membership of the local church should be regarded as facets of one act, and should be separated only by very short periods of time.[77] His booklet does add a useful, simple summary of the actions and effect of baptism:

(a) *What I do in my Baptism*
  I. I turn to God in repentance and faith
  II. I make a public confession of my personal faith in Jesus Christ as Saviour and Lord.
  III. I follow the example of the Lord Jesus Christ who was himself baptized.
  IV. I obey the command of Jesus Christ that all disciples are to be baptized.
  V. I make a vow of allegiance to Christ.

(b) *What the Lord does for me in my Conversion and Baptism*
  I. He brings me into union with the Lord Jesus Christ in his death and resurrection.
  II. He washes away all my sin, granting to me full remission and forgiveness.
  III. He clothes me with the new nature of the Lord Jesus Christ.
  IV. He gives to me the Holy Spirit, through whom I become a son of God.
  V. He incorporates me into the Body of Christ, the Universal Church.[78]

These four booklets, as we have seen, for the most part portray the same truth and cover the same subject matter, and most of the differences stem from differences of emphasis by the author. The same could also be said of the other booklets in common use,[79] and their more detailed study at this point would not add greatly to our consideration, and so we shall move to a consideration of the baptismal liturgy, a term in itself which many Baptists would dispute. In the leaflets we have seen a diversity of approach which illustrates both the independency of Baptists, and their stress on inward faith rather than outward symbol, and upon God's work in the candidate's life before baptism, expressed in the baptism rite, rather than upon what the sacrament accomplishes in itself. This same emphasis will be apparent as we consider the suggested liturgies of the period under consideration.

2. *The Liturgy of Baptism and its mystagogical explanation*

Baptist independency of action and their freedom to interpret the leading of the Holy Spirit in worship find expression in a stress upon extempore prayer and worship among many Baptists, although over the last twenty years there has been a growing interest in liturgical expressions of worship among some Baptists. This interest is by no means universal, but it is likely that most churches would use for Baptism a rite which is at least recognizable as belonging to the same species as those which we will consider.

The services which we shall consider do not include a rite of election. The equivalent action takes place at the church meeting when on the basis of the reports of the sponsors, testifying to the candidate's faith, commitment to Christ and genuine intention to serve the Church and the world, the candidate is elected to membership of the local church subject to his subsequent baptism.

The earliest service from the period under discussion comes from *Orders and Prayers for Church Worship*, published in 1960. Written by Winward and Payne, two Baptists noted for their liturgical interest, this order notes that the setting of believer's baptism should be in the context of public worship, and that it is desirable for it to be followed by communion at which the neophytes might be received into the membership of the local church.[80] The rite begins with the singing of the baptismal hymn, and is then introduced with a selection of Bible readings which relate either to Jesus' baptism by John, or baptism as practised in the New Testament.[81]. This selection is concluded with the Great Commission from Matthew 28.18–20. Other longer readings are suggested for the main

New Testament lesson,[82] but the Old Testament is not used in this list, a reminder of Baptists' stress on the New Testament, and their emphasis on the faith of the candidate rather than on the efficacy of the sacramental elements, which we saw in the Roman Catholic rite.[83]

A statement follows by the minister defining baptism as a holy sacrament[84] – one of the two dominical sacraments which Baptists accept, and have accepted since their early confessions of faith.[85] It sets forth the benefits of baptism which the believer is promised viz., union with Christ, cleansing from sin, reception of the Holy Spirit and membership of the Church universal, and continues by applying these benefits to the individual believer, describing baptism as an act of personal obedience, following the example of Christ, a public confession of faith in Christ and a pledge of personal allegiance to Christ.[86] Thus the implication of the union of the candidate with Christ, because of his response to Christ in faith, is spelt out in this public definition of baptism. These implications are stressed further in the questions to the candidates: 'Do you make profession of repentance toward God and of faith in our Lord Jesus Christ?' 'Do you promise, in dependence on divine grace, to follow Christ and to serve him for ever in the fellowship of his Church?'[87] These questions are followed by the baptismal prayer seeking the bestowal of the inward and spiritual grace of baptism upon the believers who submit themselves to its outward and visible sign. Following this prayer, the candidates are baptized by a single immersion in the baptistry with the following formula: 'N, On thy profession of repentance toward God and faith in our Lord Jesus Christ, I baptize thee in the name of the Father and of the Son and of the Holy Spirit. Amen.'[88] The rite concludes with the blessing of the candidates,[89] their emergence from the baptistry, and a concluding hymn.

The developing practice of receiving newly baptized members into the fellowship of the Church by the laying-on of hands is reflected by an appropriate rubric, which begins with an explanatory statement by the minister explaining that the laying-on of hands was practised by the apostles, and explaining its significance as an act of acceptance and commissioning.[90] This in turn is followed by one or more scripture sentences related to the function and purpose of the Church as shown in its members,[91] and a prayer which seeks the neophytes' equipment for their work as Christians and church members.

> Almighty and everlasting God, strengthen we beseech thee these thy servants with the Holy Spirit the Paraclete: the Spirit of wisdom and understanding, the Spirit of counsel and might, the Spirit of knowledge, piety, and godly fear. Grant that they may continue steadfastly in the apostles' teaching and fellowship, in the breaking of bread and the prayers. Enable them as royal priests of Jesus Christ to bring others to thee in prayer, and to take thee to others in witness. In all their vocation and ministry may they truly serve thee, through Jesus Christ our Lord.[92]

The laying-on of hands is performed by the minister and one or two other appointed representatives of the church.[93] The minister then welcomes the neophytes with the words of Ephesians 2.19–20.[94] The service continues with the administration of Communion. This service was an innovation at this period, as the more normal mode of welcome was the giving of the right hand of fellowship,[95] and this is still preferred in many churches.

Something of a development may be seen from the next service under review, one prepared by Winward in 1969 as part of his leaflet *Your Baptism* which we have seen above. He suggests that the service is meant to be illustrative and typical, but makes it plain that baptism should be performed in the presence of the worshipping community, following the service of the Word. He suggests a suitable beginning for the rite in the words of the Great Commission and then the minister proceeds with the preface to the service, as follows:

> Brethren, you have heard the command of Christ to his Church to make disciples, baptizing them in the name of the Father, the Son, and the Holy Spirit. According to the scriptures, baptism is to be administered to those who profess repentance towards God and faith in our Lord Jesus Christ. I call upon you therefore, to hear and witness the profession of repentance, the confession of faith, and the promise of allegiance which the candidates are now to make.[96]

This preface is quite considerably condensed from its predecessor and the emphasis has moved closer to the candidates' personal faith in Christ.[97] In this rite, also, the questions vary from those above[98] and the aspect of repentance and faith is spelt out more clearly:

Do you turn to God in Christ, repent of your sins and renounce evil?

Do you confess your faith in God as your Creator and Father, in Jesus Christ as your Saviour and Lord, and in the Holy Spirit as your Sanctifier and Helper?

Do you promise to follow Christ, and to serve him in the fellowship and in the world?[99]

Winward is bringing back a fourth-century emphasis in his first and second questions which are direct descendants of the renunciation and profession, and which are far more explicitly expressed than in the service examined above.

Following the questions and a time of silent prayer, the minister prays the baptismal prayer:

We give thanks to you, eternal God, our heavenly Father, for you have created all things and your compassion is over all that you have made.

We give thanks to you for your beloved Son, our Saviour Jesus Christ, who died for our sins and was buried, and was raised to life on the third day.

We give thanks to you for the Holy Spirit, the Lord, the Giver of life, who has given us a new birth and is changing us into the likeness of your Son.

Accept and bless these disciples who are now to be baptized in your name.

Grant that, being united with Christ in his death and resurrection, they may die to sin and live to righteousness. Grant that, according to your promise, they may receive the forgiveness of their sin and the gift of the Holy Spirit.

Grant that, being baptized into one body, they may always continue in the fellowship of your faithful and elect people.

Grant that, putting on the Lord Jesus Christ, they may receive out of his fullness, grace upon grace, and evermore abide in him.

Through whom, in the unity of the Holy Spirit, all glory be to you, Father almighty, for ever and ever.[100]

This is much more complex than the earlier form, and contains much of the material contained in the preface of the earlier service.[101]

The baptismal formula has been simplified, and reduced to a bare minimum: 'A .. B .. I baptize you in the name of the Father, and of the Son, and of the Holy Spirit. Amen.'[102] A rubric follows suggesting how the service might be ordered with the intercessions, notices and offering following the baptism to enable the candidates to return to the service in time to be received into membership by the laying-on of hands.[103]

Although Winward's suggested rite for the laying-on of hands is simplified, he adds the reminder that the laying-on of hands was not only an act of acceptance and commissioning, but also an act of blessing. He also transforms some of the earlier statement into his prayer:

> We are now to pray for and lay our hands upon these brothers and sisters who have been baptized, invoking the blessing of God upon them, accepting them into the membership of the Church, and commissioning them for the service of our Lord Jesus Christ. Let us stand for the prayer.
> We thank you, our God and Father, for these brothers and sisters who in baptism have made confession of their faith, and have been united with your Son and Saviour in his body the Church. Strengthen them with the Holy Spirit, the Spirit of wisdom, power and love, that they may grow up in every way into Christ. Help us by our prayers, our friendship and our example to encourage them in the Christian life, that they may continue steadfastly in the apostles' teaching and fellowship, in the breaking of bread and the prayers. Defend them in all trials and temptations, and grant that serving you faithfully here on earth, they may inherit eternal life; through Jesus Christ our Lord.[104]

The Bible passages are omitted altogether, but the procedure for the act of laying-on of hands is as above. However in Winward's service the Aaronic blessing is offered at this point, and he adds 1 Peter 2.9 to the Ephesians passage in welcoming the neophyte to membership.[105]

An indication of the changes in thinking about the whole area of Christian initiation ecumenically is to be seen in the introduction to the suggested order of service for baptism in *Praise God*.[106] Although intended as a replacement to *Orders and Prayers*, it is compiled as a collection of resource material for worship, and often the introduction is its most valuable contribution:

> Among Baptists of late there has been a growing tendency to bring closer together the act of baptism, reception into membership and admission to communion. In other branches of the church at the same time there has been a tendency to see the wholeness of the Christian Initiation in terms of strengthening the

links between baptism, confession of faith (or confirmation) and communion.

One result of this theological discussion for Baptists is that the act of baptism as a confession of faith is increasingly seen as part of a larger act of initiation which often then finds expression in one service of baptism and communion.[107]

However they note that this practice is still by no means universal and often baptism and reception into the membership of the local church are separated temporally. Whether initiation takes place in one service or not, they suggest five essential elements which should find expression in the worship.

1. Reading of Scripture (including the gospel) and our reasons for engaging in Christian initiation, including the fact that baptism bears witness to what God has done and continues to do, and that our act of baptism is our response to that love.

2. Profession of faith and commitment.

3. Prayers, including a prayer for God's action in the Spirit that those who are baptized may become children of God, entering into newness of life in Christ, becoming part of his body, and sharing his Spirit.

4. Baptism in the name of the Trinity, possibly with the laying on of hands.

5. Reception into membership and admission to communion.[108]

They then propose an order of service, and although they expand on certain items, they neither include in their order, nor in their material, a baptismal prayer. The prefatory statement[109] is simply a rendering in modern language of that from *Order and Prayers*.

The questions omit any reference to repentance or the renunciation of evil and simply require of the candidate an acknowledgement of Christ and a promise of service: 'Do you acknowledge Jesus Christ as your Saviour and Lord? Do you promise with the help of the Holy Spirit to serve him in the Church and in the world unto your life's end?'[110] These are followed by the baptismal formula which is based on the earlier order, but includes the interesting phrase 'at your own request'. 'A.B. upon profession of your faith and at your own request I baptize you in the name of the Father, the Son and the Holy Spirit.'[111] This further reminds those present that the candidates come of their own volition to make this step of commitment and faith. Once again there is no reference to any act of blessing as the candidate emerges from the water. However the following suggestion of an invitation to baptism must stand alone and would not be found in the service book of any other denomination:

> Since the act of baptism very often leads others to ask for baptism, once all the candidates are baptized the minister may then wish to invite those present who have not made this act of commitment either to come forward there and then (though not necessarily with a view to being baptized at that moment) or to meet him in the vestry afterwards.[112]

This is always a major emphasis in any celebration of believer's baptism in a Baptist church.

The introductory statement for the rite of the Reception of Candidates into Membership is basically culled from *Orders and Prayers*,[113] although we must note that Winward's concept of the laying-on of hands conferring a blessing has been abandoned in the statement. Rather it is included in the suggested prayer which has come direct from *Orders and Prayers*, save for the alteration of 'thy' to 'you': 'Bless, O Lord, this your servant. Strengthen him by the Holy Spirit, as we now in your name commission him for the service and ministry of Jesus Christ our Lord. Amen'.[114] It is also indicated that ministers who do not wish to lay hands on candidates may use the same prayers and emphasis together with the right hand of fellowship. This is a timely reminder of the built-in individuality of the Baptist minister, and of the lack of any formally agreed liturgical structure.

So we find the Baptist theology of baptism and liturgy of baptism stress the importance of the personal faith and commitment to Christ of the candidate. Although they take the view that the inward and spiritual grace is more important than the outward and visible sign, they still see baptism in sacramental terms, emphasizing the way in which baptism unites the candidate to Christ and grants his participation in the death and resurrection of Christ. But, having now reviewed the three variations to our theme individually, we shall proceed to compare them.

8

A Comparison of the Catechetical Teaching about Baptism and the Liturgy of Baptism in certain of the Orthodox, Roman Catholic and Baptist Churches 1960–1980

1 Catechetical Teaching about Baptism

The modern churches which we have considered have their roots in very different religious traditions, historical backgrounds and cultural environments, and so in one sense it is all the more surprising that two churches, historically divided for 1500 years, and a group of individual churches forming a denomination founded on the appeal of two radical reformers to a new understanding of Scripture, should actually agree to anything. However, there are a number of areas of agreement which will be discovered as we compare the teaching of the denominations about the meaning of baptism. Later we shall be able to compare the variation with the theme, although we do not seem to be considering any modern-day Chrysostom-like oratory, but rather the more sober and carefully measured catechesis of the printed word, which by its nature presupposes a higher than average degree of literacy on the part of catechumens who are used to visual rather than verbal modes of communication. Within the materials considered, we have included an attempt to encourage Orthodox Christians to rethink the meaning of baptism, and to rediscover its relevance for their lives, two very weighty and carefully written tomes containing 'clear and simple presentations', in Cardinal Conway's view of one of them 'of what the Catholic Church teaches and believes', the utterance contained in papers at conferences for the theologically aware, the simple, and not so simple, explanation of the faith in booklets aimed at candidates but more often used by the catechist as a basis for his verbal instruction, and the various rubrics and explanatory notes which are built into and around liturgy. With such a diversity of material, written for such a diverse group of readers with many and differing needs, any comparison is difficult to establish, but the enterprise must still be undertaken as fairly as possible.

The syllabi for instruction are probably one of the easier areas to compare. Bishop Kallistos asserts that the instruction of candidates in the Orthodox Church would be based upon Schmemann's book *Of Water and the Spirit*, which is basically a mystagogical explanation of the liturgy of preparation for baptism, of baptism itself, of the sacrament of the Holy Spirit, and of the entrance into the Kingdom.

The booklet *Basic Teaching for Catholic Religious Education* sets out the catechetical syllabus outlined in chapter 6 (see pp. 123–4). It is this syllabus that is closely followed in *The Teaching of Christ. A New Catechism*, on the other hand, took its syllabus from a different starting point, beginning with the mystery of man's existence (see p. 124). For a composite summary of the Baptists' material developed from my research, see pp. 146–7.

Although there are a number of parallels between the syllabuses, the Roman Catholic syllabuses are geared towards the candidate's understanding of the Church and sacraments, whilst the Baptist composite syllabus is geared towards helping the candidate to understand the implications of his conversion experience, and thus seeks to emphasize the personal response to Christ and his people.

Jesus' baptism by John the Baptist was the starting point for the explanation of baptism of a number of catechetical syllabi, and the authors of the *New Catechism* explain this ablutionary baptism as a preparation for the baptism with the Holy Spirit and with fire of 'He who comes', and Jesus' submission to John's baptism transformed it to become a symbol both of the baptism of the Spirit which would be conferred on all future believers, and a sign of Jesus' readiness to share the common lot of man.[1] John's baptism was a baptism of repentance and forgiveness, and citing the liturgy of the Easter Vigil they explain Jesus' baptism by John as the completion of a dramatic sequence of water events, so that Jesus, sinless himself, could lead his people from sin through the waters of baptism to a new covenant with the Father.[2] Clark points out that Jesus' participation in John's baptism had profoundly altered that baptism, although as we shall see below, he feels that Jesus' truest baptism was his cross, as does the *New Catechism*.[3] Inherent in John's baptism as received by Jesus were forgiveness of sins, initiation into the Israel of God, and the gift of the Holy Spirit, but all these have been transformed, and are now controlled by the redemptive act of Calvary.[4] White linked the baptism of Jesus by John to Jesus' call to the disciples to follow him, describing Jesus' baptism as a supreme instance of his unhesitating obedience to every call of God, however it came. Jesus' obedience enabled him to publicly identify himself with both his generation and ours, a point very like that made by the *New Catechism* above,[5] and suggests that in Jesus' baptism four things happened to Jesus: acknowledgement, empowering, commissioning, and temptation, and, in baptism, candidates share in some measure in the experience which came to Christ there.[6] As a result candidates should come to baptism expecting some positive, spiritual and permanent effect from it. Winward refers to Jesus' baptism at the hands of John within the context of the descent of the Holy Spirit, and thus he concludes that the baptism of the disciple, like that of the Master, is with water and Spirit.[7] He also explains that Jesus' baptism in the Jordan was in obedience to the express will of God.[8] The *New Catechism* explains that the baptizand's entry to the Church is by a new birth, a new life which he received of water and the Holy Spirit, and thus he was given a share and a place in the new creation.[9] Similarly it explains that baptism is a symbol of the resurrection, although this is not developed, but stated as the natural development of the death of Christ,[10] whilst the *Teaching of Christ* draws its teaching on baptism as a birth to newness of life from the liturgical readings for the Easter Vigil, and for Easter morning itself, reminding the candidates of the Pauline teaching from Romans 6.3–5 and Colossians 4.1–3. In addition the Old Testament points to the new creation, by promising a new heart and a new spirit to men. Thus the authors earth their catecheses firmly to the liturgy, and emphasize that both water and words symbolize the new life to which the candidate is called,[11] and further that the risen life of Christ which the baptized shares also makes him a member of the community where his risen life is celebrated.[12] Schmemann, like the *New Catechism*, seeing the resurrection of Christ as a result of his death and burial, explained baptism as the beginning of the candidate's spiritual life, as he realized the reality of life in God, as experienced by Christ. Neil suggests that baptism is the outward sign which demonstrates the new life to which the candidate comes in Christ,[13] and as a result of what Clark describes as incorporation into Christ,[14] and once again seeing the resurrection as the end result of the death of Christ. This theme of incorporation into Christ through baptism is taken up by Winward, who points out that it is only this unity with Christ through faith that makes it possible for the baptizand to share in the death and resurrection of Christ, and this oneness with Christ has revolutionary implications for the post-baptismal life of the candidate, placing him under an obligation to make this new life a reality in his daily living, by saying 'no' to the old sinful life, and 'yes' to the new life in Christ.[15] The East Midland Baptist Association booklet explains the candidate's new life in Christ in terms of the symbolism of immersion,[16] and Victor Jack thinks in terms of Romans 6.3–5 once again as he explains baptism in terms of the candidate's identification with the death, burial and resurrection of Jesus Christ.[17]

As we have seen that baptism as new life and resurrection is the obverse of the picture of baptism as death and burial, this is the next area which we shall consider. Both the *New Catechism* and *The Teaching of Christ* begin with the story of Noah, where water was the means both of salvation and destruction.[18] Moving on to Romans 6.3–5, both teach that baptism brought a share in the death and burial of Christ,[19] although the *Teaching of Christ* developed this concept to teach that this involved the candidates in a lifelong sharing in the dying of Jesus,[20] and the *New Catechism* describes the death of the Christian as his truest baptism,[21] However, although the candidate is dead to sin in Christ, he is not freed from his inclination to sin, even by his baptism, but rather begins at baptism a struggle in which steadfastness is only made possible by the healing and quickening grace of the risen

Jesus, who through his death and victory in resurrection, ensures victory to those who desire it.[22] This idea is developed by both Baptists and Orthodox. Clark interprets Jesus' baptism as ultimately his cross, and points out that only through the redemptive death and resurrection of Jesus could baptism receive its full meaning.[23] More pragmatically, White tells his candidates in the context of baptism into the death of Christ that something in them *must* die if the Christ-life is to survive and flourish,[24] and in this he is stating essentially the same point of view as Winward whom we quoted above.[25] Schmemann spends some time on the idea of baptism as the death and resurrection of Christ, pleading for a rediscovery of this as the essential meaning of the sacrament, and he poses the question of how the candidate dies in the likeness of Christ's death. He begins to answer his own question by making the point that Christ's own death was voluntary,[26] and that man however has chosen spiritual death – separation from the giver of life – which Christ came to abolish. Thus, in his baptismal death in the likeness of Christ, man chooses freely to do what Christ desires. He expresses a wish to be like Christ, thus becoming truly dead to the spiritually dead world around him, and sharing rather in that reality of life in God which Christ experienced.[27]

Allied to the concept of the Christian being baptized into the likeness of the death of Christ, and thus being dead to sin, came the related symbolism of baptism as a means of cleansing from sin. The *New Catechism* suggests that the flowing water signifies cleansing as well as birth, and states that baptism washes away the sins that a man has actually committed in his previous life, and conquers the roots of sin in a man's life, although it is careful to point that this conquest cannot be separated from man's whole life struggle.[28] Thus, the meaning of baptism is that of forgiveness of sins and of a transformation of the life of the candidate, now to be united to Christ's life of obedience.[29] So, following baptism, the candidate makes a new start in all purity, which the authors describe as the conquest of his life by light, so strengthening the connection with the illuminatory aspect of baptism. The authors of the *The Teaching of Christ* add the aspect of healing to that of forgiveness, stating that, when an adult is baptized, his sins are forgiven even as he receives the new life of grace; for divine grace, in virtue of Christ's passion and death, has a forgiving and healing effect.[30] The Baptists also pick up the symbol of water as a cleansing agent to suggest that forgiveness is the effect of baptism, and Clark states this in his two theological contributions, although he has a certain amount of agreement with Schmemann that there was over-emphasis on the aspect of forgiveness and repentance at the expense of the emphasis on baptism as the participation in the death and the resurrection of Christ.[31] Neil interprets this relationship of baptism to forgiveness into catechetical form to suggest that when baptism is seen as the outward expression of faith, the candidates can better understand the New Testament teaching that baptism results in the forgiveness of sins from Acts 2.38.[32] Although White admits that the root idea of baptism as purification was an important part of Christian thought, he prefers to describe baptism in terms of an expression of confession, repentance and pardon.[33] Winward explains to his readers that, through their union with Christ, the believers receive the promised forgiveness of sin, of which the washing of the body with water in baptism is the outward and visible sign, even though forgiveness is the province of God alone.[34]

The Roman Catholic authors move on from the concept of forgiveness to express the concept of the irrevocable nature of baptism, conferring a character upon the soul which can never be affected,[35] and they explain that even if a baptized Christian sins gravely, he can be reconciled to the Church by the sacrament of penance without a repetition of baptism.[36] White, whilst not holding a sacramental doctrine of penance, teaches the irrevocable nature of believer's baptism, which can never be undone, thus counselling the candidates of the overwhelming need for sincerity at the time of baptism,[37] a sentiment which has echoes in *A New Catechism* where the authors suggest that the character of baptism does not exist where the will not to be baptized exists during the baptism.[38] The nearest the other authors come to describing a baptismal character is when Jack describes baptism as the badge of discipleship.[39]

However, the concept of forgiveness through baptism leads on most Baptists to speak of the relationship between baptism and faith, seeing faith and belief as the essential prerequisite of baptism, and describing baptism, as Neil does, in terms of the outward declaration of the candidate's repentance and faith in Christ. He stresses the link between faith and baptism, the inside and outside of the same action, and suggests that baptism is the outward act that demonstrates the answer of God to the baptizand's response in repentance and faith, by making him at one with Christ.[40] Winward describes baptism in terms of a public confession of the candidate's personal faith in Christ,[41] and he explains the meaning of the simple confession, 'Jesus is Lord', in the light of the New Testament, creeds and subsequent confessions of faith of the various branches of the Christian Church. He stressed in his earlier booklet that hearing and believing in the act of conversion was always the essential prerequisite of baptism, and suggests that personal faith in Christ was essential even in the case of the household of the Philippian jailer.[42] White discusses this relationship between baptism and faith, interpreting it basically in terms of the Christian's acknowledgement of the lordship of Christ, but extending it to include the candidate's faith that through baptism he does share in the death and resurrection of Christ. He points out that the order in the New Testament was preaching and hearing the gospel, believing and being baptized.[43] The East Midland Baptist Association booklet suggests one reason for the importance of baptism is its nature as a prompt expression of the candidate's response of faith in Jesus Christ.[44] The *New Catechism* takes the statement 'Faith comes by hearing' and develops the concept of faith as the candidate hearing what Christ imparts from the Father through the word of the Church, and this is seen in the ceremony of the admission of catechumens as the foremost need of the candidate, recognizing that the faith that is necessary for eternal life comes from God, and cannot be reproduced by the candidate himself.[45] Baptists would agree with Beasley-Murray in his statement that conversion – defined by Winward above as hearing and believing – is a work of the Spirit,[46] which is saying something very similar to the statement made by the *New Catechism* and that made by the *Directorium Catechisticum Generale* which defines faith as a 'gift of God which calls men to conversion'[47] aided by the grace of God and the interior help of the Holy Spirit moving the heart and turning it to God.[48] However, *The Teaching of Christ* suggests that the Holy Spirit begins to dwell in the soul at baptism to implant in it faith, love and other rich gifts, to begin the process of the candidate becoming holy,[49] although this difference in emphasis is probably due, at least in part, to its selection of the Rite of Baptism for Children as their basic rite for catechetical explanation, while the *New Catechism* based its teaching on the previous rite for the baptism of adults.

Baptism is linked with the Holy Spirit, based upon the descent of the Holy Spirit at the baptism of Jesus, and this image is the thought behind the statement for the authors of the *New Catechism* that at baptism the Holy Spirit enters the candidates, gives them life, and makes them children of the Father.[50] Through the power of the Holy Spirit, the candidate is able to live in union with Christ, and to share in the new creation. However, the major sacrament of the Holy Spirit is confirmation which strengthens the gift of the Holy Spirit bestowed in baptism and lays especial emphasis upon it, and they argue for the re-establishment of the original timing of confirmation immediately after baptism.[51] *The Teaching of Christ* defines baptism as being conferred by water and the Holy Spirit, and in confirmation the Christian receives a strengthening in the power of the Holy Spirit,[52] although it sees confirmation as a sacrament of Christian maturity, and indicates a more traditional role, describing baptism as that of infants,[53] and confirmation only occasionally delayed beyond the age of seven until the days of early adolescence. Baptists have no separate sacrament of confirmation, but Clark and Winward suggest that the Holy Spirit is given in baptism and possessed through it.[54] White states that when a believer sincerely makes his baptismal confession, the Spirit comes upon him in altogether new fullness and power, and abiding with him, leads, empowers and sanctifies him, and sees him safe to glory.[55] He continues to question the practice of associating the laying-on of hands with the coming of the Spirit within the baptismal rite, describing it as a gesture of solidarity among believers, and explaining that, in Acts, the laying-on of hands was used as an exceptional supplement to an inadequate baptism.[56] Winward suggests that the activity and gift of the Holy Spirit in baptism is related to Christ, to the Church, to our vocation, and to our response to Christ, and in baptism God anoints and seals the baptizand as his own by the Holy Spirit,[57] but Winward interprets the laying-on of hands as confirmation, and interprets conversion – baptism – confirmation as the act through the whole of which God imparts his Spirit,[58] and he suggests that, when the three elements of the one act are separated, it should only be by a very short interval of time.

Baptism marks the beginning of a relationship, not just with God but with other Christians, and this relationship is described as adoption, particularly by the Catholic syllabi. The *New Catechism* describes baptism's role in building new stones into the Church, and stresses that, without distinction of race, class, or intelligence, baptism causes the adoption of the baptized into the fellowship which seeks to be a servant along with Jesus.[59] *The Teaching of Christ* stresses the community aspect of baptism, following *RCIA* and explains that baptism makes the candidates sharers in God's own life and his own adopted children, quoting once again from the Rite of Baptism for Children.[60] In terms of their catechetical material, Baptist authors do not develop the idea of the baptized as an adopted son of God, although there is one reference to it in Winward's booklet where it is a relationship based upon the union of the candidate with Christ,[61] but there are several references both in catecheses and theology to baptism in terms of the adoption of the baptized into the fellowship of the Church. Clark cited initiation into the Church as one implication of baptism in the normative New Testament period[62] and Winward ascribes to baptism the role of making members of Christ's Church.[63] Neil cites the same Galatians 3.27 passage as *The Teaching of Christ*, but interprets it to teach that through baptism the candidate is brought into the fellowship of Christ and is united with those who are Christ's disciples: thus he becomes not merely identified with the Church but committed to the life and work of the people of Christ.[64]

However, the root cause for the importance of baptism and the reason for its sacramental nature for many Christians is the way it enables a candidate to share in the life of Christ;[65] to identify with his life of service, humility and obedience. The Baptist writers have tended to underline this particular meaning of baptism. Clark suggests that baptism effects the initiation of the candidate into the life of the Trinity, and into the wholeness of redemption.[66] Neil points out that baptism is a public declaration of the union of the baptized with Christ and that immersion in water in the name of Jesus is an acted parable of the death and resurrection of Jesus Christ, by which the candidate publicly declares he has become one with Christ in his death and resurrection.[67] White makes this point in similar terms, but emphasizes that being identified with Christ was dependent upon the candidates having a real living relationship to Christ himself.[68] Winward dwells on the unity which baptism effects between the candidate and Christ, a union effected by the candidate's imperative response of obedience to the command of Christ, and as a deliberate act of discipleship.[69] Also, the candidate makes a pledge of allegiance to Christ as his response to God who through baptism unites him with Christ, cleanses him from sin, seals him with the Holy Spirit, and makes him a member of his Church.[70] The East Midland Baptist Association leaflet suggests that baptism is important because in it the candidate is following the example and command of Christ, and that in it he is both expressing and strengthening his commitment to Christ.[71] Jack describes the main reason for baptism in terms of identification with Christ: Christ's identification with man at his baptism in the Jordan and at the cross, man's identification with Christ in terms of sharing his death, burial and resurrection, through baptism.[72] Schmemann is suggesting a similar identification when, in writing of the candidate sharing in the likeness of Christ's death and resurrection, he suggests that the baptizand seeks to share that reality of life in God which Christ experienced.[73]

Our comparison of the catechetical material has produced a fair amount of similar material, of similar themes treated with the different perspectives which come from different backgrounds and different church traditions. From the Baptists we have seen an evident emphasis on the individual's response to the work of Christ in his life. This emphasis on occasions overshadows the Christian's commitment to the Church. The two Catholic catechisms differ because of the use of a different liturgy of baptism, and seem to put an emphasis on what the sacraments do for the baptized through the Church, rather than on the faith expressed by the baptized in obedience to Christ and in response to the love of God. No doubt these same differences in emphasis will show themselves as we consider the liturgical material.

2 The Liturgy of Baptism

The Orthodox Office of Holy Baptism is a telescoped rite encompassing within one service three originally separate liturgies of the reception of catechumens, the act of baptism, and the rite of confirmation and chrismation. The rite of reception of catechumens is really the heir of the service marking the election of catechumens to the proximate period for Lenten baptismal preparation. It includes within it three liturgical exorcisms as well as the rite of renunciation and profession, and the recitation of the Symbol of the Faith which would have taken place during the Lenten preparation. Schmemann's problems of mystagogy begin with the fact that he is attempting to explain a liturgy designed for adults for a church which sees infant baptism as the norm, and these problems were also acknowledged by Hapgood in a number of her explanatory notes. Schmemann uses the solution of explaining the liturgy in terms of the double rhythm of preparation and fulfilment, and suggests that preparation for baptism is always essential, even in the case of an infant only a few days old.

The first prayer of this rite depicts the candidate fleeing from captivity in a world where he has been deluded into serving the devil, and seeking refuge and protection beneath the wings of Christ and the Church, protection which is symbolized by the bishop's hand being laid upon the brow of the candidate. This prayer asks that the name of the candidate be recorded in the Book of Life and united with the flock of Christ's inheritance,[74] and describes the candidate's true life to him in terms of praise and worship. The three exorcisms describe the effect of the devil in the lives of the candidates, and Schmemann explains that evil for the Church is not merely the absence of good, but rather a real presence.[75] Realizing that evil is not to be explained, but faced and fought, the candidates begin to seek a means of being reunited with God through the exorcism,[76] and these exorcisms Schmemann describes as 'a poem', in the Greek sense of a 'performative utterance', because they are professed in the name and power of Christ, who has destroyed the enemy power from within.[77] The result of the exorcism is that the candidates are liberated, restored and purified, and ready for the rite of renunciation and profession, which the other liturgies place closer to baptism. The comparable Roman rites are described both in *A New Catechism* for the earlier pre-Vatican II rite, and in *The Rite of Christian Initiation of Adults* for the rite revised at the behest of Vatican II. The rite described by *A New*

Catechism begins by depicting the struggle between God and Satan in the candidate. The rite described as 'election' takes place at the door of the church when the candidate says the Lord's Prayer, his sponsors and the priest make the sign of the cross over him and with a sharp command, evil is bidden to depart. The candidate is then led into the church where following a moment of quiet prayer of thanksgiving, he recites aloud the Apostles' Creed and the Our Father. *A New Catechism* explains the significance of this in terms of the public nature of the statement, the public naming of God as his Father, and the public affirmation of all that he has experienced in an inner process, and in the instruction given him in private, the statement being made before God and the community. This was followed by exorcism, and then the gesture of Jesus touching the ears of the deaf man with saliva, was repeated. To further the symbolism of the healing which Christ confers in the sacrament, the priest quotes the imperative from Mark 7.34 'Be opened', and also touches the nostrils of the candidate as a sign that the candidate is to receive the good odour of Christ. The rite concludes with the anointing of the candidate with the oil of catechumens, as signifying his suppleness and strength for the combat.[78] The rite of election in *RCIA* begins with a more active role for the godparents, as, on the first Sunday in Lent, they are interrogated as to whether the candidates have been attentive to the proclamation of God's word, regular in prayer and worship and are living lives which bear testimony to their Christian commitment.[79] On the basis of the testimony of the sponsors, the whole congregation may be asked to indicate their concurrence. The candidates themselves are asked to reaffirm their intention to receive the sacraments of entry into the Church, and their names are enrolled to receive the sacrament of initiation at Easter. There is a strong stress on the continuing support of the sponsors, and of the whole community, and the Lenten period of purification and enlightenment for the whole community as *The Teaching of Christ* points out.

The spiritual and catechetical preparation of the elect is completed through the Scrutinies and Presentations which take place during the Lenten period. The Scrutinies have a two-fold purpose of revealing sins and weaknesses in the candidates so that they may be healed, and of highlighting the spiritual strengths of the candidates so that they may be strengthened,[81] and the elect are expected to progress in sincere self-appraisal and true penance during this period. At this time also the support of the sponsors and of the whole community is assured to the candidates in prayer and in physical support from the sponsors. The Presentations, placed between the Scrutinies, are occasions when the Church entrusts the elect with the documents which are considered to be a summary of its faith and prayer from ancient time, to lead the candidates to enlightenment. The Creed is given back to the Church by the candidates at their baptism, while the Lord's Prayer is said by the candidates publicly for the first time in their first Eucharist, when they say it together with the rest of the baptized. In this way the place of the community is emphasized in both presentations, the community as the place of faith and as the place of corporate prayer.

The Baptists, as we have seen, do not incorporate any rite of election into their baptismal procedure, although the candidate is prepared for baptism by a series of classes, and before he is able to be received into the membership of the local church, he is normally elected to membership at a business meeting of the church following a satisfactory report of his faith in Christ, and of his sincere desire to play a full part in the life of the local church, given to the church meeting by his sponsors.

Thus, taken as a whole, the various rites of election are the expression of a period when the candidate prepares spiritually for baptism, supported by both his sponsors and the whole worshipping community, through encouragement and prayer. The overall purpose of this preparation might be said to enable the candidate to appreciate as fully as possible the implications of baptism, given the limitations which exist due to the stage of spiritual maturity which the candidate has reached. The Orthodox and Roman Catholic rites do this by stressing the effect of sin and the influence of Satan in enslaving the lives of the candidates, and the Baptist churches would lay the stress upon the evidence of the candidate's faith in Jesus Christ as Lord.

The Orthodox Church put the rite of Renunciation and Profession in the earlier prayers rather than in the Baptismal Office, probably indicating that the Antiochene practice of this being made on Good Friday afternoon ultimately took precedence over the Jerusalem practice of the Renunciation and Profession immediately preceding baptism in the outer chamber of the baptistry. In citing the teaching of the fourth century mystagogues, Schmemann uses both Cyril and Chrysostom to explain the posture of the candidates at the Rite of Renunciation, drawing from Cyril the symbolism of facing the west as facing the region of darkness, from Chrysostom his condition of being unclad and unshod as a mark of his slavery, and his posture with uplifted hands symbolizing his desire to be the slave of Christ. Hapgood explained the uplifted hands as indicating the realm of the evil spirits of the air, although she gives no references to support this statement. The renunciation is basically unchanged even though it dates from a time when to be a Christian was to opt for a non-conformist lifestyle, and serves as a sobering reminder of man's inability to serve two masters. It is a forceful and contemptuous rejection of an entire world view built upon pride and self-affirmation. This contempt for Satan is underscored by the command to breathe and spit upon him.[82] In marked contrast, the Profession of Faith in Christ is made by the candidate facing east, making a personal statement of his unconditional commitment to Christ, pledging obedience to the Lord of Life, and the profession is in terms of the candidate uniting himself to Christ, stressing the voluntary nature of the profession, and taking up the imagery of Chrysostom, even though the Profession is threefold, and then confirmed with the same question put in the perfect tense. The symbol of faith is then given back to the Church which gave it to the candidate. The question, in the perfect tense, is repeated 'three times further', and the candidate's assurance of faith in Christ is confirmed, to signify that his knowledge *about* Christ has become knowledge *of* Christ. These acts are sealed by the candidate bowing down before the Triune God as a symbol of reverence, love, and obedience, and the prayers and foregoing actions are summed up in a prayer for God to call the candidate to enlightenment, to grant the grace of baptism, to put off the old man, to renew him to life everlasting, and to fill him with the power of the Holy Spirit in the unity of Christ.[83]

For Roman Catholic candidates, the Rites of Renunciation and Profession follow the blessing of the waters at the beginning of the celebration of the sacraments of initiation as part of the immediate preparation for the rite. The stress is put upon the candidate's free choice of personal faith and commitment to Christ. Much of the imagery of the tyrant Satan has been transformed into the image of Satan as deluder and purveyor of empty promises, although he is described as 'Father of Sin and Prince of Darkness' in Formula C.[84] This is reminiscent of the first prayer in the Orthodox Service of Prayers at the Reception of the Catechumen in which it is prayed that the candidates be far removed from their former delusions.[85] In the sense that man has to admit that he has been fooled and deluded, this is probably an effective way of dealing with man's sin of pride, and achieves the same result as the Orthodox imagery, with a more contemporary image, drawing at the same time an implicit contrast with God who keeps the promise that he makes. The Rite of Renunciation may be followed by the anointing of the candidate with the oil of catechumens to give him strength and to aid his profession of faith in Christ. The Rite of Profession, however, in spite of the stress in the introduction on the personal faith of the candidate,[86] is a précised version of the Creed, with the candidate responding to each of the three sections. This might be said to be the profession of faith in the Church, rather than of personal faith in Christ, as is present in the Orthodox service, and was present in the fourth century material, where the candidate first states that he enters the service of Christ, and then returns to the Church the Creed which he has received.

This element of personal faith is evident in the Baptist services. In the earliest of these, the questions of the candidates are posed in terms of their repentance towards God and their faith in Jesus Christ, and their allegiance to Christ and one Church.[87] Winward's service includes a question of repentance and renunciation of evil, a question posed to ascertain the candidate's confession of faith in the Triune God, and his discipleship of Christ worked out in the fellowship and the world.[88] This element of repentance is omitted in the *Praise God* service where the questions as above are an acknowledgement of Christ, and a promise of service, although this latter question adds the note of permanence and lifelong commitment.[89] Although personal faith in Christ cannot be separated from the faith of the Church which reveals Christ, the rites and statements of Renunciation and Profession seek to establish the permanent link of faith between Christ and the candidate within the limits of the cultural and ecclesiological expectations of the day and of the community. Idolatry, for example, is renounced in situations where this appears to be prevalent, and once again we see the differences in emphasis between the candidate's personal faith in Christ and the understanding of what the Church can do for the candidate through the sacrament, reflected in terms of the candidate's profession of faith in Christ or in the faith of Christ's Church.

Both Orthodox and Roman Catholics have a prayer for blessing the waters, and this plays an important part in the 'instant' mystagogy of the rite as the meaning of the baptismal action is explained through the liturgy. In the Baptist material the same function of 'instant mystagogy' is served by a statement of the purpose, meaning, and effects of baptism, and this is particularly the case in Winward's baptismal prayer.[90] Schmemann sets the baptismal rite in context by describing the festal vestments of the priest, and the light surrounding the baptistry, both symbols of the joy of the occasion, a context which he has to describe for his readers because their particular rubric, the last vestige of the paschal celebration of baptism and the baptismal celebration of the pascha, is more honoured in the breach than in the observance.[91] The deacon's prayer, also in litany form, contains some very strong echoes of the fourth century teaching, and also reveals the relationship of baptism to the world, to matter, to life and all aspects of life, and Schmemann suggests three essential dimensions in the mystery of water to show its effectiveness unto salvation, the cosmical dimension as the sacrament of the new creation, the ecclesiological dimension as the sacrament of the Church and the eschatological dimension as the sacrament of the Kingdom.[92] The priest then blesses the water in a prayer of solemn thanksgiving in which the water is signed with the cross, that the adverse powers might be crushed beneath its sign, and consecrated so that the effects of the water might be seen in the redemption, purification, sanctification, freedom, forgiveness, illumination, regeneration, renewal, adoption of sonship, and clothing in incorruption of the candidate, for whom it is the fountain of life. Thus the water is seen to mean the recreation of matter in Christ.[93] Following its blessing, the water is anointed so that it might bring not only life, but life in all its fullness. The oil is exorcized, and restored to its true function, and then the candidates and congregation are reminded of the function of oil in the history of salvation, and give thanks to God for it. Then the whole body of the candidate is anointed to show that he is reshaped, restored, and reconciled to God, and through God to the world, and prepared for combat with the devil, just as the athletes were anointed before their combat.[94]

In the Roman Catholic rite, the blessing of the font begins the paschal service, and this blessing centres the attention of the congregation upon the 'instant mystagogy' of the water. The water is blessed in a prayer which recalls to mind the wonderful works of God at the creation of the world, the cleansing effects of the flood, the rescue of the children of Israel from the Red Sea, the baptism of Jesus by John, the water and the blood which flowed from the side of the crucified Christ, and the dominical command to baptize from Matthew 28.16–20. The prayer asks for grace and the candidates were taught, as they prayed, about the new life and cleansing which came through the death and resurrection of Christ and their share in it through baptism.[95] To bless the water would be alien to the Baptists' tradition, and their emphasis is placed both on the faith of the recipient, and on the element of remembrance, an approach which is typical throughout Baptist sacramental theology. The statements, however, may be compared at this point. The Winward and Payne order begins with a statement of the nature of baptism as a sacrament with the effect of uniting the Christian with Christ, cleansing the soul from sin, sealing by the Holy Spirit, and joining the Christian into membership with the company of all Christ's faithful people. The statement applies this to the individual believer, and defines baptism in terms of an act of obedience, a following of the example of Christ, a public confession of faith, and a pledge of allegiance to Christ.[96] While Winward's preface is briefer, based upon the Great Commission, and places the emphasis on the candidate's profession of repentance, confession of faith, and promise of allegiance, his prayer for the candidates gives thanks to God for the created order and for his compassion over it, though not specifically for the water. It gives thanks for the death of Christ for the sins of mankind and for his resurrection, and for the Holy Spirit who gives Christians a new birth and who is changing them into the likeness of Christ. It asks for the acceptance of the candidates, and for their death to sin and for a life of righteousness, united with Christ in his death and resurrection, for the forgiveness of their sins and the gift of the Holy Spirit, for their continuance in the fellowship of the faithful and elect people who make up the body of Christ, and that, having put on Christ, they may receive grace upon grace out of his fulness.[97] There is a very similar prayer to this in the material from the Church of South India. The service offered in *Praise God* begins with an anamnesis of the benefits of believers' baptism and Church membership, viz., union with Christ through faith, thus sharing in his death and resurrection, the cleansing of the whole of the life and personality of the baptized, a marking of the reception of the Holy Spirit, the acknowledgement of his work in the past life of the candidate, and the reminder of his strengthening of the candidate for future endeavour. The act of baptism is an act of obedience, of confession of faith, and of association with the one holy, catholic and apostolic Church.[98]

The Baptismal act falls into two different types, depending upon the number of immersions or affusions of the candidate. The Orthodox and Roman Catholic rubrics prescribe a threefold immersion/affusion in the name of Father, Son and Holy Spirit. Baptist rubrics suggest a single immersion into the triune name, and immersion is the mode of baptism first cited in each of the three churches. The baptismal formula however varies from the simple 'I baptize you in the name of the Father, the Son and the Holy Spirit' favoured by *RCIA*, and Winward through the passive voice 'The servant of God, N, is baptized, in the name of the Father, Amen. And of the Son, Amen. And of the Holy Spirit, Amen.', the phrasing pointing away from the human and towards the divine agent of baptism, Christ himself, to the two other Baptist formulas where the formula in the active voice above is preceded by the phrase: 'On the profession of repentance toward God and of faith in our Lord Jesus Christ', in Winward and Payne, and by the addition of the phrase 'Upon a profession of your faith and at your own request...' in *Praise God*. This latter indicates once again the stress placed by Baptists on personal faith and commitment to Christ as the basic requirement for baptism. This stress on personal faith is noted from the context of the Orthodox service by Schmemann, who reminds his readers that baptism involves a personal application of the gifts which Christ makes available. He further reminds them that the Church affirms each of the three immersions with an 'Amen', concluding with Psalm 32, affirming that once again, the congregation has seen and experienced the death and resurrection of Christ, God's mercy and forgiveness, and the recreation of the world and of man in that world.

Candidates in the Orthodox Church emerge from the baptismal pool to be vested with a white garment, described variously as a robe of righteousness and a robe of light. Once again the imagery is directly from the fourth century, and very reminiscent of the robe which Chrysostom described as a shining garment, a royal robe, a garment of immortality, and Schmemann points out that it symbolizes the state of spiritual purity and righteousness which God intends for his people, as it symbolizes the new life which began at baptism.[99] Also they are given a lighted candle to hold, once again carrying the imagery of illumination over from the fourth century.[100]

The Roman Catholic service of Baptism concludes with an optional service of chrismation, if there is some reason for confirmation not following immediately, and they too use the symbolism of vesting the candidate with a white garment and giving them a light to carry. The white garment in *RCIA* symbolizes the candidates' clothing in Christ, and they are charged with bringing their garment unstained to the judgement seat of Christ. The garment is actually placed on the candidates by the sponsors, and it is the sponsors who light a candle from the paschal candle, and give it to the neophytes to remind them of their enlightenment by Christ, and of the flame of faith alive in their heart.[101] Confirmation should follow as part of the same liturgical office. The theologians are still working out the implications of this requirement in relation to the role of the bishop, although *RCIA*[102] is quite plain that the presbyter who conferred baptism may confirm the candidates in the absence of the bishop, as can the parish priest of the candidate. It is explained to the neophytes that through their new birth they have become members of Christ and his priestly people, and at confirmation they are to receive the outpouring of the Holy Spirit to strengthen them, making them more like Christ, enabling them to be witnesses to his suffering, death and resurrection, and strengthening them to be active members of the Church. Following a prayer for the benefits of the Holy Spirit to be granted to the neophytes, they are sealed with the gift of the Holy Spirit by the signation of the cross with chrism on their foreheads. It is intended that the service should proceed immediately to the Eucharist.[103] The Orthodox service moves to its third office, that of chrismation, beginning with a prayer in which God's help is invoked for the newly baptized to maintain his baptismal purity, and then the neophyte is signed with the cross on the forehead, eyes, nostrils, lips, ears, breast, hands and feet, with the purpose of enabling the neophyte to receive the gifts of the Holy Spirit to rear and strengthen him in the spiritual life. Chrismation admits the neophyte to communion. Following chrismation, the priest, the sponsors, and the neophyte process around the font three times symbolizing that the neophyte has entered into an eternal union with Christ the Light of the World through baptism.[104] The service concludes now with the rites of the eighth day. Earlier, as their name signifies, these took place following a week's mystagogical instruction one week after baptism, but now the time lapse has been disregarded, However, the Christian still has to return into the world, and these rites signify the beginning of Christian life as mission and witnessing. The first rite is the Washing Off of Holy Chrism, as the external symbols of the rite can be removed, and only the inner appropriation of the gift of grace and of faith will sustain man in the real struggle in the world.[105] The white garment can also be removed, and the neophyte's hair may be cut and offered to God, even as the firstfruits were offered to God in the Old Testament.

Because Baptists have returned so recently to the rite of laying-on of hands following baptism, Payne and Winward have to explain carefully both the rite and its significance in terms of its use in the New Testament, and they describe it as an act of acceptance and commissioning. It assures the candidates of their strengthening and equipment for their vocation as priests and servants of Jesus Christ, and the explanation concludes with a charge to the church members, to encourage, help, and build them up in the Lord. Following the reading of one or more scripture sentences, prayer is offered asking that the neophytes be strengthened by the Holy Spirit, described in terms of Isaiah 11.2, as it is described in the chrismation prayer in *RCIA*,[106] and be equipped for their vocation, and their continued presence within the fellowship of the Church. The laying-on of hands is performed by the minister and two others, and this is followed by a welcome to the neophyte as a member of the local church and of the Church universal.[107] Winward simplified his version of this rite, but adds the idea of laying-on of hands as an act of blessing as well as of acceptance, and commissioning. He omits the scripture passages, and puts the Aaronic blessing at this stage rather than immediately following baptism.[108] *Praise God* produces a further minor variant on the theme but one of litle basic significance.

Thus the essential common element in all the offices for the post-baptismal rite is one of the equipment of the neophyte for the task of witnessing to the gospel of Christ in word and deed. Approaching this point from their own standpoints, the offices arrive at a very similar expression of the basic task of the Christian. Throughout each of the offices of baptism there have emerged a number of similarities about the basic rite of entry to the Christian Church, regardless of the tradition or culture from which they emanate, and these similarities and variations help us to see the way in which the liturgies we have considered have emerged from their fourth-century ancestors.

9
Conclusion

Any comparison which is made between the fourth-century material, delivered in the golden age of catechesis, and that of two decades of the recent twentieth century (1960–1980), can only be made subject to the differences which we have noted between the various church situations, cultural backgrounds, and ecclesiological understanding, and to the differences of personality and style of those who have produced the material. The fourth-century material was delivered to be listened to by the catechumens and neophytes, whereas the twentieth-century material, which we have been able to locate, is designed to be read or for reference purposes. The fourth-century material has crystallized into a formal presentation based on the transcription of the materials, whilst the modern material is in process of transition from a gaseous to a fluid state, and so is difficult to analyse conclusively. So our final step will be to compare a number of catechetical themes, and to observe the twentieth-century variations in the liturgy from the fourth-century. Thus, we shall highlight the tendency in the last two decades of this century to revert towards the 'golden age' of catechesis.

1) *Six Major Catechetical Themes*

A natural starting point for most catechetical material in relation to baptism is the narrative and implications of Jesus' baptism by John the Baptist. The theme from the fourth century was that Jesus submitted to the baptism of John, which was intended as a baptism of repentance for confessed sins, and in so doing gave dignity to that baptism. In his submission to that baptism, he identified himself with sinful man and demonstrated his obedience to God. He was enabled to conquer the 'dragon in the waters', to use Cyril's image of the dreadful power of sin and death and thus of chaos, and thus he gave his dignity to baptism itself. John's baptism was abrogated by the baptism instituted by Christ. The descent of the Spirit upon Christ indicated that he would also descend upon the candidates at their baptism. The variations from this theme current in the twentieth century material are not particularly significant. Emphasis is still placed on the readiness and willingness of Jesus both to obey God and to share the common lot of man. Thus Jesus, in his baptism of preparation for his ministry of obedience and love for man, profoundly altered baptism. By his participation in it, he transformed it to become the symbol of the baptism of the Spirit. Hence Christian baptism is both a baptism of water and the Spirit.

In dealing with the theme of the Christian's baptism as a death, burial and resurrection, based on the Pauline teaching in Romans 6.2–5, the Fathers described the Christian beginning his new life in Christ at baptism, a life in which he was dead to sin, but a life which it was the candidate's responsibility, with the help of the Holy Spirit, to preserve in a clean and unsullied state. At baptism the Christian had become one person in place of another, and so a radical transformation was expected in the behaviour of the candidate. They saw baptism as a once for all sacrament, and did not all suggest the possibility of the renewal of the baptismal life by penance. The life begun at baptism was to be a symbol of the life which is to come at the resurrection of the dead, and so was to be a life of constant effort. However, it was a life lived at one with Christ, and, even though the sacrament was an imitation of the death, burial and resurrection of Christ, that which it accomplished was the creation of a bond of unity, between the candidate and Christ. Their twentieth-century successors stress the candidate's unity and identification with Christ in baptism, the sacramental point at which the candidates outwardly receive new life by water and the Holy Spirit, and as they realize the reality of the life of God. This places upon them the obligation to make their new lives a reality by regularly and habitually following the way of Christ. However, the emphasis on the baptismal character has shifted from the fourth-century pattern of a once for all character which could never be repeated or replaced if spoiled, to the twentieth-century variant that baptism can never be undone.[1] Baptism is still seen as permanent and indelible, but the element of fear lest the soul be spoiled has been replaced by an emphasis on the forgiving nature and grace of God which should not be taken for granted. In baptism the candidate shares in the death and burial of Jesus, and thus is dead to sin, although life is still a daily struggle, because the natural inclination of the human being to sin remains. Baptism receives its full meaning in the death of Christ, and in the voluntary obedience with which he submitted to that death, and so the candidate in baptism demonstrates a desire to be at one with Christ, freely obeying the will of God, and baptism itself is the application of the truth that something in the candidate must die if the Christ-life is to flourish. Schmemann's thesis that the emphasis shifts from baptism as the death and resurrection of Christ to baptism as the means of grace seems to be being reversed in terms of the emphasis which we find in the former aspect of baptism in this recent material.

The fourth-century material considered the water as a means of cleansing from sin by allusion in the catechetical material, describing the baptistry as the bath of grace and the bath of regeneration which brought the remission of sins to the candidates, and by a closer description in some of the mystagogical material, depicting the flowing waters cleansing the candidate from sin, and drowning Satan as surely as Pharaoh was drowned in the Red Sea. The more recent material takes up the idea of flowing waters washing away sins and granting forgiveness, purity, and healing to the candidates, although some are aware of an over-emphasis on forgiveness and repentance at the expense of the idea of baptism as participation in the death and resurrection of Christ. Others would want to make the point that the cleansing waters of baptism are the outward sign of the repentance and pardon of the candidate.

The relationship between baptism and the faith of the candidate in the fourth century came across in the stress which was put on the need for the candidate to be sincere about his desire for baptism, and to have a heart genuinely enlightened by the Spirit. It was the communication of the Holy Spirit to the candidate which would produce a variety of gifts varying according to the fervour of faith and the intensity of his love for God, and so the candidate was encouraged to prepare for baptism by fostering both piety of soul and also a good conscience. The faith of the candidate was plainly the gift of the grace of God, and the candidate had to affirm his faith in and commitment to Christ before he was baptized. So faith – the work of grace – was necessary before the candidate was baptized. In much of the modern material there is a similar emphasis upon faith as the essential pre-requisite of baptism, but faith is always seen as the gift of God calling men to conversion which is the work of the Spirit. Through the Spirit at work in the life of the candidate, he is enabled to acknowledge the Lordship of Christ, and to declare his faith in Christ. The material based upon infant baptism, however, shows a difference in emphasis to delineate baptism as the time when the Holy Spirit begins to dwell in the soul, to implant in it faith, love and other rich gifts, rather than the expression of the commitment of the life of the candidate to Christ. Often the instrument which God uses to lead men to faith in Christ through the Spirit is the Church, and there is a relationship between the individual's faith in Christ and the faith of the Church expressed through the creeds and statements of faith which formed the basis of much of the catechetical material which we have considered.

In the fourth century, the relationship between the Holy Spirit and baptism was described in terms of baptism bestowing the Holy Spirit upon the candidate as a guarantee of his Christian hope, to enlighten him spiritually, and to give him the power to overcome temptation. The candidate was sealed through the operation of the Holy Spirit, with the seal of belonging to Christ, which was also described as a spiritual circumcision, the mark of the new covenant which the candidate made with Christ. So the candidates were described as both temples and instruments of the Holy Spirit, indicating the presence of the Spirit in the lives of the baptized. The twentieth-century catechists take the descent of the Spirit at the Baptism of Jesus as their basis for the link between the baptism of the candidate and the Holy Spirit, and they teach that baptism is the sacrament of water and the Spirit. This imparts to the candidate the power to live in union with Christ, and at baptism, the candidate receives a new fullness of the Spirit. The Spirit is given in baptism and possessed through it, and is strengthened at confirmation, which is described in the Roman Catholic material as the major sacrament of the Holy Spirit.

Linked with the Holy Spirit is the theme of baptism as a rite of spiritual adoption. The fourth-century Fathers explained that the adoption of the candidates as children of God was marked by the imposition of hands, and the candidates were reminded of the statement at the descent of the Spirit 'you are my beloved Son' which for them was rendered 'you now become my Son'. This adoptive sonship had implications for their relationship with other Christians, relating them to each other through Christ as brothers and members of Christ and of one another and making them heirs together of the promise of God. This relationship has been taken up more strongly in the Roman Catholic syllabi which stress the element of baptism into a community. Baptism's role is described as building new stones into the Church, and as causing the adoption of the baptized into the servant Church, without distinction of race, class, or intelligence. Baptism effects the spiritual adoption of the candidate as a child of God by adoption, but the stress has moved away from the personal relationship to Christ towards the relationship of the candidate to his fellow Christians as a result of his relationship to Christ. This is expressed in terms of initiation into the Church, and membership of the Church, the emphasis being upon commitment to the life and work of the people of Christ.

Catechesis and mystagogy have completely merged and this merging of material has meant that, on occasions above, material classified as mystagogy in our previous analysis has been considered under the catechetical themes. As we reach the modern material, it becomes impossible to differentiate between mystagogy and catechesis, and so, as we progress to consider the liturgy of baptism, we shall compare the fourth century liturgy drawn from the mystagogical material with the rubrics of the published services of the last two decades of this century.

2) *Liturgy of Baptism*

In much of the material which has been our concern, the baptismal process begins with the rite of election or enrolment for the proximate period of baptismal preparation. In the fourth century this rite took place at the beginning of Lent when the catechumens intending to be baptized at Easter were presented by their sponsor to the bishop for their names to be enrolled, together with that of the sponsor, following the interrogation of the sponsor by the bishop regarding the moral standard and good intentions of the catechumen. Names were enrolled in the church register, with the sponsor acting both as guide and guarantor, and the candidate was admitted to the Lenten period of proximate preparation for baptism, and he was accompanied to the instruction and exorcisms by his sponsor. In preparation for full membership of the Church at baptism, the candidates were instructed in the Creed which they had to recite back to the bishop before baptism. In the Orthodox liturgy this process marks the beginning of the first of the rites which, telescoped together in temporal terms together from the Office of Holy Baptism, and is in the form of a service of prayers for the reception of catechumens. In prayer this recalls the enrolment of the candidates in the Book of Life, and is followed by three prayers of exorcism. In the earlier Roman Catholic rite of election, the candidate moves from the door of the church were he is signed with the cross by the priest and sponsors, and evil is bidden sharply to depart from him by the priest. In the Church he recites the creed, summing up his private instruction and making public declaration of this, and of the fact that God is his Father. This is followed by exorcism, and then the candidate is anointed with the oil of catechumens. *RCIA*, on the other hand returns, to the fourth-century emphasis on the sponsor, and begins its rite of Election by an interrogation of the sponsor by the bishop, followed by the election of the candidate by the Church. After this the candidate reaffirms his intention to receive the sacraments of initiation at the paschal season. The anointing is replaced by a gesture of blessing from the bishop. The period between Election and Initiation is spent in the three Scrutinies and the two Presentations of the Lord's Prayer and the Creed, a formal practice suggested for fixed Sunday and weekday Masses based upon the fourth-century liturgy by a process of conscious reversion to that period. Throughout there is a stress on the support of the ecclesial community for the candidate, not least in that the whole community is exhorted by *Sacrosanctum Concilium* to spend each Lenten season in recalling their own baptism. The Baptists do not include any rite of election within their worship structure, but each candidate desiring to join the local church is elected to membership of that local church by the regular meeting of members of that church, following classes and upon receipt by the church of a satisfactory report from two members concerning the faith of the candidate and his willingness to play a full part in the life of the local church. The emphasis here is placed upon the personal faith and commitment of the candidate.

As they moved closer to Easter in the fourth century the rite of Renunciation and Profession took place, at which the candidate confronted Satan to renounce him, and pledged allegiance to Christ as Lord. The imagery of the rite, the gestures prescribed for the candidate, the posture he was to adopt, all were combined to give the candidate an experience of what was involved in the act of repentance and of faith. The mystagogy forcefully made him aware of the reality of evil, and the rite was concluded with anointing as a mark of belonging and of appointment to service. This rite has survived in each of the rites which we have considered. The Orthodox probably come closest to retaining the former emphasis of a contemptuous rejection of an entire world-view based upon pride and man's self-assertion to which man was in bondage although, even in this liturgy, the stress is placed upon the profession of faith and the assurance which that profession brings to the candidate. In *RCIA* the stress is placed upon the free choice of the candidate and his personal faith and commitment and much of the imagery of the tyrant Satan has been replaced by the image of Satan as deluder and purveyor of empty promises in the rite of Renunciation. The candidate may then be anointed to give him the strength to aid his profession of faith in Christ, but the rite of profession is a précised version of the Creed, with little reference to the personal faith of the candidate, apart from his faith emanating from the faith of the Church. The Baptists formulate the first question to the candidate in their service as a formal renunciation of evil and sin, and a profession of personal faith in Jesus Christ, although this formula is omitted in the most recent suggested version of the service. The liturgical position of the question points to the emphasis placed upon personal faith and commitment of the candidate.

Following this rite, came the rite of Baptism itself, sometimes separated by about 36 hours in the fourth century. Candidates in the fourth century at this point removed their remaining garments, and received an anointing of the whole body. These two elements were explained to them in terms of laying aside the old life and putting on Christ, the anointing symbolizing also his healing power, his protection of the candidate, and the union of the candidate with Christ. Then followed the triple immersion/emersion of the candidates into the name of Father, Son and Holy Spirit, and one of the ways in which this was explained was to remind the candidate of the three days Christ spent in the tomb between the crucifixion and resurrection. So it was a natural step, and the logical conclusion of the catechetical stress on baptism as a participation in the death and resurrection of Christ, to explain coming out of the pool in terms of sharing in the Resurrection of Christ. This was linked with the possession by the candidate of the new life of Christ, and the Fathers made much of the way in which the baptismal font was both tomb and womb at one and the same time. By this century the symbolism of clothing and nakedness has been replaced by the need to observe decency and decorum.[2] The rite begins for the most part with the blessing of the waters, a prayer which corresponds with the statement of the effects of baptism given by the Baptist liturgies. For the Orthodox this prayer celebrates the recreation of matter in Christ, for the Roman Catholics it celebrates the place of water in creation. The Orthodox and Roman Catholic services practice triple immersion, the Baptists a single immersion, although they use the trinitarian formula. For the Orthodox Church this takes the form of a statement to the Church made in the passive voice, whilst for the other two, the candidate is addressed in the active voice. Personal faith, and the image of baptism as a means of participation in the death and resurrection of Christ, are the areas stressed in this section of the various offices.

In the fourth century, upon his emergence from the baptismal font, the candidate was anointed with chrism, signifying the presence of the Holy Spirit, and the christlikeness of his new life, which was protected by chrismation to incorruptibility. The other rite which is mentioned in the material in connection with baptism is that of the union of the candidate with the risen Christ, a symbol of the joy to which by baptism he was admitted. Stress is laid upon the ongoing responsibility to keep the baptismal robe clean and radiant, so that, through the influence of the Christ-like life which it symbolizes, others might be attracted to Christ. Frequently, the twentieth-century celebrations of baptism lack the symbolism of illumination that was so readily available as part of the paschal vision in the fourth century, so we find that frequently the image of light has been added to this part of the services. The white garment with which Orthodox baptizands are vested is explained to them in the liturgy as the robe of light, and they are given a lighted candle to hold, these being explained by imagery from the fourth century. Then follows their chrismation, sealing the body with the seal of the gift of the Holy Spirit, and into this office are incorporated the rites of the eighth day, to which there appears to be scant reference in the fourth-century material which we considered, and on which Schmemann is vague.[3] These rites of the eighth day appear only in the Orthodox material, and their significance is not replaced in the other services which we have considered. In *RCIA*, the chrismation of the candidate is optional, for situations in which confirmation is not to follow immediately, but the garment and candle are given. The intention of the rite for the celebration of the sacrament of initiation is that confirmation should be part of the same rite, and arrangements are specified to cover the absence of the bishop as the minister of confirmation. The purpose of confirmation is to strengthen the candidate to make him more like Christ, to enable him to witness to the death and resurrection of Christ, and to assist him in becoming an active member of the Church. The Baptist services refer to the acceptance of the baptizands into the membership of the Church by the laying on of hands, symbolizing his acceptance, commissioning, strengthening, and his equipment for the vocation and ministry to which God has called him. The services also include a similar charge to the other Church members to support and encourage the candidate.

Thus the last twenty years have seen a re-emergence of baptism to its place within the witnessing community of the Church. The accepting community has grown in importance in the liturgy, as has the public acceptance of the lordship of Christ by the candidate. Baptism has emerged from its place as a sacramental 'mystery' celebrated only in the presence of the faithful, and from its concealment behind the disinterest of the community in which it was seen as a private and discreet ceremony for two or three interested people, which Robert Hovda alludes to in *Made, Not Born*.[4] *RCIA* is described by several of my correspondents as the contribution of the missionary Church to the older and more established churches, and those using the new liturgy seem to be discovering something of the power of the sacrament of baptism in the context of the missionary situation of the universal Church. This variation has been evident in each of the offices which we have considered and is perhaps the most significant reversion to the practice of the fourth century which has emerged from this study.

Thus we have seen that the thread of the theme is present throughout the variations which we have considered. Sometimes, in the twentieth-century material, this has been discerned only as a thread of a similar hue, whilst on other occasions it has been plain that there is an unbroken chain linking theme and variations. We have found that the theme itself was interpreted by the personalities and situations in which the lectures were given, and by the interplay between preacher and congregation. Each of the Fathers laid his own stress upon various areas of the baptismal teaching which they gave and interpreted the liturgy of their particular church to emphasize those aspects which they considered important in their own situation. The Roman Catholic Church has shown a tendency to canonize the theology and catechesis of baptism, and to interpret the reform of the liturgy in terms of a return to the theology of the ancient Church, but this is posing problems in re-establishing the adult rite as normative in communities long used to the baptism of infants. The Orthodox church retains both the liturgy and the theology of the fourth century, regardless of the difference in age of the subjects of baptism, and the telescoping of nearly two months' liturgical processing into a brief service taking place on one day. Theologians are striving to encourage a deeper understanding of baptism and its effects, but there does not seem to be any way of assessing the effects of their efforts upon that church. The Baptist churches show an unconscious reversion to the fourth century because of a limited number of ways of expressing the truths of baptism to those undergoing catechetical and mystagogical training, but in considering samples of their material we have seen interesting differences in ecclesiology between Baptist and Roman Catholic Churches.

Over the next twenty year period, to the end of the century, it will be interesting to consider further developments in the variations upon the theme of the Baptism of the Christian Adult. During this future period, the fluidity of baptismal practice evidenced from the Roman Catholic responses to my letter will no doubt progress towards the solid state of either disinterest, or of a changed emphasis on the life of the baptized believer in the community of the baptized. There seems to me little chance of any change in the Orthodox service. Baptists will probably continue to adhere rigidly to the principle of their independence, and no material produced in response to the review of the life of the denomination undertaken at the 1980 Assembly has yet come to light.

Notes

Introduction

1. Lactantius: *On the Deaths of the Persecutors* 48.2.4.
2. Lactantius: *op cit.* 7–10.
3. Eusebius: *Hist. Eccle.* 4.38ff.
4. W. K. Reischl and J. Rupp: *S. patris nostri Cyrilli opera quae supersunt omnia*, 2 vols. (Munich 1848, 1860), translated as A.A. Stephenson and L. P. McCauley: *The Works of St Cyril of Jerusalem*, 2 vols. (Fathers of the Church 61, 64) (Washington, D.C. 1969, 1970); F. L. Cross: *St Cyril of Jerusalem's Lectures on the Christian Sacraments* (*Texts for Students* 51) (London 1951).
5. Translated as J. Wilkinson: *Egeria's Travels* (London 1971).
6. Antoine Wenger: *Jean Chrysostome: Huit catéchèses baptismales inédites* (*Sources Chrétiennes* 50 bis) (Paris 1970); A. Papadopoulos-Kerameus: *Varia graeca sacra. Sbornik greceskikh neisdannikh bogoslovskikh tekstov I–IV vekok* (St Petersburg 1909) pp. 154–183; B. Montfaucon: *Catechesis illuminandos prima et altera (PG* 49:223–240) (Paris 1862); collected as St John Chrysostom: *Baptismal Instructions* trans. P. W. Harkins (*Ancient Christian Writers* 31) (New York 1963).
7. R. Tonneau and R. Devréesse: *Les Homélies Catéchétiques de Théodore de Mopsueste* (*Studi e Testi* 145) (Vatican City 1949); A. Mingana: *Commentary of Theodore of Mopsuestia on the Nicene Creed* (*Woodbrooke Studies* 5) (Cambridge 1932); *Commentary of Theodore of Mopsuestia on the Lord's Prayer and the Sacraments of Baptism and the Eucharist* (*Woodbrooke Studies* 6) (Cambridge 1933).
8. A. Kavanagh: 'Christian Initiation of Adults: The Rites', a chapter in Murphy Center for Liturgical Research: *Made not Born* (Notre Dame, Indiana 1976) p. 118. See also *Sacrosanctum Concilium* 66ff.

9. *Sacrosanctum Concilium* 64.
10. I. F. Hapgood: *Service Book of the Holy Orthodox-Catholic Apostolic Church* (New York 1922)
11. There are in fact eleven Baptist Union Areas in England and Wales, but problems of timing and re-organization meant that two of them were not able to be included in the survey.
12. V. Jack: *Believe and Be Baptized* (Bury St Edmunds 1970).

Chapter One
1. See W. Telfer: *Cyril of Jerusalem and Nemesius of Emesa* (*Library of Christian Classics* 4) (London 1955) pp. 36–38; J. Quasten: *Patrology* III (Westminster MD 1960) p. 362 ff.
2. This note is appended to the older of the Munich Mss at the close of Lecture 18.
3. At *Cat.* 18.7 ('The season is winter...'), E. H. Gifford said that this passage and the reference to winter in *Cat.* 4.30 'show that the lectures were delivered in a year when Easter fell early', but cf. *Cat.* 14.10 which commented upon the arrival of spring and of the spring flowers.
4. See F. L. Cross: *St Cyril of Jerusalem's Lectures on the Sacraments* (*Texts for Students* 51) (London 1951) pp. xxxvi–xxxix where the main objections are summarized. Hereafter textual references to this work are given as FLC. See also A. A. Stephenson: *Were the Cat. Myst. delivered in Jerusalem at all?*: A communication delivered at the Eighth International Conference on Patristic Studies (Oxford 1979).
5. cf. W. J. Swaans: 'À propos des Catéchèses mystagogiques attribuées à saint Cyrille de Jérusalem in *Muséon* 55) (1942) p. 1–43.
6. W. K. Reischl & J. Rupp: *S. Patris nostri Cyrilli opera quae supersunt omnia* (Munich 1848, 1860). Hereafter textual references to this work are given as RR.
7. J. P. Migne: *Patrologia Graeca* 33.331–1180.
8. See note 4 above.
9. A. A. Stephenson and L. P. McCauley: *The Works of St Cyril of Jerusalem* Vols I & II (*Fathers of the Church* 61, 64) (Washington DC 1969, 1970). Hereafter textual references to this translation are given as FaCh.
10. P. Devos: 'La date du Voyage d'Égérie' in *Analecta*

Bollandiana 85 (1967) pp. 165–194.
11. J. Wilkinson: *Egeria's Travels* (London 1971), a recent translation of *Peregrinatio Aetheriae*.
12. J. Wilkinson: *op. cit.*, 46.2
13. W. Telfer: *op. cit.*, p. 42.
14. *Cat.* 3.6 (RR 1.70; FaCh 61.111).
15. Matthew 11.11 although Cyril was using a variant reading of his own; see J. H. Greenlee: *The Gospel Text of Cyril of Jerusalem* (*Studies and Documents* 17) (Copenhagen 1955) p.51.
16. Luke 1.44.
17. *Cat.* 3.6 (RR 1.72; FaCh 61.112).
18. *Cat.* 3.7.
19. *Cat.* 3.9 (RR 1.76; FaCh 61.114) quoting Matthew 3.11.
20. *Cat.* 3.11 (RR 1.78; FaCh 61.115).
21. *Cat.* 12.15 (RR 2.18; FaCh 61.235).
22. *Cat.* 17.9 (RR 2.260; FaCh 64.101).
23. *Cat.* 3.11.
24. cf. Job 40.18, 26; 41.13, and Jonah's choice of a sea journey rather than obedience to God's command.
25. *Cat.* 3.11 (RR 1.80; FaCh 61.115).
26. *Cat.* 3.14.
27. *Cat.* 3.13 (RR 1.80; FaCh 61.116).
28. *Procat.* 2 (FLC 1; FaCh 61.71) see also Origen: *Hom. in Num.* 3.1 in which he illustrated the hypocrisy of Simon.
29. *Procat.* 3.4 cf. Matthew 22.11–13.
30. *Cat.* 3.2.
31. *Cat.* 3.4 (RR 1.68; FaCh 61.110) cf. Hebrews 10.22.
32. *Procat.* 9.
33. *Cat.* 1.5 (RR 1.34; FaCh 61.94).
34. *Cat.* 17.37.
35. *Procat.* 15 (FLC 9; FaCh 61.81) referring to Psalm 138.12.
36. cf. Acts 10.46.
37. *Cat.* 3.4 (RR 1.68; FaCh 61.110, 111) quoting Acts 10.48.
38. *Procat.* 1.
39. See above, note 29.
40. *Cat.* 13.21.
41. *Cat.* 18.32 (RR 2.336; FaCh 64.137).
42. See J. Ysebaert: *Greek Baptismal Terminology* (*Graecitas Christianorum Primaeva*: Fasciculus Primus) (Nijmegen

1962) p. 173 ff; p. 376, 378.

43. *Procat.* 16 (FLC 10; FaCh 61.82).
44. *Cat.* 3.14 (RR 1.82; FaCh 61.116, 117).
45. *Cat.* 11.9 (RR 1.300; FaCh 61.215) quoting John 1.12–13.
46. *Procat.* 16 (FLC 10; FaCh 61.82).
47. *Cat.* 1.2 (RR 1.30; FaCh 61.92) cf. also *Cat.* 7.3 and *Cat.* 17.26.
48. *Cat.* 17.36 (RR 2.294; FaCh 64.118).
49. *Cat.* 4.32.
50. *Cat.* 5.6 (RR 1.142; FaCh 61.143).
51. *Cat.* 3.4 (RR 1.68; FaCh 61.110).
52. cf. Acts 10.4.
53. *Procat.* 17 (FLC 11; FaCh 61.84).
54. *Cat.* 3.12 (RR 1.80; FaCh 61.115).
55. *Cat.* 4.32 (RR 1.24; FaCh 61.134), See also *Cat.* 3.11.
56. *Cat.* 3.11.
57. *Procat.* 16 (FLC 10; FaCh 61.82).
58. G. W. H Lampe: *Patristic Greek Lexicon* (Oxford 1961) p. 815.
59. Mark 10.45.
60. Romans 6.3–4.
61. Titus 3.5; Matthew 19.28.
62. Basil: *De Baptismo* 1.2.27.
63. G. W. H. Lampe: *PGL* p. 1417.
64. See above p. 5f.
65. cf. *Cat.* 1.6; 2.9; 3.2, 4, 5, 13.
66. *Cat.* 17.35.
67. *Cat.* 17.36 (RR 2.294–296; FaCh 118).
68. *Cat.* 3.4, 16.
69. *Cat.* 1.4 (RR 1.34; FaCh 61.93) cf. *Cat.* 17.37.
70. *Cat.* 15.23 (RR 2.94; FaCh 64.69).
71. Hebrews 6.4–6; Romans 2.17–21; cf. Irenaeus; *Adv. Haer.* IV.42.4; Tertullian *De Baptismo* 8.
72. F. L. Cross in his introduction pointed out that a phrase in *Cat.* 18.33 seemed to look forward to a sixth catechesis, and that it would be more natural for every day of the Paschal week to have its lecture, but there is no evidence to decide this matter. See *op. cit.*, p. xxiv.
73. *Cat. Myst.* 1.1 (FLC 12; FaCh 64.153).
74. *Cat. Myst.* 1.2.
75. *Cat. Myst.* 1.3.

76. H. M. Riley: *Christian Initiation* (*Studies in Christian Antiquity* 17) (Washington DC 1974).

77. *Cat. Myst.* 1.3 (FLC 13; FaCh 64.154).

78. *Cat. Myst.* 1.4, 5, 6, 8. A. Piédagnel (ed); *Cyrille de Jérusalem: Catéchèses Mystagogiques* (*Sources Chrétiennes* 126) p. 92 notes that most manuscripts have 'his' rather than 'thy' in the third phrase (*Cat. Myst.*) 1.6) but due to the free style of the Catecheses he does not consider this significant. Cross's Greek text has 'and all thy pomp' without a notation, but the translation of Church which he used has 'and all his pomp'.

79. *Cat. Myst.* 1.4 (FLC 13–14; FaCh 64.155)

80. *Cat. Myst.* 1.8 (FLC 16; FaCh 64.158).

81. See e.g. Chrysostom: *Stav.* 2.14, 27; *Stav.* 3 = P–K 4.24; Theodore: *Homily* 12.19, 23.

82. *Cat. Myst.* 1.8 (FLC 16; FaCh 64.158).

83. *Cat. Myst.* 1.9 (FLC 26; FaCh 64.158–9).

84. *See Procat.* 15 (FLC 9; FaCh 61.81).

85. See also H. M. Riley: *op. cit.* p. 63.

86. *Cat. Myst.* 1.4 (FLC 14; FaCh 64.115).

87. *Cat. Myst.* 1.9.

88. *Cat. Myst.* 1.6 (FLC 15; FaCh 64.156) cf. also Chrysostom: *Stav.* 6.1.

89. *Cat. Myst.* 1.7.

90. *Cat. Myst.* 1.8.

91. *Cat. Myst.* 1.4.

92. H. M. Riley: *op. cit.* p. 95.

93. *Cat. Myst.* 1.5.

94. *Cat. Myst.* 2.1.

95. *Cat. Myst.* 2.2 (FLC 18; FaCh 64.161) although F. Dölger: *Der Exorzismus im altchristlichen Taufritual* (Paderborn, 1909) points out that the word 'naked' need not mean total nakedness, but can still apply if an undergarment is being worn (see p. 107ff).

96. *Cat. Myst.* 2.3.

97. *Cat. Myst.* 2.4.

98. H. M. Riley: *op. cit.* p. 62.

99. Colossians 3.9.

100. *Cat. Myst.* 2.2 (FLC 18; FaCh 64.161).

101. *Cat. Myst.* 2.2 (FLC 18; FaCh 64.161).

102. H. M. Riley: *op. cit.* p. 173.

103. *Cat. Myst.* 2.2 (FLC 18; *Cat.* 64. 162).

104. Colossians 2.14
105. *Cat. Myst.* 2.2 (FLC 18; FaCh 64. 161–2).
106. *Cat. Myst.* 2.2 (FLC 18; FaCh 64.162).
107. *Cat. Myst.* 2.3 (FLC 19; FaCh 64.163).
108. *Cat. Myst.* 2.3 (FLC 19; FaCh 64.163).
109. A. Piédagnel: *op. cit.* SC 126 p. 109 n. 1.
110. See also *Tradition Apost.* 20 (SC 11 p. 48).
111. *Cat. Myst.* 2.3 (FLC 18; FaCh 64.162), *Cat.* 1.4.
112. See H. M. Riley: *op. cit.* p. 198.
113. See H. M. Riley: *op. cit.* p. 228.
114. *Cat. Myst.* 2.4.
115. *Cat. Myst.* 2.4 (FLC 19; FaCh 64.164).
116. Matthew 12.40; Jonah 2.1 (TEV).
117. See e.g. *Procat* 2; *Cat.* 3.12; *Cat. Myst.* 2.8.
118. *Cat. Myst.* 2.6 (FLC 20; FaCh 64.165–6).
119. See H. M. Riley: *op. cit.* pp. 235–236.
120. *Cat. Myst.* 2.7 (FLC 21; FaCh 64.167).
121. *Cat. Myst.* 2.4 (FLC 19; FaCh 64.165).
122. See H. M. Riley: *op. cit.* p. 303.
123. Hebrews 3.14.
124. *Cat. Myst.* 3.1 (FLC 22; FaCh 64.169).
125. *Cat. Myst.* 2.4.
126. *Cat. Myst.* 3.2 (FLC 23; FaCh 64. 170).
127. *Cat. Myst.* 3.3 (FLC 23; FaCh 64.170–1).
128. H. M. Riley: *op. cit.* p. 370 n. 64.
129. John 13.8–11.
130. cf. 2 Corinthians 3.18; *Cat. Myst.* 3.4 (FLC 24; FaCh 64.171–2).
131. 2. Corinthians 3.18.
132. Isaiah 50.4; Matthew 11.15.
133. Ephesians 6.14.
134. Isaiah 11.4.
135. Philippians 4.13; *Cat. Myst* 3.4 (FLC 24; FaCh 64.172).
136. H. M. Riley: *op. cit.* p. 376.
137. *Cat. Myst.* 3.5.
138. *Cat. Myst.* 3.7.
139. *Cat. Myst* (FLC 25; FaCh 64.173).
140. Ecclesiastes 9.7 LXX.
141. *Cat. Myst.* 4.8 (FLC 29; FaCh 64.184–5).

Chapter Two

1. P. W. Harkins (ed): *John Chrysostom: Baptismal Instructions*

(Ancient Christian Writers 31) (Westminster, Md. and London 1963), referred to hereafter as *ACW* 31.

2. J. P. Migne: *Patrologia Graeca* 49.221–40 (Paris 1857–1866), referred to as Mf. 1 and Mf. 2. Page reference given as *PG*.

3. A. Papadopoulos-Kerameus: *Varia Graeca Sacra* Vol. 6 (*Subsidia Byzantine*) (Leipzig 1975) pp. 154–183. The original with the same pagination was published in St Petersburg 1909. These are referred to as P-K2, 3 and 4, and pages as *Vgs*.

4. A. Wenger (ed): *Jean Chrysostome; Huit catéchèses baptismales inédites* (*Sources chrétiennes* 50 bis) (Paris 1970), designated hereafter as *Stav.* 1.8. Page references are given as *SCh* 50 bis.

5. *ACW* 31.13.

6. *ACW* 31.13.

7. *Mf* = *P-K* 1.12 (*PG* 49.225) cf. *P-K* 2.8, 9, 11 where he further developed these ideas (see *ACW* 31.135).

8. *Mf* = *P-K* 1.16–26 (*PG* 49.226f; *ACW* 31.137–140).

9. *De bap. Christi* (*PG* 49.366c) cf. *Mf1* = *P-K* 1.16; (*ACW* 31.137).

10. *Mf* = *P-K* 1.20; (*ACW* 31.138).

11. *In Matt.* 12 (*PG* 57.206A; *ACW* 31.294).

12. *Stav.* 4.1 (*SCh* 50 bis. 183 *ACW* 31.66) cf. *Mf1* = *P-K* 1.19. (*PG* 49.226A–227A) *In prin. act.* 3. (*PG* 51.96D).

13. See *Stav.* 3 = *P-K* 4.19.

14. *Stav.* 1.17 (*SCh* 50 bis. 117–118; *ACW* 31.29–30).

15. cf. *Stav.* 4.14.

16. *Stav.* 2.25 (*SCh* 50 bis. 147; *ACW* 31.52).

17. *Stav.* 4.14 (*SCh* 50 bis. 190; *ACW* 31.72).

18. *Stav.* 4.16 (*SCh* 50 bis. 191; *ACW* 31.72).

19. *Mf.* 2.8 (*PG* 49.233A; *ACW* 31.175).

20. *Mf* = *P-K* 1.21–22 (*PG* 49.227B *ACW* 31.138–139) cf. in John 11 (*PG* 59.75D–76A).

21. Psalm 2.9; Jeremiah 18.4.

22. *Mf* = *P-K* 1.26 (*PG* 49.228A; *ACW* 31.140) cf. *Stav.* 3 = *P-K* 4.23; *Stav.* 4.14.

23. See *ACW* 31.239 n. 49 for a fuller examination of this point.

24. *Stav.* 5.19 (*SCh* 50 bis. 209; *ACW* 31.88) but cf. the order of events in Acts 9 where the illumination comes at v.3 and baptism only at v.17!

25. *Stav.* 5.20 (*SCh* 50 bis. 209).
26. *Stav.* 4.19 (*SCh* 50 bis. 192; *ACW* 31.73).
27. Cf. *Stav.* 7.24.
28. *Stav.* 4.12(*SCh* 50 bis. 189; *ACW* 31.71).
29. *Stav.* 2.11 (*SCh* 50 bis. 139; *ACW* 31.47).
30. *P–K* 2.8–11.
31. *In Rom.* 10 (*PG* 60.480A).
32. *P–K* 2.9 (*Vgs.* 158–9; *ACW* 31.151).
33. *P–K* 2.11 (*Vgs.* 159; *SCh* 31.152).
34. *Stav.* 7.22 (*SCh* 50 bis. 240; *ACW* 31.113).
35. *Stav.* 7.22 (*SCh* 50 bis. 240; *ACW* 31.113) cf. *In Col.* 7.
36. *Mf.* = *P–K* 1.29 (*PG.* 49.228; *ACW* 31.141).
37. *Stav.* 3 = *P–K* 4.20–21 (*SCh* 50 bis. 163; *ACW* 31.63).
38. See *In Col.* 6 (*PG* 62.340A; *ACW* 31.292), and *In II Cor.* 11 (*PG* 61.475C-76; *ACW* 31.249).
39. *Mf.* = *P–K* 1.5–6 (*PG* 49.224C; *ACW* 31.133).
40. *P–K* 3.13–14 (*Vgs.* 170.6–10; *ACW* 31.165).
41. *P–K* 3.14 (*Vgs.* 170.6–10; *ACW* 31.165).
42. *Mf.* 2.36 (*PG* 49.238A; *ACW* 31.184) cf. *Stav.* 2.1.
43. *Stav.* 1.26.
44. *Stav.* 3 = *P–K* 4.20 (*SCh* 50 bis. 193; *ACW* 31.62).
45. *Stav.* 6.21 (*SCh* 50 bis. 225; *ACW* 31.101).
46. *Stav.* 4.2 (*SCh* 50 bis. 183; *ACW* 31.66).
47. *Stav.* 6.25.
48. See *Stav.* 7.24 (*SCh* 50 bis. 241; *ACW* 31.114).
49. *Stav.* 2.31 (*SCh* 50 bis. 150; *ACW* 31.54–55).
50. *Mf.* 2.21 (*PG* 49.234; *ACW* 31.179).
51. See above p. 39.
52. *Mf.* = *P–K* 1.22.
53. *Stav.* 5.20 (*SCh* 50 bis. 210; *ACW* 31.89).
54. *Stav.* 1.3 (*SCh* 50 bis. 110; *ACW* 31.23–24).
55. *Stav.* 1.6 (*SCh* 50 bis. 111; *ACW* 31.25) cf. *Stav.* 1.8.
56. *Mf.* 2.36–37 cf. *In paralyticum* (*PG* 51.52c–53a) when Chrysostom developed this teaching in his comments on John 5.14.
57. Ephesians 5.31–32, also *In Eph.* 20 (*PG* 62.140B–C, 141A–142B), *Qual. duc. ux.* (*PG* 51.130A).
58. *Stav.* 1.1 (*SCh* 50 bis. 108; *ACW* 31.23) Chrysostom is sidetracked away from developing his other analogy to military enlistment.
59. See Harkins: *ACW* 31.207–208.
60. *Stav.* 6.24–25 (*SCh* 50 bis. 227) cf. also parallel passage

in *De res. dom.* (*PG* 50.441A) Chrysostom developed the theme of the baptismal robe at *Stav.* 4.3, 4.31, stressing the honour of wearing it, and stressing the need to keep it untarnished by sin.

61. *SCh* 50 bis. 227 n. 2.
62. *P–K* 3.26 (*Vgs.* 173; *ACW* 31.168).
63. Matthew 22.11–14. cf. Cyril of Jerusalem *Procat.* 3.
64. *Mf.* 2.19 (*PG* 49.234B; *ACW* 31.178).
65. *Stav.* 3 = *P–K* 4.7 (*SCh* 50 bis. 154; *ACW* 31.57–58).
66. *Stav.* 1.44 (*SCh* 50 bis. 131; *ACW* 31–41). See also *Mf* 1.1.
67. *Stav.* 5.23 (*SCh* 50 bis. 212; *ACW* 31.90).
68. *Mf* 2.8 (*PG* 49.232C; *ACW* 31.175) cf. *Stav.* 5.19–23; *Stav.* 4.7–16.
69. For the analysis of the liturgy, I am indebted to H. M. Riley: '*Christian Initiation*' (*Studies in Christian Antiquity* 17) (Washington 1974), a very useful work, which has been invaluable in preparing this material.
70. *P–K.* 3.10–20. See H. M. Riley's note in *Christian Initiation*, p. 28 n. 29, regarding the time of the act of renunciation and profession.
71. *Stav.* 2.18, *P–K* 3.20.
72. *P–K* 3.21, *Stav.* 2.18.
73. From the way Chrysostom uses the term 'priest' it seems clear that it is the bishop who received the act of renunciation and profession, assisted by the priests. See T. Finn: *The Liturgy of Baptism in the Baptismal Instruction of St John Chrysostom* (*Studies in Christian Antiquity* 15) (Washington 1967) pp. 18–21.
74. *Stav.* 2.18.
75. *P–K* 3.27.
76. *Stav.* 2.20 (*SCh* 50 bis. 145; *ACW* 31.51). See also *P–K* 3.22, 24 and *Mf* 2.48, 60 where partial formulas are quoted by Chrysostom.
77. *Stav.* 2.21 (*SCh* 50 bis. 145; *ACW* 31.51) cf. *P–K* 3.24; *Mf* 2.60.
78. *Stav.* 2.22 (*SCh* 50 bis. 145; *ACW* 31.51).
79. *P–K* 3.27.
80. *Stav.* 2.22 (*SCh* 50 bis. 146; *ACW* 31.51).
81. *Stav.* 2.18.
82. *Stav.* 2.20.
83. *P–K* 3.24.

84. *Stav.* 2.23.
85. *Stav.* 2.22–23; *P–K* 3.27.
86. *Stav.* 2.23.
87. *Stav.* 3 = *P–K* 4.23–24.
88. *Stav.* 3 = *P–K* 4.24 (*SCh* 50 bis. 164–5; *ACW* 31.64).
89. *Stav.* 3 = *P–K* 4.15 (*SCh* 50 bis. 159; *ACW* 31.61).
90. *Stav.* 2.14 (*SCh* 50 bis. 141; *ACW* 31.48); although this refers to exorcism the concept is the same for the act of renunciation and profession.
91. *P–K* 3.21.
92. *Stav.* 2.18.
93. *P–K* 3.21.
94. *P–K* 3.19–20 (*Vgs.* 171; *ACW* 31.166–7).
95. *P–K* 3.24.
96. *Stav.* 3 = *P–K* 4.9.
97. *Stav.* 3 = *P–K* 4.11.
98. 1 Corinthians 7.23.
99. *Mf.* 2.50.
100. *Stav.* 3 = *P–K* 4.21–22 (*SCh* 50 bis. 163–4; *ACW* 31.63).
101. *Mf.* 2.50 (*PG* 49.239; *ACW* 31.188).
102. *P–K* 3.26.
103. *Stav.* 4.31 (*SCh* 50 bis. 198; *ACW* 31.78).
104. *P–K* 3.27.
105. *Stav.* 2.22.
106. *Stav.* 2.23 (*SCh* 50 bis. 147; *ACW* 31.52).
107. H. M. Riley: *op. cit.* p. 121.
108. *Stav.* 2.23 (*SCh* 50 bis. 146–7; *ACW* 31.52).
109. *Mf.* 2.60 (*PG* 49.240; *ACW* 31.191).
110. *P–K* 3.28; for 'bishop', 'priest' may be read here and subsequently.
111. *Stav.* 2.24.
112. *Stav.* 2.24.
113. *P–K* 3.28, *Stav.* 2.25.
114. *Stav.* 2.26, *P–K* 3.12–14.
115. H. M. Riley: *op. cit.* p. 154.
116. *Stav.* 2.24–26 (*SCh* 50 bis. 147; *ACW* 31.52). Riley refers to paragraphs 24–25.
117. *Stav.* 2.11 (*SCh* 50 bis. 130; *ACW* 31.47) and see Colossians 3.9–10.
118. *Stav.* 2.25.
119. *Mf.* 2.15–20.
120. See above p. 35 and p. 42.

121. *Mf.* 2.41 (*PG* 49.237; *ACW* 31.185).
122. *Mf.* 2.43 (*PG* 49.237; *ACW* 31.186).
123. *Stav.* 1.37 (*SCh* 50 bis. 127; *ACW* 31.38).
124. *Stav.* 1.38.
125. *P–K* 3.28–29 (*Vgs.* 173–4; *ACW* 31.170).
126. See above p. 44.
127. H. M. Riley: *op. cit.* p. 351 cites evidence from Proclus to suggest that the baptized probably received a lamp or candle and a ritual white garment. To both of these Chrysostom referred, although he did not mention their moment of reception within the liturgy.
128. *Stav.* 2.27 (*SCh* 50 bis. 148; *ACW* 31.53).

Chapter Three

1. Quoted by J. Quasten: *Patrology* Vol. III (Westminster, Md. 1960) p. 408.
2. A. Mingana: *Commentary of Theodore of Mopsuestia on the Nicene Creed* (*Woodbrooke Studies* 5) (Cambridge 1932) hereafter referred to as 'WS.5'; *Commentary of Theodore of Mopsuestia on the Lord's Prayer and the Sacraments of Baptism and the Eucharist* (*Woodbrooke Studies* 6) (Cambridge 1933), hereafter referred to as 'WS. 6'. A phototypic version of this MS was produced and translated into French by R. Tonneau and T. Devréesse: *Les Homélies Catéchétiques de Théodore de Mopsueste.* (*Studi e Testi* 145) (Vatican City 1949) hereafter referred to as *SeT.* 145.
3. J. Quasten: *op. cit.* p. 409.
4. H. Lietzmann: *Die Liturgie des Theodor von Mopsuestia* (*Sonderausgabe aus den Sitzungberichten der preussischen Akademie der Wissenschaft, Phil-Hist, Klasse* 23) (Berlin 1933). Reprinted in H. Lietzmann: *Kleine Schriften III; Studia zur Liturgie und Symbolgeschichte.* (*Texte und Untersuchung* 74) (Berlin 1962) p. 72.
5. H. M. Riley: *op. cit.* p. 16.
6. *Homily* 1.7 (*SeT.* 145.12; *WS.* 5.21).
7. *Homily* 6.1 (*SeT.* 145.132; *WS.* 5.63).
8. *Homily* 6.8 (*SeT.* 145.144; *WS.* 5.67).
9. Romans 6.1–5 *et al.*
10. *Homily* 6.11 (*SeT.* 150.151; *WS.* 5.69).
11. *Homily* 6.11 (*SeT.* 145.152; *WS.* 5.69–70).
12. *SeT.* 145.153.
13. *Homily* 6.12.

14. *Homily* 6.12 (*SeT.* 145.152; *WS.* 5.70).
15. Romans 6.3–4.
16. Romans 7.4, although Theodore has added the word Jesus.
17. *Homily* 6.12 (*SeT.* 145.152.154; *WS.* 5.70–71).
18. H. M. Riley: *op. cit.* p. 40.
19. Ephesians 1.13.
20. *Homily* 6.14–15 (*SeT.* 145.158; *WS.* 5.72).
21. *Homily* 9.3–4 (*SeT.* 145.218.220; *WS.* 5.95).
22. *Homily* 9.5 (*SeT.* 145.220.222; *WS.* 5.96).
23. *Homily* 9.5 (*SeT.* 145.222; *WS.* 5.96).
24. *Homily* 9.12, 13, 14.
25. *Homily* 9.15 (*SeT.* 145.236; *WS.* 5.101).
26. 1 Corinthians 12.13; Ephesians 4.4–6; cf. *Homily* 9.16.
27. *Homily* 9.17 (*SeT.* 145.242; *WS.* 5.103).
28. *Homily* 9.18 (*SeT.* 145.242; *WS.* 5.103).
29. *Homily* 10.1 (*SeT.* 145.244; *WS.* 5.104).
30. *Homily* 10.14 (*SeT.* 145.266.268; *WS.* 5.111–12).
31. *Homily* 10.16 (*SeT.* 145.270; *WS.* 5.113).
32. *Homily* 10.17–18 (*SeT.* 145.270.272; *WS.* 5.113–14) Mingana noted the absence of the Credal article: 'We acknowledge one baptism for the remission of sins', and explained that this phrase did not appear in the first edition of the Creed but came from the Council of Constantinople in 381.
33. *Homily* 10.22 (*SeT.* 245.278.280; *WS.* 5.115–16).
34. *Homily* 13. Text, 2.
35. *Homily* 13.2.
36. *Homily* 13.4 (*SeT.* 145.372; *WS.* 6.37).
37. *Homily* 13.5 (*SeT.* 145.372; *WS.* 6.37).
38. *Homily* 13.17 (*SeT.* 145.396; *WS.* 6.46).
39. *Homily* 13.19.
40. *Homily* 13.5–12.
41. Philippians 2.11.
42. *Homily* 13.3 (*SeT.* 145.370; *WS.* 6.36).
43. See above pp. 40–1.
44. *Homily* 13.19 (*SeT.* 145.398.400; *WS.* 6.47).
45. *Homily* 13. Text, 3.16 (*SeT.* 145.366.368.370.394; *WS.* 6.35.36.45).
46. *Homily* 13.4 (*SeT.* 145.372; *WS.* 6.36–37).
47. *Homily* 13.16 (*SeT.* 145.394; *WS.* 6.45).
48. *Homily* 13.17 (*SeT.* 145.394; *WS.* 6.45).

49. See H. M. Riley: *op. cit.* p. 76–77.
50. *Homily* 13.5–6 (*SeT.* 145.374; *WS.* 6.37–38) but at *Homily* 12.23 (*SeT.* 145.358.360; *WS.* 6.31) he had used similar imagery to portray exorcism in terms of a dramatic courtroom scene.
51. *Homily* 13.5 (*SeT.* 145.374; *WS.* 6.38).
52. *Homily* 13.6 (*SeT.* 145.376; *WS.* 6.38).
53. *Homily* 14.1 (*SeT.* 145.404; *WS.* 6.49).
54. *Homily* 13.17–18 (*SeT.* 145.396.398; *WS.* 6.46–47).
55. W. C. van Unnik: 'De semitische achtergrond van *Parrēsia* in het Nieuwe Testament' in: *Mededelingen der Koninklijke Nederlands Akadamie van Wetenschappen, afd Letterkunde,* N.R. XXV.II (1962).
56. *Homily* 11.7 (*SeT.* 145.296; *WS.* 6.6).
57. *Homily* 12.27 (*SeT.* 145.366; *WS.* 6.34).
58. *Homily* 7.13 (*SeT.* 145.180; *WS.* 5.80).
59. *Homily* 12.9 (*SeT.* 145.336; *WS.* 6.22).
60. W. C. van Unnik: '*Parrēsia* in the 'Catechetical Homilies' of Theodore of Mopsuestia' in *Melanges offerts à Mlle Christine Mohrmann,* (Utrecht 1963) pp. 12–22.
61. *Homily* 15.34 (*SeT.* 145.514; *WS.* 6.90).
62. *Homily* 16.30 (*SeT.* 145.582; *WS.* 6.115).
63. *Homily* 16.38 (*SeT.* 145.494; *WS.* 6.119–120).
64. W. C. van Unnik: *art. cit.* pp. 16–17.
65. 1 Corinthians 13.12; 2 Corinthians 3.18.
66. W. C. van Unnik: *art. cit* p.19.
67. See also in this connection *Acta Thomae* 26; A. F. J. Klijn ed. *The Acts of Thomas* (Leiden 1962) p. 76ff and commentary p. 205ff.
68. *Homily* 13.20 (*SeT.* 145.400; *WS.* 6.47).
69. *Homily* 14.8 (*SeT.* 145.418; *WS.* 6.54).
70. *Homily* 14.14, 18–19 (*SeT.* 145.430.440.442; *WS.* 6.58.62.63).
71. *Homily* 14.8 (*SeT.* 145.418; *WS.* 6.54).
72. *Homily* 14.8 (*SeT.* 145.416; *WS.* 6.54).
73. *Homily* 14.8 (*SeT.* 145.418; *WS.* 6.54).
74. *Homily* 14.17 (*SeT.* 145.438; *WS.* 6.62).
75. *Homily* 12.6 (*SeT.* 145.330.332; *WS.* 6.20).
76. *Homily* 12.7 (*SeT.* 145.332; *WS.* 6.20).
77. *Homily* 12.6 (*SeT.* 145.330; *WS.* 6.20).
78. See further: R. Greer, *Theodore of Mopsuestia: Exegete and Theologian* (London 1961) pp. 66–85; T. M. Finn:

'Baptismal Death and Resurrection: A study in Fourth Century Eastern Baptismal terminology' *Worship* 43 (1969) pp. 184–185, concerning Theodore's Doctrine of the Two Ages which formed the basis of his sacramental theology.

79. *Homily* 14.5 (*SeT.* 145.412; *WS.* 6.52) quoting Romans 6.3.
80. *Homily* 14.5 (*SeT.* 145.412; *WS.* 6.52).
81. *Homily* 14.11 (*SeT.* 145.424; *WS.* 6.56–57).
82. *Homily* 14.11 (*SeT.* 145.414; *WS.* 6.57) quoting Job 33.6 and 4.19.
83. H. M. Riley: *op. cit.* p. 286.
84. *Homily* 14.6 (*SeT.* 145.412.414; *WS.* 6.52).
85. *Homily* 14.21–22 (*SeT.* 145.446.448; *WS.* 6.64–65) quoting Phil. 3.20–21.
86. *Homily* 14.22 (*SeT.* 145.448; *WS.* 6.65).
87. *Homily* 14.25 (*SeT.* 145.454; *WS.* 6.67).
88. *Homily* 14.15–16 (*SeT.* 145.434.436; *WS.* 6.60).
89. *Homily* 14.21–22 (*SeT.* 145.446.448; *WS.* 6.64–65).
90. *Homily* 14.2 (*SeT.* 145.404.406; *WS.* 6.49–50); see also H. M. Riley: *op. cit.* p. 327.
91. *Homily* 14.3 (*SeT.* 145.406; *WS.* 6.50).
92. *Homily* 14.5–6 (*SeT.* 145.412.414; *WS.* 6.52) see also above p. 98f.
93. *Homily* 14.3 (*SeT.* 145.406.408; *WS.* 6.50) quoting John 3.3, 4, 5.
94. *Homily* 14.4 (*SeT.* 145.410; *WS.* 6.51).
95. *Homily* 14.7 (*SeT.* 145.416; *WS.* 6.53–54).
96. *Homily* 14.7 (*SeT.* 145.416; *WS.* 6.53).
97. H. M. Riley: *op. cit.* p. 333.
98. *Homily* 14.9–10 (*SeT.* 145.420.422.424; *WS.* 6.55–56) quoting John 3.4–5; 1 Corinthians 15.42–44.
99. cf. Matthew 19.28.
100. Jeremiah 18.1–6; Job 33.6 (*LXX*); Job 4.19 (*LXX*).
101. See *Homily* 14.11 and above p. 6f.
102. Genesis 2.7.
103. *Homily* 14.12–13 (*SeT.* 145.428; *WS.* 6.57–58).
104. *Homily* 14.14 (*SeT.* 145.430; *WS.* 6.58).
105. *Homily* 14.26 (*SeT.* 145.454; *WS.* 6.68).
106. *Homily* 14.27 (*SeT.* 145.456; *WS.* 6.68).
107. *Homily* 14.27 (*SeT.* 145.458; *WS.* 6.68–69) quoting Luke 8.18 and Acts 10.38.

108. *Homily* 14.26 (*SeT*. 145.454.456; *WS*. 6.68).
109. See above p. 64.

Chapter Four
1. Chrysostom: *P–K* 3.18 (Harkins *ACW* 31.166).
2. *Stav*. 8.1 (*ACW* 31.119); *Mf*= *P–K* 1 (*ACW* 31.140) *et al*.
3. *Mf*= *P–K* 1.29 (*ACW* 31.140).
4. *Hom. in Genesis* 6 (PG.54, 616 C–D).
5. *Luke* 1:44; Cyril of Jerusalem: *Cat*. 3.6; *Cat*. 3.7, see also *Cat. Myst* 2.6, *Cat*. 3.11, 12.15; Chrysostom: *Mf*= *P–K* 1.13; *De Bap Christi* (*PG* 49.366c), *In Matt*. 12 (PG.57.206a) *ACW* 31.294.
6. Theodore: *Hom*. 6.8 (*SeT* 145.144; *WS*. 5.6.7).
7. Cyril: *Cat*. 17.9.
8. Chrysostom: *P–K* 3.13.
9. *P–K* 3.14.
10. Theodore: *Homily* 9.3–4 (*SeT* 145.218, 220; *WS* 5.95).
11. Cyril: *Cat*. 3.11; *Job* 40.23ff.
12. Cyril: *Cat*. 3.15.
13. Chrysostom: *Stav*. 6.21 (*SCh* 50 bis. 193; *ACW* 31.101).
14. *Cat*. 3.4; See also Cyril: *Procat*. 2 and *Procat*. 3.4. cf. *Matthew* 22.11–13.
15. Chrysostom: *Stav*. 4.16.
16. *Procat*. 2–4.
17. *Mf*. 2.19.
18. Cyril: *Cat*. 17.37.
19. *Procat*. 15.
20. *Procat*. 2.
21. Chrysostom: *Stav*. 5.19.
22. Cf *Stav*. 7.24.
23. Cyril: *Cat*. 3.14; 11.9.
24. Chrysostom: *Stav*. 2.26.
25. Cyril: *Cat*. 3.14.
26. *Cat*. 1.2; 7.3; 17.26; 17.36.
27. *Cat*. 5.6.
28. Chrysostom: *Mf*= *P–K* 1.12.
29. *In Col*. 6.
30. *In II Cor*. 11.
31. Cyril: *Cat*. 3.4.
32. *Cat*. 3.12.
33. *Cat*. 4.32.
34. *Procat*. 16.

35. Chrysostom: *Stav.* 2.11.
36. *Mf* = *P–K* 1.12.
37. *P–K* 2.8–11.
38. *In Rom.* 10.
39. *P–K* 2.11, *Stav.* 4.1.
40. *Stav.* 7.22.
41. *Stav.* 2.25.
42. *Mf* = *P–K* 1.21–22.
43. *Mf* = *P–K* 1.26; *Stav.* 3 = *P–K* 4.23; *Stav.* 4.14.
44. *P–K* 3.23.
45. *Stav.* 3 = *P–K* 4.7.
46. *P–K* 3.26.
47. Theodore: *Homily* 6.12.
48. *Homily* 6.12.
49. *Homily* 6.14 (*SeT* 145.158; *WS.* 5.72).
50. Cyril: *Cat.* 1.6; 2.9; 3.2, 4, 5, 13.
51. *Cat.* 3.4, 16.
52. *Cat.* 1.4; 17.37; 15.23.
53. Chrysostom: *Mf* = *P–K* 1.5–6; *P–K* 3.13, 14.
54. *P–K* 3.21.
55. *Mf* 2.21.
56. *Mf* 2.36, *Stav.* 1.26, 2.1; *Stav.* 3 = *P–K* 4.20.
57. Cyril: *Cat. Myst.* 1.9.
58. Theodore: *Homily* 13.3; Chrysostom: *Stav.* 2.14.
59. Chrysostom: *P–K* 3.21.
60. Cyril: *Cat. Myst.* 1.8.
61. Theodore: *Homily* 13.19.
62. Cyril: *Cat. Myst.* 1.4.
63. Chrysostom: *Stav.* 2.18; *P–K* 3.21.
64. Theodore: *Homily* 13.16.
65. Cyril: *Cat. Myst.* 1.9.
66. Chrysostom: *P–K* 3.20–21.
67. See Theodore: *Homily* 13.16.
68. Cyril: *Cat. Myst.* 1.2, 3; *Cat. Myst.* 1.4.
69. Chrysostom: *P–K* 3.24; Theodore: *Homily* 13.5–6.
70. *Stav.* 3 = *P–K* 4.21–22.
71. *Stav.* 2.20; Cyril: *Cat. Myst.* 1.5.
72. *P–K* 3.26.
73. Cyril: *Cat. Myst.* 1.4; Theodore: *Homily* 13.6.
74. Chrysostom: *Stav.* 3 = *P–K* 4.9–11.
75. *P–K* 3.27.
76. Theodore: *Homily* 13.17.

77. Chrysostom: *Stav.* 2.23.
78. Theodore: *Homily* 14.1.
79. See H. M. Riley: *Christian Initiation* (*Studies in Christian Antiquity* 17) on the anticipatory nature of Theodore's words here.
80. Theodore: *Homily* 13.17–18.
81. Chrysostom: *P–K* 3.19–20.
82. Cyril: *Cat. Myst.* 2.1.
83. Chrysostom: *Stav.* 2.24.
84. Theodore: *Homily* 13.20.
85. Cyril: *Procat.* 4.
86. Chrysostom: *Mf* 2.15–20.
87. Cyril: *Cat. Myst.* 2.2; Chrysostom: *Stav.* 1.3.
88. Chrysostom: *Stav.* 1.34–38; *Mf* 2.39–47.
89. Cyril: *Cat. Myst.* 2.2.
90. Theodore: *Homily* 14.8.
91. Cyril: *Cat. Myst.* 2.2; Chrysostom: *P–K* 3.29; Theodore: *Homily* 14.8.
92. Cyril: *Cat. Myst.* 2.3.
93. Theodore: *Homily* 14.8.
94. *Stav.* 3 = *P–K* 4.9.
95. H. M. Riley: *op. cit.* p. 209.
96. Cyril: *Cat. Myst.* 2.3.
97. Chrysostom: *Stav.* 3 = *P–K* 4.9.
98. Theodore: *Homily* 14.8.
99. Cyril: *Cat. Myst.* 2.4.
100. *Cat. Myst.* 2.4.
101. Chrysostom: *P–K* 3.28, 29; *Stav.* 7.21–23.
102. Theodore: *Homily* 14.5, 11.
103. Cyril: *Cat. Myst.* 2.7.
104. Chrysostom: *P–K* 2.9.
105. *Stav.* 3 = *P–K* 4.16.
106. *P–K* 2.11.
107. Theodore: *Homily* 14.6.
108. Chrysostom: *Stav.* 1.16.
109. Theodore: *Homily* 14.3, 7.
110. Cyril: *Cat. Myst.* 2.4.
111. Chrysostom: *Stav.* 4.1; *Stav.* 3 = *P–K* 4.19.
112. *P–K* 3.16–17.
113. Theodore: *Homily* 14.9.–10.
114. Chrysostom: *Mf* = *P–K* 1.26; *Stav.* 3 = *P–K* 4.23; *Stav.* 4.14.

115. Theodore: *Homily* 14.11.
116. H. M. Riley: *op. cit.* p. 348.
117. Cyril: *Cat. Myst.* 3.2
118. Theodore: *Homily* 14.27.
119. Cyril: *Cat. Myst.* 3.1.
120. *Cat. Myst.* 3.3.
121. *Cat. Myst.* 3.7.
122. Theodore: *Homily* 14.27.
123. Cyril: *Cat. Myst.* 3.1.
124. e.g. Chrysostom: *Stav.* 4.18.
125. *Stav.* 4.4.
126. Theodore: *Homily* 14.26.
127. Cyril: *Cat. Myst.* 4.8.
128. Chrysostom: *Stav.* 7.24; 2.25; *P–K* 3.6–7.
129. *Stav.* 5.18; 8.25; 5.24–26; 6.24–25.
130. Cyril: *Cat. Myst.* 4.8.
131. Theodore: *Homily* 14.26.

Chapter Five
1. A. Schmemann: *Of Water and the Spirit* (London 1976) hereafter referred to as AS.
2. I. F. Hapgood: *The Service Book of the Holy Orthodox Catholic Apostolic Church* (New York, 1922) hereafter referred to as IFH.
3. IFH p. 601.
4. AS p. 15.
5. AS p. 53ff.
6. See AS p. 54.
7. AS p. 55.
8. See T. R. Ware: *Eustratios Argenti* (Oxford 1964).
9. AS p. 55.
10. Mark 8.34.
11. e.g. the immersion/sprinkling debate.
12. AS p. 58.
13. See R. F. G. Burnish: *The Doctrine of Grace from Paul to Irenaeus* (unpublished thesis, Univ. of Glasgow, 1973).
14. AS p. 60.
15. John 10.17–18.
16. 1 Corinthians 15.54ff.
17. The Corinthians do not appear to have found it all that easy either!
18. John 1.2.

19. AS p.63.
20. 1 Corinthians 15.56.
21. As p. 64.
22. Philippians 121.
23. AS p. 65.
24. 1 John 2.16.
25. AS p. 66.
26. IFH p. 271.
27. see above p. 78 *et al.*
28. IFH p.271.
29. IFH pp. 601–2 (underlined parenthesis mine).
30. AS p. 18.
31. See above pp. 28ff.
32. See my thesis 'The Baptism of the Christian Adult' (Nottingham 1983) pp. 40, 120 for a further examination of the role of sponsors.
33. IFH p. 271.
34. IFH p. 271.
35. IFH p. 271.
36. IFH p. 271.
37. AS p. 23.
38. AS p. 23.
39. AS pp. 23–24.
40. AS p. 24.
41. AS p. 273.
42. IFH pp. 273–4. Miss Hapgood notes that the phrase 'reason-endowed sheep' is used to distinguish the candidate from dumb animals.
43. See above pp. 5, 38.
44. IFH p. 274.
45. IFH p. 603 cf. Cyril: *Cat. Myst.* 1.4.
46. AS p. 27–8 cf. Chrysostom *Bapt. Inst.* 10; 14.15.
47. AS p. 29.
48. IFH p. 274.
49. AS p. 30.
50. IFH p. 274.
51. cf Cyril *Cat. Myst.* 1.9. See T. M. Finn: *The Liturgy of Baptismal Instructions of St John Chrysostom* (Washington 1967) p. 116.
52. AS p. 31.
53. AS p. 33.
54. IFH p. 275.

55. IFH p. 276; AS p. 37.
56. AS p. 38.
57. AS p. 38.
58. IFH p. 276–7.
59. AS p. 40.
60. IFH p. 278.
61. IFH p. 279.
62. AS p. 51.
63. John 10.10.
64. IFH p. 279.
65. IFH pp. 279–80.
66. IFH p. 280.
67. AS p. 70.
68. AS p. 70.
69. IFH p. 280. Dr Schmemann deals with this at the beginning of his section on 'The Sacrament of the Holy Spirit'.
70. See above p. 97.
71. IFH p. 281.
72. IFH p. 281.
73. IFH p. 603.
74. AS p. 78.
75. AS p. 79.
76. AS p. 79.
77. AS p. 81.
78. AS p. 94.
79. AS p. 98.
80. Genesis 3.8.
81. AS p. 102.
82. AS p. 107.
83. IFH p. 281.
84. Romans 6.3–11; Matthew 28.16–20 respectively.
85. IFH p. 282–3.
86. See above p. 78.
87. IFH p. 283.
88. IFH p. 284.
89. AS p. 126.
90. IFH p. 284.
91. IFH p. 603.
92. See AS p. 127.
93. IFH p. 284.
94. AS p. 128.

95. AS p. 129.

Chapter Six

1. *A Catechism of Christian Doctrine* (London 1971) referred to hereafter as *CCD*.
2. *CCD* 259 p. 44 (emphasis mine).
3. The approved translation is: Sacred Congregation for the Clergy: *General Catechetical Directory* (London 1971) referred to hereafter as *DCG*.
4. *DCG* 7 p. 17.
5. *DCG* 9 p. 19.
6. See *DCG* 10 p. 21; *DCG* 18 p. 27. See also *DCG* 19 p. 27.
7. *DCG* 20 p. 28. See also *Christus Dominum* 14; *Ad gentes* 14.
8. *DCG* 57 pp. 49–50. See also *Lumen Gentium* 31.
9. *DCG* 57 p. 50, cf. *CCD* 262 p. 45.
10. *Lumen Gentium* 11; *Ad gentes* 11.
11. Basic Teaching for Catholic Religious Education (London 1975).
12. *ibid.* Section headings.
13. *A New Catechism with Supplement*: trans. Kevin Smyth 8th edn. (London 1980).
14. *Sacrosanctum Concilium* 64.
15. *op. cit.* pp. ix–xviii; see also p. iv.
16. See *op. cit.* p. 69.
17. *op. cit.* p. 91.
18. *op. cit.* pp. 91–92, 246.
19. *op. cit.* pp. 92–3.
20. *op. cit.* p. 93.
21. *op. cit.* p. 242.
22. *op. cit.* p. 242.
23. *op. cit.* p. 243.
24. *op. cit.* p. 243.
25. Mark 7.34.
26. See above p. 39 and *Stav.* 2.23.
27. *op. cit.* p. 244.
28. See *op. cit.* p. 246.
29. *op. cit.* p. 246.
30. E. Dhanis & J. Vissen: *The Supplement to a New Catechism* (London 1969).
31. *Supplement* p. 49.
32. *op. cit.* p. 246.
33. *op. cit.* p. 247.

34. *op. cit.* p. 247.
35. *op. cit.* p. 247.
36. See *op. cit.* p. 248.
37. *op. cit.* p. 249.
38. *op. cit.* p. 248.
39. *op. cit.* p. 249.
40. *Supplement* p. 49.
41. *op. cit.* p. 257.
42. *op. cit.* p. 252.
43. R. Lawler, D. W. Wuerl, T. C. Lawler: *The Teaching of Christ* (Dublin 1976).
44. See above pp. 123–4.
45. *op. cit.* p. 272.
46. Dated 15 May 1969.
47. *op. cit.* p. 457.
48. *op. cit.* p. 459.
49. Romans 6.6.
50. Colossians 4.1–3; see *op. cit.* p. 459.
51. *op. cit.* p. 460.
52. *op. cit.* p. 461.
53. *op. cit.* p. 463.
54. Council of Trent: *Decree on Justification* ch.7. See *op. cit.* p. 464.
55. *Rite of Baptism for Children*: General Introduction n. 6.
56. Council of Trent: *Decree on Original Sin* n. 5.
57. *Rite of Baptism for Children*: General Introduction n. 5.
58. 1 Peter 2.9.
59. *Teaching of Christ* p. 467.
60. *Rite of Baptism for Children*: General Introduction 4.
61. See *A New Catechism* p. 252.
62. *op. cit.* p. 471.
63. *op. cit.* p. 474.
64. Murphy Center for Liturgical Research: *Made Not Born* (Notre Dame, Ind. 1976) p. 151.
65. Sacred Congregation for Divine Worship: *Prot.* n. 15/72. Sacred Congregation for Divine Worship: *Ordo Initiationis Christianae Adultorum* (Vatican City 1972), translated by International Commission on English in the Liturgy: *Rite of Christian Initiation of Adults* (London 1974) Preface; referred to hereafter as *OICA*.
66. *Sacrosanctum Concilium* 64, in Walter M. Abbott: *Documents*

of Vatican II (London 1967) p. 159, referred to hereafter as *DVII*.

67. *Ad gentes* 14 (*DVII* pp. 600–601); see also *Lumen Gentium* 14, 17; *Sacrosanctum Concilium.* 64–5.
68. *DCG* 7 p. 17.
69. *Christus Dominus* 14 (*DVII* p. 406).
70. *Christus Dominus* 14 (*DVII* p. 406).
71. See also *OICA* 4 p. 1.
72. *Ad gentes* 13 (*DVII* p. 600).
73. *OICA* 6 pp. 1–2.
74. See *Sacrosanctum Concilium* (*DVII* pp. 169–170).
75. *OICA* 8 p. 2.
76. See *OICA* 22 p. 5.
77. Sometimes meeting in a deliberation on the suitability of the candidates, which involves presbyters, deacons, catechists, godparents, and delegates of the local community; see *OICA* 137 p. 36.
78. *OICA* 143 p.37.
79. See *OICA* 154 p. 43.
80. *OICA* 25(1) p. 6.
81. *OICA* 156 p. 44.
82. *OICA* 25(2) p. 6.
83. See *Sacrosanctum Concilium* 110 (*DVII* p. 170).
84. *OICA* 26(2) p. 6.
85. *OICA* 198 p. 60.
86. *OICA* 206 p. 62. This passage indicates the transient state of the Roman Catholic Church's liturgical revision.
87. *OICA* 310 p. 63.
88. *OICA* 30 p. 7.
89. *OICA* 19(2) p. 4; *OICA* p. 64.
90. *OICA* 317 p. 67 (Formul A & B).
91. *OICA* 213 p. 64.
92. *OICA* 219 p. 69.
93. See *OICA* 32 p. 7.
94. M. Dujarier: *The Rites of Christian Initiation* (New York 1979) p. 176.
95. *OICA* 220, 221 p. 70.
96. See *OICA* 33 p. 7. This does not take place if the rite continues to confirmation. *OICA* 224 p. 71; *OICA* 225 p. 71; *OICA* 226 p. 72.
97. *OICA* 34, 35 p. 8.

98. A. Kavanagh: 'Christian Initiation of Adults: The Rites' in Murphy Center for Liturgical Research: *Made not Born* (Notre Dame, Ind. 1976) p. 128. Also in *Worship* 48 (1974) pp. 318–335.

99. *OICA* 46 pp. 10–11.

100. A. Kavanagh: *art. cit.* p. 129.

101. A. Kavanagh: *art. cit.* p. 128.

102. A. Kavanagh: *art. cit.* p. 128.

103. C. Kiesling quoted in E. Braxton: *art. cit.* p. 182.

104. A. Kavanagh: quoted in E. Braxton: *art. cit.* p. 182.

105. E. Braxton: *art. cit.* p. 183.

106. *OICA* 36 p. 8; M. Dujarier: *The Rites of Christian Initiation* (New York 1979).

107. *OICA* 234 p. 74.

108. Murphy Center: *op. cit.* p. 155.

109. cf. Murphy Center: *op. cit.* p. 143. 'Baptism took place quietly in a corner, even more quietly in a corner for the rare adults, so as not to cause embarrassment by the perceived incongruity of submitting people to something which ought to have been done in infancy.'

110. *OICA* 235 p. 74.

111. *OICA* 39 p. 8.

112. Murphy Center: *op. cit.* p. 141.

113. *OICA* 237 p. 74.

114. R. B. Kemp: *op. cit.* p. 158.

115. R. B. Kemp: *op. cit.* p. 159.

116. R. B. Kemp: *op. cit.* pp. 159–60.

117. J. B. Dunning: *New Wine, New Wineskins* (New York 1981) p. 98; *OICA* 237 p. 74.

118. *OICA* 238 p. 74.

119. M. Dujarier: *The Rite of Christian Initiation* (New York 1979) p. 220.

120. J. B. Dunning: *op. cit.* p. 9.

121. M. Dujarier: *op. cit.* p. 14.

122. Murphy Center: *op. cit.* p. 138; R. Lewinski provides an excellent summary of the changes introduced by *RCIA* in: *Welcoming the New Catholic* (Chicago 1978) pp. 7–9.

123. As part of this research a letter was written to key liturgical and catechetical personnel in each diocese. Eleven dioceses replied, and both national commissions.

124. Letter from Rev. M. C. Fewell, CMF, 13 January 1982.

125. R. B. Kemp: *op. cit.* p. 161.

Chapter Seven

1. Constitution of Baptist Union of Great Britain and Ireland Baptist Union Handbook, 1984–5 p. 9.
2. E. A. Payne: 'Baptists & Christian Initiation' in *Baptist Quarterly* XXVI (October 1979) p. 147.
3. As part of this research, a questionnaire was given to each minister attending an Area Minister's Conference in Spring 1981. 330 Ministers returned them and the results are published in R. F. G. Burnish: 'The Baptism of the Christian Adult; Theme and Variation' PhD Thesis, Nottingham 1983, Appendix C, pp. 387ff.
4. The ministers who responded to this section form approximately one third of all the cases surveyed. Included for analysis are those who indicated a more general response, specifying a New Testament basis, or a series based on the Apostles' Creed; and some used published material for one part of the course, and their own material for other parts of their catechetical preparation. To enable a picture to be built up of this third, I list some of the significant responses and compare them with the responses to the whole sample as a fraction.

Age of Respondent

21–30	14/31	**31–40**	32/95	**41–50**	28/87
51–60	14/64	**61–70**	21/43	**70+**	4/9

Length of Ministry

1–10 yrs	38/114	**11–20 yrs**	31/93
21–30 yrs	12/32	**40+ yrs**	9/13

Numbers of meetings before Baptism

1–4	17/52	**5–6**	45/140
7–10	41/109	**10+**	11/20

Duration of Prebaptismal Classes

1 month	17/41	**3 months**	73/206		
6 months	14/40	**Others**	8/26	**Varies**	1/4

Numbers of meetings after Baptism

1–2	24/72	**3–4**	25/72	**over 4**	18/38
Never	29/95	**Other**	5/15		

Duration of Post-Baptismal Course

1 month	16/55	**2 months**	2/4	**3 months**	27/78
6 months	15/35	**6+ months**	7/17		

Appointment of Visitors

Yes	103/285	**No**	12/43

5. On the basis of answers to questions re syllabus on the quesionnaires.
6. However, one syllabus intended for post-baptismal instruction does not mention it in the chapter headings.
7. Constitution of the Baptist Union of Great Britain and Ireland.
8. A. C. Underwood: *A History of English Baptists*. Baptist Union (London 1961) pp. 268ff.
9. A. C. Underwood: *op. cit.* p. 269.
10. A. C. Underwood: *op. cit.* p. 270.
11. J. McClendon: 'Why Baptists do not Baptize Infants', in *Concilium* IV No. 3 p. 4.
12. A. Gilmore (ed.): *Christian Baptism* (London 1959) p. 307.
13. *op. cit.* p. 308.
14. He refers to A. Benoît: *Le Baptême chrétien au second siècle* 36ff., 121ff., 148ff., 188ff.; Clark: *op. cit.* pp. 308–9.
15. *op. cit.* p. 309.
16. G. R. Beasley Murray: *op. cit.* p. 83.
17. *op. cit.* p. 89.
18. R. L. Child: *A Conversation about Baptism* (London 1963).
19. *op. cit.* p. 13.
20. *op. cit.* p. 14.
21. *op. cit.* pp. 63–4.
22. *op. cit.* p. 64.
23. *op. cit.* pp. 64–5; see also p. 72.
24. B. S. Moss (ed.): *Crisis for Baptism* (London 1965); the papers given at the Parish and People Conference at Swanwick on 'The Baptismal Life'.
25. Rev. A. Gilmore, S. Winward and N. Clark.
26. See above n. 12.
27. *op. cit.* p. 62.
28. Quoted in *op. cit.* p. 63.
29. *op. cit.* p. 64.
30. *op. cit.* p. 73.
31. *op. cit.* p. 74.
32. *op. cit.* p. 123.
33. *op. cit.* p. 124.
34. *op. cit.* p. 125.
35. *op. cit.* pp. 126–7.
36. D. Bridge, D. Phypers: *The Water that Divides* (Leicester 1977).
37. *op. cit.* p. 21.

38. p. 27.
39. D. F. Neil: *The Way of Christ* (London 1973). This publication is one selected by the Joint Publications Committee of Baptist Missionary Society, Baptist Union of Great Britain and Ireland, Baptist Union of Scotland and Baptist Union of Wales.
40. Matthew 28.18–20.
41. *op. cit.* p. 8; see also Romans 6.3–4.
42. *op. cit.* p. 9.
43. See also 1 Corinthians 12.13.
44. R. E. O. White: *Invitation to Baptism* (London 1962).
45. *op. cit.* p. 13.
46. John 4.1–3.
47. *op. cit.* pp. 15–16.
48. *op. cit.* p. 17.
49. e.g. Acts 2.38; 22.16; Ephesians 5.25–27; Titus 3.5.
50. *op. cit.* p. 26.
51. *op. cit.* p. 41.
52. *op. cit.* p.44.
53. Romans 6.1–11.
54. *op. cit.* p. 56.
55. *op. cit.* p. 56.
56. *op. cit.* pp. 64–5.
57. Acts 8.14–17.
58. Acts 19.1–7.
59. *op. cit.* p. 68.
60. *op. cit.* p. 75, quoting Matthew 3.1.
61. S. F. Winward: *Your Baptism* (London 1969).
62. *op. cit.* p. 17.
63. Galatians 3.26–27.
64. Romans 6.3–5.
65. See above pp. 155–6.
66. *op. cit.* p. 19; *op. cit.* p. 20.
67. *op. cit.* p. 22.
68. *op. cit.* pp. 22–3.
69. Matthew 28.16–20.
70. *op. cit.* p. 28.
71. *op. cit.* p. 30, cf. Tertullian's imagery in *De Baptismo*.
72. *op. cit.* p. 31.
73. S. F. Winward: *The N. T. Teaching on Baptism* (London 1952). Although this publication date is before 1960, the booklet is still in regular use, and had reached a tenth

impression by 1977.

74. John 3.22; 4.1–2.
75. *op. cit.* pp. 16–17.
76. *op. cit.* p. 22.
77. *op. cit.* p. 23.
78. *op. cit.* pp. 63–64.
79. EMBA: '*Church Membership*' (Nottingham 1972). A completely revised edition entitled '*To be a Christian*' was produced in 1981. V. Jack: *Believe and be Baptized* (Bury St Edmunds 1970); B. Gilbert: *New Horizons* (Lutterworth 1979).
80. E. A. Payne, S. F. Winward: '*Orders and Prayers for Church Worship*' (London 1960).
81. E. A. Payne & S. F. Winward: *op. cit.* p. 127.
82. Matthew 3.13–17; Luke 3.21–22; John 3.5–8; Acts 2.38, 41, 42; Romans 6.3–4; 10.9–11; 1Corinthians 12.12–13; Galatians 3.26–28; Colossians 2.12; 1 Timothy 6.12; 1 Peter 3.21–22.
83. *op. cit.* p. 130.
84. See above pp. 126ff.
85. 'Ordinance' is the term which most Baptists would prefer to use.
86. *op. cit.* pp.131–2.
87. *op. cit.* p. 132.
88. *op. cit.* p. 133.
89. Numbers 6.24–26. Baptismal sentences in the *Baptist Hymn Book* are Num. 6.24–26; Revelation 5.13; 2.10.
90. *op. cit.* pp. 135–6.
91. 1 Peter 2.9; 4.10–11; Romans 12.11–12; Matthew 5.14a, 16; John 13.34–35.
92. *op. cit.* p. 137.
93. *op. cit.* p. 137.
94. *op. cit.* p. 138.
95. The author was received into the membership of his first Church in December 1960 by the right hand of fellowship.
96. *op. cit.* pp.44–45.
97. Cf. above note 4.
98. Cf. above note 5.
99. *op. cit.* p. 45.
100. *op. cit.* p. 46.
101. Winward is committed to a policy of so ordering worship

that there is no scope for repetition. This makes demands on his congregation if none of the impact of the worship is to be lost. Its disadvantage is that it makes little allowance for the outsiders who are frequently attracted by the witness of a baptismal service.

102. *op. cit.* p.46.
103. *op. cit.* pp. 47–48.
104. *op. cit.* p.48.
105. *op. cit.* p. 49.
106. A. Gilmore, E. Smalley, M. Walker: *Praise God* (London 1980).
107. *op. cit.* p. 137.
108. *op. cit.* p. 137.
109. *op. cit.* p. 139.
110. *op. cit.* p. 139.
111. *op. cit.* p. 139.
112. *op. cit.* p. 139.
113. *op. cit.* p. 140.
114. *op. cit.* p. 140.

Chapter Eight
1. *A New Catechism* p. 93.
2. *The Teaching of Christ* p. 459.
3. N. Clark: 'The Theology of Baptism' in A. Gilmore (ed.): *Christian Baptism* p. 307; and see below p. 127.
4. N. Clark: 'Baptism and Redemption' in B. S. Moss (ed.) *Crisis for Baptism* p. 73.
5. See above, pp. 154 and 125.
6. R. E. O. White: *Invitation to Baptism* p. 17.
7. S. F. Winward: *Your Baptism* p. 17.
8. *ibid.* p. 27.
9. *A New Catechism* pp. 244–245.
10. *op. cit.* p. 247.
11. *The Teaching of Christ* pp. 460–463.
12. *ibid.* p. 466.
13. D. F. Neil: *The Way of Christ* p. 8.
14. N. Clark: 'The Theology of Baptism' in A. Gilmore (ed.) *op. cit.* p. 309.
15. S. F. Winward: *Your Baptism* p. 19.
16. EMBA: *Church Membership* (Nottingham 1972) p. 8.
17. V. Jack: *Believe and Be Baptized* (Bury St Edmunds 1970) pp. 15–18.

18. *A New Catechism* p. 247; *The Teaching of Christ* p. 458.
19. *A New Catechism* p. 246; *The Teaching of Christ* p.459.
20. *The Teaching of Christ* p. 466.
21. *A New Catechism* p. 466.
22. *The Teaching of Christ* p. 466.
23. N. Clark: 'Baptism and Redemption' in B. S. Moss (ed.) *op. cit.* p. 73.
24. R. E. O. White: *op. cit.* p. 44.
25. See above p. 170.
26. A. Schmemann: *Of Water and the Spirit* p. 50.
27. A. Schmemann: *op. cit.* p. 65.
28. *A New Catechism* pp. 245–246.
29. *op. cit.* p. 246.
30. *The Teaching of Christ* p. 465.
31. N. Clark: 'The Theology of Christian Baptism' in A. Gilmore (ed.): *op. cit.* pp. 308–9, citing A. Benoît: *Le Baptême chrétien au second siècle* (Paris 1953) pp. 36ff., 121ff., 188ff.
32. D. F. Neil: *op. cit.* p. 9.
33. R. E. O. White: *op. cit.* p. 26.
34. S. F. Winward: *Your Baptism* p. 20.
35. *A New Catechism* p. 246.
36. *The Teaching of Christ* p. 471.
37. R. E. O. White: *op. cit.* p. 26.
38. *A New Catechism* p. 246.
39. V. Jack: *op. cit.* p. 8.
40. D. F. Neil: *op. cit.* p. 9.
41. S. F. Winward: *Your Baptism* p. 28.
42. S. F. Winward: *The N. T. Teaching on Baptism* p. 23.
43. R. E. O. White: *op. cit.* p. 32.
44. EMBA: *op. cit.* pp. 8–9.
45. *A New Catechism* p. 242.
46. G. R. Beasley Murray: *Baptism Today and Tomorrow* (London 1966) p. 89.
47. *DCG* 22.
48. *Dei Verbum* 5.
49. *The Teaching of Christ* p. 245.
50. *A New Catechism* p. 245.
51. *op. cit.* p. 257.
52. *The Teaching of Christ* p. 169.
53. *op. cit.* p. 476.
54. N. Clark: 'The Theology of Baptism' in A. Gilmore

(ed.): *op. cit.* pp. 308–9; S. F. Winward: 'Baptism, Confirmation and the Eucharist, a Comment' in B. S. Moss (ed.) *op. cit.* p. 125.

55. R. E. O. White: *op. cit.* pp. 64–65.
56. R. E. O. White: *op. cit.* p. 68.
57. S. F. Winward: *Your Baptism* pp. 22–23.
58. S. F. Winward: *The N. T. Teaching on Baptism* p. 22.
59. *A New Catechism* p. 247.
60. *The Teaching of Christ* pp. 466–7.
61. S. F. Winward: *Your Baptism* pp. 18–19.
62. N. Clark: 'Theology in Baptism' in A. Gilmore (ed.): *op. cit.* pp. 308–9.
63. S. F. Winward: 'Baptism, Confirmation and the Eucharist, a Comment' p. 125.
64. D. F. Neil: *op. cit.* p. 9.
65. *A New Catechism* p. 247.
66. N. Clark: 'Theology of Baptism' in A. Gilmore (ed.) *op. cit.* p. 309.
67. D. F. Neil: *op. cit.* p. 8.
68. R. E. O. White: *op. cit.* p. 41ff.
69. S. F. Winward: *Your Baptism.* p. 25.
70. S. F. Winward: *Your Baptism* pp. 30–31.
71. EMBA: *op. cit.* p. 8.
72. V. Jack: *op. cit.* pp. 14–18.
73. A. Schmemann: *op. cit.* p. 66.
74. I. F. Hapgood: *op. cit.* p. 271.
75. A. Schmemann: *op. cit.* p. 22.
76. A. Schmemann: *op. cit.* p. 23.
77. A. Schmemann: *op. cit.* p. 25.
78. *A New Catechism* pp. 243–4.
79. *OICA* 144 p. 38.
80. *The Teaching of Christ* p. 46.
81. *OICA* 25(1) p. 6.
82. A. Schmemann: *op. cit.* pp. 27–29; I. F. Hapgood: *op. cit.* pp. 274, 603.
83. A. Schmemann: *op. cit.* pp. 32–35; I. F. Hapgood: *op. cit.* pp. 274–275.
84. *OICA* 217 pp. 67–68, although it is permitted for Episcopal Conferences to adapt the formulas to take account of the need to renounce superstitions, divinations, magical arts, bearing in mind the missionary situation.

85. I. F. Hapgood: *op. cit.* p. 271.
86. *OICA* 30 p. 7.
87. E. A. Payne & S. F. Winward: *op. cit.* p. 132.
88. S. F. Winward: *Your Baptism* p. 45.
89. A. Gilmore, E. Smalley, M. Walker: *op. cit.* p. 139.
90. S. F. Winward: *Your Baptism* p. 46.
91. A. Schmemann: *op. cit.* p. 37.
92. A. Schmemann: *op. cit.* p. 40.
93. A. Schmemann: *op. cit.* p. 51; I. F. Hapgood: *op. cit.* p. 279.
94. I. F. Hapgood: *op. cit.* pp. 279–280.
95. *OICA* 215 p. 66.
96. E. A Payne & S. F. Winward: *op. cit.* pp. 131–2.
97. S. F. Winward: *Your Baptism* p. 46.
98. A. Gilmore, E. Smalley, N. Walker: *op. cit.* p. 139.
99. A. Schmemann: *op. cit.* pp. 71–72.
100. A. Schmemann: *op. cit.* p. 109.
101. *OICA* 225, 226, pp. 71–72.
102. *OICA* 46, 228.
103. *OICA* 229–231.
104. I. F. Hapgood: *op. cit.* p. 603.
105. A. Schmemann: *op. cit.* p. 126.
106. *OICA* 230 p. 73.
107. E. A. Payne & S. F. Winward: *op. cit.* p. 138.
108. S. F. Winward: *Your Baptism* p. 48.

Chapter Nine

1. Baptists would agree with this, but for them the question of rebaptism occurs following infant baptism, which, with their emphasis on individual faith and commitment, many would feel was an act of blessing only, at least until the infant's personal faith was confirmed in the sacrament of confirmation.
2. See *OICA* 220 p. 69. This is further illustrated by the practice for female Baptist candidates, whereby the baptismal robe is provided by the Church, worn immediately before and during the service, and then given back to the church, either dripping wet, or one week later suitably washed and pressed. Male candidates provide their own shirt and white or grey trousers.
3. Cardinal Daniélou refers to the concept of the eighth day in *The Bible and the Liturgy*, but in the context of the

eschatology of the Cappadocian Fathers and of Augustine, and he does not refer to the rites of the eighth day *per se*. The earliest reference in Dr Schmemann's footnotes is to Symeon of Thessalonica (d. 1429).

4. Murphy Center for Liturgical Research: *Made, not Born* (Notre Dame, Ind. 1976); R. W. Hovda: 'Hope for the Future: A Summary' p. 155.

Select Bibliography

Abbott, W. M. *The Documents of Vatican II* (London 1967)

Barrett, J. O. *Suggestions for Visitors to Candidates* (rev. edn.) (London 1979)

Baur, J. C. *John Chrysostom and His Time* (2 vols.) tr. M. Gonganza (Westminster, Md., 1960–1)

Beasley Murray, G. R. *Baptism Today and Tomorrow* (London 1966)

Benoît, A. *Le Baptême chrétien au second siècle* (Paris 1953)

Bingham, J. *Origines Ecclesiasticae, and other works* Vols 1 & 8 (London 1840)
A Scholastic History of Lay Baptism (London 1842)

Bridge, D. & Phypers. D. *The Water that Divides* (Leicester 1977)

Buckingham, D. *Caring for New Christians* (Ilkeston 1980)

Child, R. L. *A Conversation about Baptism* (London 1963)

Church, R. W. *The Catechetical Lectures of St Cyril (Library of Church Fathers* Vol. 2) (Oxford 1839)

Conybeare, F. & Maclean, J. *Rituale Armenorum* (Oxford 1905)

Cross, F. L. (ed.) *St Cyril of Jerusalem's Lectures on the Christian Sacraments (Texts for Students* 51) (London 1951)

Daniélou, J. *The Bible and the Liturgy* (Ann Arbor, Mich. 1956)

Devos, P. 'La date du Voyage d'Égérie' in *Analecta Bollandiana* 85 (1967) pp. 165–194

Dhanis, E. & Vissen J. *The Supplement to a New Catechism* (London 1969)

Dolger, F. *Der Exorzismus im altchristlichen Taufritual* (Paderborn 1909)

Dujarier, M. *A History of the Catechumenate* (New York 1979)
The rites of Christian Initiation (New York 1979)
'Sponsorship' in *Concilium* Vol. 2 No. 3 (1967)

Dunning, J. B. *New Wine, New Wineskins* (New York 1981)

East Midland Baptist Association *Church Membership* (Nottingham 1972)

   To be A Christian (Nottingham 1981)

Finn, T. M. *The Liturgy of Baptism in the Baptismal Instructions of St John Chrysostom (Studies in Christian Antiquity* 15) (Washington 1967)

   'Baptismal Death and Resurrection: A Study in Fourth Century Theology' in *Worship* 43 (1969)

Gifford, E. H. (tr.) *St Cyril, Archbishop of Jerusalem: Catechetical Lectures (Nicene and Post-Nicene Fathers* Vol 7) (London 1894)

Gilbert, B. *New Horizons* (Lutterworth 1979)

Gilmore, A. (ed.) *Christian Baptism* (London 1959)

Gilmore, A., Smalley, E. & Walker, M. *Praise God* (London 1980)

Greenlee, J. H. *The Gospel Text of St Cyril of Jerusalem (Studies and Documents* XVII) (Copenhagen 1955)

Greer, R. *Theodore of Mopsuestia: Exegete and Theologian*

Haidacher, S. 'Neun Ethica des Evangeliumkommentars von Theodor Meliteniotes und deren Quellen' in *Byzantinische Zeitschrift* 11 (1902) pp. 370–387)

   'Chrysostom-Fragmente im Maximon-Florilegium und in den Sacra parallela' in *Byzantinische Zeitschrift* 16 (1907) pp. 172–173)

   'Eine unbeachtete Rede des hg. Chrysostomus an Neugetaufte' in *Zeitschrift für katholische Theologie* 28 (1904) pp. 168–186

Hapgood, I. F. *Service Book of the Holy Orthodox-Catholic Apostolic Church* (New York 1922)

Harkins, P. (tr.) *St John Chrysostom: Baptismal Instructions (Ancient Christian Writers* 31) (Westminster Md., 1963)

International Commission on English in the Liturgy *The Rite of Christian Initiation of Adults* (London 1974)

Jack, V. *Believe and Be Baptized* (Bury St Edmunds 1970)

Kemp, R. B. *A Journey in Faith* (New York 1979)

Lampe, G. W. H. *The Seal of the Spirit* (London 1951)

   A Patristic Greek Lexicon (Oxford 1961)

Lawler, R., Lawler, T. C. & Wuerl D. W. *The Teaching of Christ* (Dublin 1976)

Lewinski, R. *Welcoming the New Catholic* (Chicago 1978)

Lietzmann, H. *Die Liturgie des Theodor von Mopsuestia (Sonderausgabe aus den Sitzungsberichten der Preussischen Akademie der Wissenschaft* Phil. Hist. Klasse 23) (Berlin 1933)

McClendon, J. 'Why Baptists do not baptize Infants' in *Concilium* Vol. 4 No. 3 (1967)

Mingana, A. (ed.) *Commentary of Theodore of Mopsuestia on the Nicene Creed (Woodbrooke Studies 5)* (Cambridge 1932)
Commentary of Theodore of Mopsuestia on the Lord's Prayer and the Sacraments of Baptism and the Eucharist (Woodbrooke Studies 6) (Cambridge 1933)

Montfaucon, B. (ed.) *Catechesis prima et altera (Patrologia Graeca* 49, 223–240) (Paris 1862)

Moss, B. S. (ed.) *Crisis for Baptism* (London 1965)

Murphy Center for Liturgical Research *Made, not Born* (Notre Dame, Ind. 1976)

National Conference of Catholic Bishops of the U.S.A. *Basic Teachings for Catholic Religious Education* (London 1975)

Neil, D. F. *The Way of Christ* (London 1973)

Papadopoulos-Kerameus, A. (ed.) *Varia graeca sacra. Sbornik greceskikh Neissdannikh bogoslovskikh tekstov I–IV vekov* (St Petersburg 1909)

Payne, E. A. 'Baptists and Christian Initiation' in *Baptist Quarterly* XXVI (1979) pp. 145–158

Petre, H. (ed.) *Ethérie: Journal de voyage (Sources chrétiennes* 21) (Paris 1948)

Piédagnel, A. (ed.) *Cyrille de Jérusalem: Catéchèses Mystagogiques (Sources chrétiennes* 126) (Paris 1966)

Quasten, J. *Patrology* Vol. 3 (Westminster, Md. 1960)

Reedy, W. J. (ed.) *Becoming a Catholic Christian* (New York 1974)

Reischl, W. K. & Rupp, J. (eds.) *S. patris nostri Cyrilli opera quae supersunt omnia* 2 vols. (Munich 1848, 1860)

Riley, H. M. *Christian Initiation (Studies in Christian Antiquity* 17) (Washington D.C. 1974)

Sacred Congregation for the Clergy *A Catechism of Christian Doctrine* revised edn. (London 1971)
General Catechetical Directory (London 1971)

Sacred Congregation for Divine Worship *Ordo Initiationis Christianae Adultorum* (Vatican City 1972)

Schmemann, A. *The World as Sacrament* (London 1965)
Of Water and the Spirit (London 1976)

Smyth, K. (tr.) *A New Catechism* 8th edn. (London 1980)

Stephenson, A. A. & McCauley, L. P. *The Works of St Cyril of Jerusalem* 2 vols. *(Fathers of the Church* 64, 64) (Washington D.C. 1969–70)

Swaans, W. J. 'A propos des Catéchèses mystagogiques attribuées à Saint Cyrille de Jérusalem' in *Muséon* LV (1942) pp. 1–43

Telfer, W. *Cyril of Jerusalem and Nemesius of Emesa* (*Library of Christian Classics* 4) (London 1955)

Tonneau, R. & Devréesse, T. (eds.) *Les Homélies Catéchétiques de Théodore de Mopsueste* (*Studi e Testi* 145) (Vatican City 1949)

Underwood, A. C. *A History of English Baptists* (London 1961)

Unnik, W. C. van *'De semitische ashtergrond van* parrhésia *in het Nieuwe Testament'* in *Mededelingen der Koninklijke Nederlanse Akademie van Wettenschappen afd. Letterkunde* N.R. XXVII (1962)
'Parrhésia in the 'Catechetical Homilies' of Theodore of Mopsuestia' in *Mélanges offerts à Mlle. Christine Mohrmann* (Utrecht 1963) pp. 12–22

Ware, T. R. *Eustratios Argenti* (Oxford 1964)

Weaver, J. *Catechetical Themes in the Post-Baptismal Teaching of St John Chrysostom* (Thesis, Catholic University of America, Washington 1964)

Wenger, A. (ed.) Jean Chrysostome: *Huit catéchèses baptismales inédites* (*Sources chrétiennes* 50 bis) (Paris 1970)

Westcott, B. F. *The Gospel according to St John* (London 1894)

White, R. E. O. *Invitation to Baptism* (London 1962)

Wilkinson, J. (tr.) *Egeria's Travels* (London 1971)

Williamson, J. A. (tr.) *Eusebius: The History of the Church* (London 1965)

Winward, S. F. *Your Baptism* (London 1969)
The New Testament Teaching on Baptism (London 1952)

Ysebaert, J. *Greek Baptismal Terminology* (*Graecitas Christianorum Primaeva: Fasciculus Primus*) (Nijmegen, 1962)

1.38 46, 91
1.44 38
2.1 33, 84
2.11 29, 45, 46, 82
2.14 10, 40, 85
2.18 38, 39, 41, 86
2.20 39, 87
2.21 39
2.22 39, 43
2.23 39, 43, 89, 126
2.24 44, 45, 90
2.25 26, 44, 45, 46, 82, 98
2.26 44, 45, 81
2.27 10, 47
3.7* 37, 83
3.9 41, 88, 92, 93
3.10 88
3.11 42, 88
3.15 40
3.16 94
3.19 26, 95
3.20 20, 31, 33, 84
3.21 31, 37, 42, 87
3.22 42, 87
3.23 28, 39, 83, 96
3.24 10, 39
4.1 26, 82, 95
4.2 33, 34
4.3 36
4.4 97
4.7 38
4.8 38
4.9 38
4.10 38
4.11 38
4.12 29, 38
4.13 38
4.14 26, 27, 28, 38, 83, 96
4.15 38
4.16 27, 38, 80
4.18 97
4.19 29
4.31 36, 43
5.18 98
5.19 28, 38, 81

5.20 29, 34, 38
5.21 38
5.22 38
5.23 38
5.24 98
5.26 98
6.1 11
6.21 11, 80
6.24 36, 98
6.25 34, 36, 98
7.21 93
7.22 30, 82
7.23 93
7.24 29, 34, 81, 98
8.1 78
8.25 98

Papadopoulos-Kerameus series†
1.1 38
1.5 32, 84
1.6 32, 84
1.12 24, 25, 82
1.13 79
1.16 25
1.17 25
1.18 25
1.19 25, 26
1.20 25
1.21 25, 27, 28, 82
1.22 25, 27, 28, 34, 82
1.23 25, 27, 28
1.24 25, 27, 28
1.25 25, 27, 28
1.26 25, 27, 28, 83, 96
1.29 30, 79
2.8 25, 29, 82
2.9 25, 29, 30, 82, 94
2.10 29, 82
2.11 25, 29, 30, 82, 94
2.14 111
2.15 111
3.6 98
3.7 98
3.10 38
3.11 38
3.12 38, 44
3.13 32, 38, 44, 79, 84

3.14 32, 33, 38, 44, 79, 84
3.15 38
3.16 38, 95
3.17 38, 95
3.18 38, 78
3.19 38, 41, 90
3.20 38, 86, 90
3.21 38, 40, 41, 84, 85, 86
3.22 39
3.23 83
3.24 39, 41, 87
3.26 37, 42, 83, 88
3.27 38, 43, 89
3.28 44, 47, 93
3.29 47, 92, 93

Montfaucon series
2.8 27, 38
2.15 46, 90
2.16 46, 90
2.17 46, 90
2.18 46, 90
2.19 37, 46, 80, 90
2.20 46, 90
2.21 34, 84
2.36 33, 35, 84
2.37 35
2.41 46
2.43 46
2.48 39
2.50 42
2.60 39, 44

Hom. in Genesis 6 79
Hom. in Matthew 12 25–6, 79
Hom. in John 11 28
Hom. in Romans 10 30, 82
Hom. in 2 Corinthians 11 31, 82
Hom. in Ephesians 20 36
Hom. in Colossians 6 31, 82
                        7 30
In paralyticum 35
In prin. act. 3 26
Qual duc. ux. 36

---

* This is also included as Papadopoulos-Kerameus 4: see p. 24 above.
† The first Montfaucon lecture has been discovered to be one of a series discovered by
  A. Papadopoulos-Keraneus: see p. 24 above

Index of Subjects

Themes which recur frequently throughout the book are not listed comprehensively.

239